SAMENESS AND SUBSTANCE

SAMENESS
AND
SUBSTANCE

David Wiggins

HARVARD UNIVERSITY PRESS
CAMBRIDGE, MASSACHUSETTS
1980

Library of Congress Cataloging in Publication Data
Wiggins, D.
　Sameness and substance.

　Bibliography: p.
　Includes index.
　I. Identity.　II. Individuation.　III. Essence.
(Philosophy)　IV. Conceptualism.　V. Substance
(Philosophy)　I. Title.
BD236.W53　1980　　110　　79-25134
ISBN 0-674-78595-9

Printed in Great Britain

Preface

Although this is a new book, it began in an attempt to expel error, gratuitous compression, and obscurity from the author's 1967 *Identity and Spatio-Temporal Continuity*, which has been out of print for a number of years. The revision was undertaken in the idealistic belief that, at a time when philosophy is in danger of caving in under the weight of its own productions, it would be a good thing if authors neither printed nor reprinted that which they saw as standing in need of correction. Unluckily, however, and in defiance of all the maxims against overproduction that are implied by the said belief, the outcome of the revision process has proved to be a new and longer book. Symbolism, conventions of nomenclature, one extended smaller print tract of Chapter One, and isolated pages of Chapters Two and Three are all that will be literally reidentifiable.

The theory of individuation defended in this new book is the same as that advanced in *Identity and Spatio-Temporal Continuity*. But it has appeared necessary to remove not only plain blunders but also the several sources of misunderstanding for which expressions in the earlier text were to blame—not least the title even. With that removed, let me now reaffirm a proposition that is common to both books: that nothing whatever is to be made of bare continuity. *A fortiori,* neither identity, nor even the identity relation as restricted to material objects, is the same relation as continuity. *Identity and Spatio-Temporal Continuity* was intended as the first engagement in the war *against* this idea. And it has always been the purpose of Proposition **D** (that is the Thesis of Sortal Dependency, now freshly stated and argued in Chapter Two), implying that behind every true identity there is an identity sentence covered by a substance concept for some particular *kind* of thing, to show that the idea of mere continuity is just as dispensable as it is incoherent.

Many of the amplifications and refinements of the original theory have been explained and justified, sometimes less summarily and dogmatically than has been possible in a book whose purpose is to organize them into one consolidated statement, in journals and collections:

1. 'On Being in the Same Place at the Same Time', *Philosophical Review* January 1968.
2. 'Reply to Mr Chandler', *Analysis* 1969.
3. 'Continuity, Identity and Essentialism', *Synthèse* 1974, some of whose conclusions are further modified in 4.
4. 'Frege's Problem of the Morning Star and the Evening Star' in M. Schirn, ed., *Studies on Frege II: Logic and Philosophy of Language*, Stuttgart, Bad Canstatt, 1976.
5. 'The *De Re* "Must": A Note on the Logical Form of Essentialist Claims' (with an Appendix by C. A. B. Peacocke) in Evans and McDowell, eds, *Truth and Meaning: Essays in Semantics*, Oxford, 1976.
6. 'Locke, Butler, and the Stream of Consciousness: and Men as a Natural Kind', *Philosophy* April 1976.
7. 'Identity, Necessity and Physicalism' in Stefan Körner, ed., *Philosophy of Logic* (Proceedings of 1974 Bristol Conference), Blackwell, 1976.
8. Reply to Richard Wollheim on 'Are the Criteria of Identity of Works of Art Aesthetically Relevant?' (for Bristol Conference on the Philosophy of Art, 1976, *Ratio* 1978).
9. 'Contingency, Identity, and *de re* and *de dicto* Necessity', forthcoming in *Proceedings of the 1979 Keele Conference on the Philosophy of Language*, J. Dancy ed., published by Dept. of Philosophy, University of Keele.

I am grateful to the appropriate editors for permission to reproduce certain passages. But in accordance with the belief that I mentioned at the beginning I have corrected these passages too, sometimes substantially.

From the 1967 monograph that this book is to replace I must carry forward a grateful acknowledgement of the advice and assistance of Professor P. T. Geach and Dr W. A. Hodges; and an acknowledgement of my special indebtedness to the views and writings of Professor B. A. O. Williams, who has also made comments on two of the new chapters. Among those who have read and helped me with comments on tracts of new text that have varied from chapters to notes or single paragraphs are M. K. Davies, E. L. Hussey, D. W. Hamlyn, R. A. Wollheim, C. A. B. Peacocke, D. F. Cheesman, J. A. W. Kamp, N. Tennant, J. H. McDowell. I am extremely grateful to them, and have tried to acknowledge in the text or notes all the original points that they made to me. My greatest debts, however, are to my coeditor P. F. Strawson and to J. Hornsby, each of whom, at some moment when I was almost resolved to postpone publication *sine die,* came to my rescue, read through the bulk of the manuscript and offered encouragement usefully qualified with detailed criticism and advice.

In trying to clarify in the new book two points that seemed to many people to have been left in a state of great obscurity, viz. the notion of a principle of individuation and the doctrine of essentialism, I have greatly profited by studying the writings of Hilary Putnam, Saul Kripke and Richard Cartwright, and most particularly the book, *Leibniz's Philosophy of Logic and Language* (London, Duckworth, 1972), by Hidé Ishiguro. In various and different ways (for which, whenever they deem the result unfortunate, they are not to be blamed—and, having heard Saul Kripke talk once on this subject, I know that this *caveat* is called for), these authors have helped me toward the expression of convictions more extreme than any I previously dared formulate about the mutual dependence of substance, causality and law, and metaphysical *de re* necessity. (Causality and nomological considerations were previously accorded an important and explicit role only in the discussion of persons.) Where identity of artifacts is concerned, these convictions have served to temper somewhat the vehement anti-conventionalism of the original monograph. Where natural things and people are concerned they have fortified that anti-conventionalism.

In *Identity and Spatio-Temporal Continuity* certain dark claims were made about the relevance and importance for the theory of individuation of the philosophy of biology. As the present book was going to press I was pleased to make the discovery that, in response to all the facts that confront the biological scientist, Professor J. Z. Young has arrived in chapters five and six of *An Introduction to the Study of Man* (Oxford, 1971) at a conception of identity over time substantially similar where living things are concerned to my own conception:

> The essence of a living thing is that it consists of atoms of the ordinary chemical elements we have listed, caught up into the living system and made part of it for a while. The living activity takes them up and organizes them in its characteristic way. The life of a man consists essentially in the activity he imposes upon that stuff . . . it is only by virtue of this activity that the shape and organization of the whole is maintained.

A reader who wishes to begin by seizing the main essentials of the theory advanced here should omit the Preamble, which is largely methodological, and look back at this only for explanations later referred to. He should begin with Chapter One, sections 1–5, then skip to section 9 of that Chapter, then read Chapters Two and Three omitting passages in smaller type. A summary is given at Chapter Three, section 5 of just this material. The chief aim of these sections is to place questions of individuation and identity or persistence through time on a firmer and broader basis of theory which will determine better the point that is at issue in particular problems of identity, and suggest securer standards of relevance and irrelevance to each case of the empirical information that is collateral with it.

Individuation, real essence, and identity through change, I have come to see, are matters on which it is easy to be misunderstood, and especially perhaps by those who give the appearance of instantaneous understanding and agreement. For the one aim of being understood, mistakes and all, every aspiration to grace, expedition or economy of expression has in this new book been ruthlessly sacrificed. As a result it is now a long book. It would have been a fine thing to have arrived, by making it so, at the point where one could echo Nelson Goodman's complaints against critics who suppose they do him a favour by thinking that he does not mean what he says. But in truth there are miserably few sections where I could dispense with the readiness, which that realist Frege so earnestly required of his reader, to meet the writer half way and not begrudge a pinch of salt.

Bedford College (University of London),   D.W.
Regent's Park,
London NW1.

Contents

Preamble

1. *Purpose*

It is the aim of this book to propose and elaborate a theory of the individuation of continuants, both living substances and other substances.

It would appear that a theory of individuation must comprise at least three things: first, an elucidation of the primitive concept of identity or sameness; second, some however abstract account of what it is for something to be a substance that persists through change; and third (supervening in my treatment upon the first two things) the beginnings of some lifelike description, however schematic, of what it is for a thinker at one time and then another to single out the same substance *as* the same substance.

From a philosopher's attitude towards the logical and methodological ordering of these three tasks there is much to be learned about his attitude and orientation to the idea that the meaning of a word is a function of its use. I take myself to accept, without cavil or qualification of any sort, that the meanings of such words as 'same', 'substance', 'change' and 'persists' depend on their use. Indeed it is several times insisted in the course of the argument that the activity of singling out or individuating is what gives to these words their whole life and semantic identity. But the thesis of meaning as use is fully consistent with two converse or complementary theses, on which philosophical reflection will confer an equal relevance to what is to be attempted and an equal claim upon rational acceptance. The first is that the relation between the meaning and the use of such words as 'same', 'substance', 'change', 'persists' is reciprocal; rather, once the temptation to Platonize the description of meaning is resisted, meaning and use can be seen as two aspects of one and the same thing. The second is that, just as understanding the relations and transactions between the participants of some culture and the features that they respond to in the world is a better way to start to peer into the minds of these persons than to mount a frontal assault on the inner states of some secret something (or try to take mental states in abstraction from all the features of the world to which they are intentionally directed), so the interpretation and comprehension of a set of linguistic uses or conceptual practices involves understanding the *subject matter* to which they relate.

In the second sentence of this Preamble mention was made of three concerns. It is the third concern which affords the framework for our inquiry: but it is the first and second which will determine the whole content of any description of the link between objects in the world and the individuative practices that presuppose or require these objects. And this form and content relationship entitles me, I believe, to try to subsume under the elucidation of the concepts *identical, substance, change, persistence, continuant* the main burden of devising a theory of individuation and, at the same time, to insist—in deference to the third concern and the doctrine of meaning as use—that our understanding of these concepts cannot be completely characterized otherwise than by reference to the observable commerce between things singled out and the thinkers who think or find their way around the world precisely by singling them out.

When the reciprocities and mutual interdependencies of concept, custom and thing-singled-out are acknowledged and likened to those of some seamless web, and when the primitiveness of all the relevant notions is acknowledged, how much genuine clarification is it reasonable to expect a philosophical theory of individuation to be able to achieve? To this question I would reply that we have rudimentary pretheoretical ideas of identity, of persistence through change, and of the singling out of changeable things. These are ideas that we can put together to arrive at a provisional or first elucidation and understanding, not only of what 'same' means (that is the first and easiest thing), but also of the actual applicability of this two-place predicate. But then, I claim, so soon as this first understanding is achieved, it can be a basis from which first to scrutinize afresh, and second to advance and consolidate, our logical and participative understanding of the individuative practices that a thinker's grasp of the concepts of substance, sameness and persistence through change makes possible for him. It is my hope that at the end of this second phase, even though nothing recognizable as a *philosophical analysis* of ' = ' will have been achieved, there will be no mystery left about how a notion of the exigency that we are disposed *a priori* to ascribe to the identity relation can find application in the uncertain and ever changing world of our experience. When this phase is complete, we shall be able to describe, admittedly in terms no different in principle from the terms of ordinary untheoretical individuation and reidentification of particulars, both what regulates the principled employment of ' = ' and what it *is* for a thinker who is bent on singling out objects to segment or articulate the world of his experience in such a way as to isolate within it things that persist through change.

This last does not mean (what it might seem to mean if more than due priority or emphasis were accorded to the third of the three tasks enumerated in the second sentence of this preamble) that, for the benefit of his deluded subjects, the theorist is to find a way to see a world in which nothing really persists through change *as if* some of the things in that world did persist through change—a sort of make-believe. For there is persistence through change, and no inquiry of the kind here envisaged could take leave of a datum so fundamental and so deeply entrenched. It means that, arriving at the point I have programmatically described, the theorist is to understand as well as he can—discursively, and in the same sort of terms as those who individuate them—what it is for an object to count as a continuant; and then he is to describe how the charge that something did *not* persist is to be considered and, in the appropriate fashion (on its merits, that is, and in terms accessible in principle to those who take themselves to believe in genuine continuants), either countered as false or conceded as true.

Where there is reciprocity or mutual presupposition between concepts, analytical philosophy is often tempted into violence or arbitrariness. We find it hard to endure the thought that in the important substantive questions of philosophy there is rarely or never some unique and manifest starting place, or some single master thread to pull upon to unravel everything else. It may appear that the chapters which follow are not exempt from the illusion of the master thread. For the formal properties of identity (contrast the application of the concept) are treated here as enjoying a special status. Indeed it may appear that the whole method of proceeding depends first upon my making the assumption that these formal properties of 'the same' are given from altogether outside the investigation, and then depends upon my insulating from all criticism the opinion that they not only determine what can count as someone's singling out or tracing an entity in the world, but also condition and regulate, by reference to a claim they make upon rationality, the very interpretation of thought and conduct *as* thought and conduct.

Someone who takes issue with the claims I make about the formal properties of 'the same' and 'the same f' will find this a particularly question-begging attitude. Something is done in the course of Chapter One to justify my view of the formal properties of ' = ' (which is not so much that they are given *ab extra*, as that answerability to the Leibnizian principle is immanent in any linguistic and conceptual practices that we can recognize as reference and individuation). But, apart from what I offer at section 2 of Chapter One to liken their status to that of the Law of Non-Contradiction, I can only say that the issue between this opponent and me, however plain it lies to view in certain details, is in the end both holistic and dialectical. It will not be resolved until an opposing theory of individuation is developed to the same point as the theory developed here, and the two descriptions of individuation are compared with one another against the background of all the practices that they purport to describe. I am convinced, however, that the internal difficulties of the ontology and ideology of the position that results from the abandonment of Leibnizian identity are overwhelmingly greater than any which attach to the position I recommend.

2. Notions

Corresponding to three tasks mentioned in the first paragraph there are the notions *identical, continuant* and *individuate.*

(i) The notion of sameness or identity that we are to elucidate is not that of any degree of qualitative similarity but of coincidence as a substance—a notion as primitive as predication, and correlative with it in the following way: if and only if Socrates is a man then Socrates is identical with some man, and so, we shall argue, shares all his properties with him. No reduction of this relation has ever succeeded. (*Vide* Chapter One, note 7, Longer Note 2.03, both offered without prejudice to the model-theoretic or other utility of certain partial reductions.) Nor is it called for, once we realize how much can be achieved in philosophy by means of elucidations which *use* a concept without attempting to reduce it, and, in using the concept, exhibit the connexions of the concept with other concepts that are established, genuinely collateral and independently intelligible.

(ii) We have to explicate what it is to be a substance or continuant. This explication will not amount to a definition, or be achieved without the ineliminable demonstration of ordinary perceptible individuals of common experience; but it will go some way beyond mere demonstration of these. Indeed to set out, as so many philosophers have done in emulation of Book VII of Aristotle's *Metaphysics,* with the high-minded aspiration to achieve an altogether purer kind of definition of substance, and then, because the result does not satisfy, to abandon the concept of substance, is to end up doing philosophy that is at once ill-tempered and needlessly bad. (It represents the inability to learn from Aristotle's experiment.)

Kant writes at § 46 of *Prolegomenon to Any Future Metaphysic:* 'People have long since observed that in all substances the proper subject, that which remains after all the accidents (as predicates) are abstracted, remains unknown.' I protest that the substances or subjects we begin with are not unknown but known, and that the only abstraction which we need be interested in is utterly distinct from that which is supposed to result from the notional (mythical) removal of properties from a substance. The abstraction we need is what results from the ascent from particular kinds of substance to the determinable *substance of some kind.* (Ascent to what Wittgenstein in *Tractatus Logico-Philosophicus* called a formal concept.) This form of abstraction cannot part us from our conviction that substances are things which are known to us.

(iii) The Oxford English Dictionary defines 'individuate' in terms of 'single out' or 'pick out', and this definition suits well what is meant here. That which individuates, in the sense in which the word will be used in this book, is in the first instance a thinker, and derivatively a substantive or predicate. By 'single out' I mean to isolate x in experience; to determine or fix upon x in particular by drawing its spatio-temporal boundaries and distinguishing it in its environment from other things of like and unlike kinds (at this, that and the other times during its life history); to articulate or segment reality in such a way as to discover x there. To single out, however, is not yet to refer or to designate. And one may well refer to x without in our primary sense singling x out at all. (Though, if there were no singling out of anything by anyone at any time, it seems there could be no referring.)

The verbs 'individuate' and 'single out' are not intensional. If a thinker singles out or individuates x, and $x = y$, then, whether he knows that or not, he singles out or individuates y. Such verbs do, however, permit of a complementation that is intensional. A Greek could have singled out Socrates simply, singled out Socrates as Socrates, singled out Socrates as a man or philosopher, or singled out Socrates as the Athenian married to Xanthippe who was represented by Plato to have stressed (*Phaedrus* 265^e) the equal importance in classification and carving of 'dividing where the joints are'. What then is the relation of singling out and singling out *as*? We shall discover reason in due course to think that there could be no singling out *tout court* unless there could also be singling out *as*. It will be claimed that not just any attempt at singling out counts as singling *something* out; and that what is required in a given case derives from what the thing in question is—from what it *would be* to single that particular thing out *as* whatever it is. It will be a consequence of our theory that, for a thinker to single out or individuate a substance *s*, there must be something about what he does and about his *rapport* with *s*, or his relational state towards *s*, which (regardless of whether he knows this or not, or whether or not it is a singling out *as*) sufficiently approximates to, or sufficiently tends towards, the singling out of *s* either as *s* or as a thing of a kind f such that membership in f entails some correct answer to the question 'what is *s*?'. It will be particularly insisted that the singling out at time *t* of the substance *s reaches backwards and forwards* to times before and after *t*; and categorically denied that a case where it is indeterminate what was singled out is the singling out of something indeterminate. But at this point we get beyond explanation of terminology and deep into the philosophy of the matter. (It will not be possible until Chapter Five to complete or justify this account of what singling out is, or of the way in which the singling something out at *t* reaches backwards and forwards, as I claim, to times before and after *t*.)

3. *Terminological matters*

It will probably be best now for the reader to turn straight to Chapter One. But, for the record and for subsequent use, certain terminological and methodological provisions must be set down.

The illusion of some single starting point for all questions, or of some minimum knowledge of certain and evident truth from which everything else should be somehow deducible, is not the only illusion to which we are subject. In the twentieth century, analytical philosophy has also been prey to the illusion, most likely produced by an irrelevant admiration of what is admirable in science, that by judicious enrichment of the object language the theorist can rise to some vantage point on a higher plane of theory and then inspect and describe from on high, in his own theoretical way, the subject matter of ordinary thought and discourse. Perhaps it is almost enough to put this hope into words to see that, almost by definition, philosophy is the place where its disappointment is nearly inevitable, and to conclude that technical terms whose sole advertised purpose is to achieve this are to be shunned (as Leibniz so quaintly and vehemently put it in *Preface to Nizolius*) as worse than dog or snake.

Ideally, all technical terms in philosophy should surely belong in that part of the metalanguage which does not overlap with the object language. Where there is no alternative but to allow technical terms to penetrate into the object language (e.g. because the object language is poor in schematic devices or devices of generalization), they should serve the sole purpose of summarizing or systematizing, in terms not essentially different from the expressions indigenous to the object language, the matters of which the object language already speaks. The semi-technical uses in this book of 'concept', 'continuant', 'substance', 'coincidence', 'coincidence under a concept' will stand condemned unless they conform to this requirement. They do not quite always live up to this ideal in fact, and do to that extent stand condemned. But what they aspire to be are *determinables* of which ordinary English provides countless *determinations*. (This is everywhere important, but it is a particularly important stipulation in connexion with the term 'substance'. If we forget it then we shall unintentionally restore the unwanted associations of 'substance' with doctrines of bare particulars and qualityless substrate.)

In Chapter One, for instance, at the very outset of the inquiry, the question is put whether x can be the same f as y without being the same g. To make a question in English out of this schema, replace the letters 'x' and 'y' by names of substances and the letters 'f' and 'g' by predicates denominating kinds of thing, e.g. 'donkey', 'horse', 'tree'.

4. *Sortal predicates and sortal concepts*

A technical term that is associated with 'substance' but belongs in the metalanguage is 'sortal predicate'. Any predicate whose extension consists (and is determined by a good theory of truth to consist) of all the particular things or substances of one particular kind, say horses, or sheep, or pruning knives, will be called here a sortal predicate. I use this Lockean term in roughly the manner of the second part of P. F. Strawson's *Individuals* (London: Methuen, 1959), see especially pp. 168–9. (For a discrepancy not of philosophical purpose but of detail see Chapter Two, section 8 below.) Locke's usage, Strawson's usage and my own are all focused or organized by Aristotle's distinction of the categories of substance and quality. See *Categories, ad init.*, especially the two passages I have prefixed to Chapter One. For Locke's usage see *Essay* III, iii, 15:

. . . it being evident that things are ranked under names into sorts or species only as they agree to certain abstract ideas, to which we have

annexed those names, the essence of each *genus,* or sort, comes to be
nothing but that abstract idea which the general, or *sortal* (if I may have
leave so to call it so from *sort,* as I do *general* from *genus*) name stands
for.[1]

What a particular sortal predicate stands for may be called a *sortal
concept.* Following Frege, I shall explain 'sortal concept' in object
language terms by generalizing from the following stipulation: the
concept *horse* is what it is to be a horse. Bracketing the problem about
the predicational tie that Frege himself brackets by calling concept-
words or predicates 'unsaturated', we may say that a sortal concept is
what a sortal predicate stands for. It would be good some day to show
that this kind of talk is fully compatible with nominalism in that
reasonable acceptation of the term in which both Aristotle and
Leibniz are to be reckoned nominalists, or held (in effect) that they
were.

On the subject of 'f' and 'g', I am sorry to say that they do multiple
duty in this book. They are sometimes variables ranging over kinds
(as in 'for any x and any kind f, if f is a substance kind, then if x
belongs to f, x always belongs to f') and sometimes variables ranging
over *concepts* (as in the quantification '$(\exists f)(f(Socrates))$', read as
'there is something Socrates is' or 'there is a sortal concept Socrates
falls under'); but occasionally they operate in a different way and
serve as schematic letters whose substituends are substantives (as in 'x
is an f' or 'x is the same f as y', or as in 'in the case of an f, to exist is to
be f'). In opting for this economy (and sparing the reader certain
symbolic complexities that would otherwise have been required to
preserve the links between predicate, concept and extension), I trust
that I have not subjected him to any task of contextual disambigua-
tion he cannot perform almost without thinking. Let him who sus-
pects that some argument trades on confusion of these usages first
decide the questions I have preferred to leave open in the next section,
and then consider the suspect contention in some corresponding
reformulation.

1. At § 19 ('Divided reference') of *Word and Object* (MIT, Cambridge, Massachus-
sets, 1960), Quine notes the following variants for 'sortal predicate': (1) individuative
predicate; (2) articulative predicate; (3) substance-name; (4) shared, or multiply deno-
tative, name; (5) predicate which divides its reference (extension). Another variant that
has had some currency, cf. Michael Woods, *Substance and Quality* (B.Phil., Oxford,
1959), is (6) boundary drawing predicate. (Cf. Frege, *Foundations of Arithmetic,* § 54.)
All six terms serve to illuminate the difference, partially but only imperfectly reflected
in the grammatical division of noun and adjective or verb, between Aristotle's onto-
logically basic question *What is x?* and less basic questions such as *What is x like?
Where is x? What is x doing?*

5. *Formal notations*

There occur in the ensuing chapters a number of locutions that may give the impression that I am engaged in the business of constructing a formal system. Nothing could be further from the truth. The only function of these notations is to effect abbreviation where abbreviation is needed or to make fixed and transparent what are taken in the context to be the logical and inferential character of certain antecedently familiar forms and locutions.

In the case of notations like '$a \underset{\text{donkey}}{=} b$' this disclaimer is to be borne particularly in mind. In proofs and associated text this simply abbreviates 'a is the same donkey as b', in full cognizance of the fact that the logical character of this particular form is a matter of dispute and that, until the conclusion of the argument is reached (an argument that cannot, however, be conducted at all without using the locution), it is not even clear what the issue is when we try to choose between the four following options:

(i) 'a is the same donkey as b' abbreviates and is semantically equivalent to 'a is a donkey and b is a donkey and $a = b$';[2]

(ii) 'a is the same donkey as b' is a *sui generis* complex form, built up from the form 'ξ is the same ζ as η' where ξ and η hold places for names of individuals and ζ for a sortal concept name, the filling being 'donkey' in this case, and the final result being the predication of a particular congruence relation between a and b which, though logically equivalent, is neither syntactically equiform nor synonymous with 'a is a donkey and b is a donkey and $a = b$';

(iii) —a proposal that institutionalizes all the second level suggestions implicit in (ii)—'a is the same donkey as b' means 'a has to b the relation of identity as restricted to *donkey* (i.e. as restricted to the concept of what it is to be a donkey)';[3]

(iv) 'a is the same donkey as b' represents, as Geach says it does, the ascription of a primitive non-Leibnizian relation between a and b; this relation being that underlying the allegedly semantically *more* complex predicate 'donkey'; and 'a is a donkey' being held to mean the same as '$(\exists x)(x$ is the same donkey as $a)$'.[4]

---

2. See *Longer Note* 0.02.   3. See *Longer Note* 0.03.
4. See *Longer Note* 0.04.

In the face of all these contestants, it will be best not to go beyond '*a* is the same donkey as *b*' in reading '$a \underset{\text{donkey}}{=} b$' and to consult intuition about whether this does (as I say) or does not (as Geach and Griffin and Noonan say) entail that donkey *a* has all and only the same properties as donkey *b*. The reader can make up his own mind between these different options at any point he chooses between now and when he has read as far as the end of Chapter Three. My own provisional preference ranking would be (i), (ii), (iii). ((iv) is not for me an option at all.) But for purposes of the theory of individuation as a whole it does not matter whether (i) or (ii) is right; and it does not matter whether (ii) entails (iii). Nor would (iii) be impossible to accommodate to any important claim advanced in this book.

6. *Real and nominal*

Finally, a word on the terminology of 'real' and 'nominal'. My own use of these terms turns on the distinction between a predicate whose elucidation makes ineliminable allusion (or must *begin* by making ineliminable allusion) to members of its actual extension (real) and a predicate whose elucidation can dispense with such allusion (nominal).[5] In the second kind of case the elucidation can often be made fully explicit or articulate, and it never needs to involve the deictic or demonstrative element that is so typical of the real definition (at least until the completion of a science, cf. Chapter Three, section 5, point (vii)). A typical nominal definition would be Aristotle's formula '*x* is a house $\equiv$ *x* is a shelter against destruction by wind, rain and heat'. A typical real definition would be '*x* is a vole just if *x* is relevantly similar to *that* [demonstrated] *animal* (and let the criterion of "relevantly" depend at least in part on the nature, whatever it may prove to be, of the animal just demonstrated)'.[6] Not only does the real definition depend on real specimens; the question of its application and correctness or incorrectness also depends crucially on the facts about these specimens. Nevertheless real definitions lie within the province of semantics, as well as of empirical fact. No

5. Compare the way in which the elucidation of the sense of a proper name is *designatum*-involving. Cf. here 'On the Sense and Reference of a Proper Name', *Mind* 1977, by John McDowell, to whom this Preamble is indebted also in other ways.

6. A definition can be real with respect to *genus* and nominal with respect to *differentia*. The philosophers' favourites like 'sibling', 'oculist' and 'bachelor' have definitions like this. For some refinements of this pattern of elucidation, see Chapters Three and Six, and *Longer Note* 3.24.

lifelike elucidation of ordinary discourse could be contrived without them.[7]

I would stress that the foregoing explanation is independent of the intelligibility or truth of essentialism.

The *Longer Notes* are an integral part of the final defences of the theory. But the reader will find a little goes a long way; and I hope he will be grateful that these notes have been exported from the foot of the page. As a general policy I have aimed to relegate in this way both polemical and supplementary topics. The Chapter footnotes too are meant to be dispensable to the basic understanding of the argument. One conspicuous and regrettable departure from this policy is footnote 2 of Chapter Three.

For frequently cited examples, and for principles that are given special names or abbreviations of any sort, the Index will serve as a key.

The *Bibliography* includes all the major and minor classics of the theory of individuation known to me, and works, whether or not they have a claim to be classic, on which this book very heavily leans or depends. But it is selective. To have included all the numerous fascinating and useful items referred to in text or footnotes and others happened upon in the course of writing these notes, or to have

7. There is a measure of injustice to Locke (as well as to certain other philosophers) implicit in this usage. By using terms that are commonly conceived of as Locke's property, and by stressing constantly the importance of the real, I may seem to be claiming that, in his adherence to what he called the nominal, he failed to see things which it has recently been pointed out that he did see. Locke's doctrine of ektypes and archetypes, and the way he contrasts ideas of mixed modes with ideas of substance, both suggest, not only that he had a grasp of the question whether a given predicate has an extension-involving or not extension-involving sense; but also that he anticipated the ideas of onus of match and direction of fit which, following Michael Woods (*op. cit.*, in footnote 1) and David Shwayder (cf. 'Man and Mechanism', *Australasian Journal of Philosophy* 1963, p. 9), I have adapted from J. L. Austin ('How to Talk: Some Simple Ways', *P.A.S.* 1952–53) and allowed to influence the exposition I have given of certain thoughts that now have fresh currency in philosophy about substantives and kinds. I have traced these back to Leibniz. But it should be remarked that the germ of all this may be found in Aristotle's account at *Posterior Analytics* 93a21 (cf. Robert Bolton 'Essentialism and Semantic Theory in Aristotle', *Philosophical Review* Oct. 1976) of how we may effect a preliminary determination of a phenomenon and then, having picked it out, gradually refine our description of its nature. And equal or comparable credit is due perhaps to Locke if he is correctly interpreted. See, generally, on these matters Martha Brandt Bolton, 'Substance, Substrate and Names of Substances in Locke's *Essay*', *Philosophical Review* Oct. 1976; J. L. Mackie, 'Locke's Anticipation of Kripke', *Analysis* June 1974; and Douglas Lewis, 'The Existence of Substances and Locke's Way of Ideas', *Theoria* 1969.

included literature on subordinate themes, might have cast gloom on the serious minded who would wish philosophy to remain accessible and intelligible to itself as a single and unbroken strand in the more and more inextricable fabric of human knowledge.

Only [species and genera, among predicables,] reveal the primary substances [e.g. Socrates]. For if one is to say of the individual man *what he is,* it will be in place to give the species or the genus (though more informative to give man than animal); but to give any other thing would be out of place—for example to say 'white' or 'runs' or anything like that. (Aristotle, *Categories* 2^{b30-7}, as translated by J. L. Ackrill, Clarendon Press, 1963, but with italics and square bracket additions.)

[*Man* or *animal*] does not signify simply a certain qualification, as *white* does. *White* signifies nothing but a qualification, whereas species and genus mark off the kind of substance—they signify what sort of substance. (Aristotle, *Categories* 3^{b17-21}, translation and paraphrase based on J. L. Ackrill, *op. cit., vide* p. 88.)

CHAPTER ONE

The Absoluteness of Sameness

1. *A central problem of identity; and the theses of absoluteness and relativity of identity*

If somebody claims of something named or unnamed that it moves, or runs or is white, he is liable to be asked the question by which Aristotle sought to define the category of substance: *What is it* that moves (or runs or is white . . .)? Perhaps the man who makes the claim that something moves does not need to know the answer to this question, and one may envisage circumstances in which he can know that it moves without knowing what the thing is. Yet it seems certain that, for each compliant of a predicate like 'moves', 'runs' or 'white', there exists a known or unknown named or nameable kind to which the item belongs and by reference to which the 'what is it' question *could* be answered. Everything that exists is a *this such*.

If the man reports that the thing that runs is the same as the thing that is white, then his judgement has no chance of being true unless at least two preconditions are satisfied: (a) there exists some known or unknown answer to the question 'same *what?*'; and (b) this answer affords some principle by which entities of this particular kind—some kind containing things that are such as to run or be white—may be traced through space and time and reidentified as one and the same.

These two requirements will represent one part of what will be called **D**, or the Thesis of the Sortal Dependency of Individuation. But in some readers these and all other neo-Aristotelian formulations will instantly arouse grave misgivings. In due course, and by simply following out the implications of the classical conception of identity, such suspicions will be allayed. That is the work of later chapters. But, at the beginning of the search for a theory of individuation, it will be better to focus first on a non-Aristotelian and much more general question, which requires nothing more of the reader than that he should understand English sentences that employ familiar locutions like 'the same horse', 'the same donkey', 'the same tree'. The universally accessible un-Aristotelian question is whether *a* can be the same f as b without being the same g as b. (Better and more precisely, the question is whether a can be the same f as b, and not the same g as b, even where a or b is itself a g.)

This is the topic of Chapter One. My own answer to the question is negative. But the absoluteness I ascribe to identity will in the end carry many consequences, at least some of which have the interest of being unexpected, e.g. the consequence that a single portion of space may be co-occupied at a time by distinct entities (provided that they belong to different kinds). Indeed I can conceive that some of these consequences are strange enough to prompt one who agrees too quickly with the absolute view to re-examine carefully all the virtues of the affirmative or relative answer to our question.

The thesis of the *Relativity of Identity*, which I shall denominate **R** and shall steadfastly oppose, may be held in several distinct forms.[1] It will convey the general spirit of at least one relative position, however, to rehearse a few of the different and equally correct sortal answers that may be given to the question 'What was the thing that ran?' Suppose the answers are *man, soldier, greybeard, Greek, philosopher, official of the state, the chairman (epistates) for day d, 406 B.C., the subject of a certain portrait bust in the Vatican Museum, stonemason, victim of the wit of Aristophanes, the person who owned the only human body that was to be discovered at place p at time t in the agora of ancient Athens.* Then an **R**-theorist may suggest that it makes all the difference to the project of tracing continuants through space and time which of the concepts in such a list one subsumes something under. For a particular a may coincide with some specified material particular b when individuated under some of these concepts and not coincide with b, but be distinct from it, when individuated under others. From this the defender of **R** concludes that the notion of

---

1. The label is suggested by W. V. Quine's review (*Philosophical Review* LXXII, Jan. 1964, p. 102) of P. T. Geach *Reference and Generality* (Cornell, 1962), and Quine's characterization of the doctrine given at page 157, where Geach says: 'I could not object in principle to different As' being one and the same B ... as different official personages may be one and the same man.' Cf. also Geach's later articles at *Review of Metaphysics*, vol. 21, no. 1, 1967, and vol. 22, no. 3, 1969. Also 'Ontological Relativity and Relative Identity' in Milton K. Munitz ed., *Logic and Ontology*, New York University Press, 1973.

Among those who have followed Geach in one way or another are Eddy M. Zemach 'In Defence of Relative Identity', *Philosophical Studies* 26, 1974, pp. 207–218; D. Odegard, 'Identity through Time', *American Philosophical Quarterly* 9, 1972, pp. 29–38; Nicholas Griffin, *Relative Identity*, Oxford, 1977; Harold Noonan, *Objects and Identity*, Cambridge Ph.D. thesis, 1977 (see the extracts published in *Mind* LXXXV, 1976, 'Wiggins on Identity' and LXXXVII, 1978, 'Sortal Concepts and Identity'); and Tobias Chapman, 'Identity and Reference', *Mind* LXXXII, 1973.

identity is concept- or sortal-relative, i.e. relative to different possible answers to the question '*a* is the same what as *b*?'.

D and **R**, the theses of Sortal Dependency and Relativity of Identity, may seem to be made for one another. For this reason they have sometimes been confused or assimilated; and sometimes, because **R** appears to entail **D**, **R** has been taken to be the one good reason for maintaining **D**.[2] Occasionally philosophers have gone so far as to argue from the falsity of **R** to the falsity of **D**, but this is a formally fallacious procedure.

R and **D** are utterly distinct. The falsity of **R** is argued in the present chapter, on the justified basis of the principle commonly known as Leibniz's Law, which says that if *a* is *b* then whatever may be true of *a* is true of *b*. It will be argued that both '*a* is *b*' and '*a* is the same f as *b*' are exceptionlessly subject to the Leibnizian principle. In Chapter Two, with **R** put out of the way, **D** itself will be amplified and corrected. **D** will then be applied to the task of finding a schematic or formal characterization of the notions of substance and sortal concept. Chapter Three will relate the abstract requirements upon sortal concepts to the sortal concepts that we actually possess.[3]

In addition to **R** and **D** there will be occasion to mention a thesis

2. Some may have held that the reverse dependence exists between Relativity of Identity and Sortal Dependency, others that they are equivalent doctrines. But the supposition that **D** depends for its rationale on its being possible for *a* to be the same f and not the same g as *b* was certainly made by Professors Geach and Quine in their original controversy about these matters. Professor Geach insisted on the universal legitimacy of pressing the *same what?* demand (see *Reference and Generality* §§ 31–4, and Chapter Six); and one of his arguments for it rested on the doctrine that it was logically possible for *a* to be the same f as *b* without being the same g as *b*. Professor Quine in his review rejected out of hand the possibility of *a*'s being the same f as *b* without being the same g as *b*. But it was apparently on the strength of that rejection that he strongly questioned the legitimacy of Geach's *same what?* demand and what he took to be Geach's proposals for the treatment of quantified sentences. The one and only point on which Geach and Quine seem to have been agreed is that the possibility of *a*'s being the same f but not the same g as *b* is what provides the principal rationale of **D**. This is a point on which I am to disagree with them both.

3. For other support of **D**, or for related theses, see e.g. A. Prior, *Analysis*, vol. 17, June 1957; S. Hampshire, 'Identification and Existence' in H. D. Lewis, ed., *Contemporary British Philosophy*, 3rd series, London, 1957; D. Wiggins, 'Individuation of Things and Places', *P.A.S. Supp.* XXXVIII, 1963, printed in its correct form in M. Loux, ed., *Universals and Particulars*, New York, Doubleday, 1969.

Thesis **D**, as will again be emphasized in Chapter Two, carries no commitment either to some semantical incompleteness in plain '*a* is *b*' (this is a claim made nowhere in this book or in *Identity and Spatio-Temporal Continuity*), or to the possibility of discrepant answers to the question of what *a* and *b* are. Note also that to believe in the existence of a three-place relation '*x* is the same f as *y*', the relation manifestly presupposed to the *same what* question, to the project of appraising doctrine **R**, and to the English idiom 'Cicero is the same man as Tully' that is symbolized in this book as '$x \overline{\overline{f}} y$', is not in itself that I shall call the Counting thesis, or **C**. It says that to specify the something or other under which *a* and *b* coincide is to specify a concept f which qualifies as adequate for this purpose *only* if it yields a principle of counting for fs. **C** is no more to be confused with **D** than **R** is. I shall submit that **C** is false, though a near miss. (See Chapter Two, section 8.)

The realistic discussion of the thesis of the Relativity of Identity requires not only formal argument, as in the ensuing section, but also the detailed and in some cases lengthy and difficult analysis of examples.

2. *Leibniz's Law and the difficulties of relative identity*

The fact that there are many different sortal concepts under which one may single out some individual *a* does not in itself imply that there is any possibility of getting different answers to the question whether *a* coincides with some mentioned individual *b* in the way relevant for *a*. For all the alternative procedures of individuation under alternative covering concepts might, when they yielded *any* answer, yield the same answer to that question.[4] My contention is precisely that they must do so. The reflexivity and congruence of identity provide logically compelling reasons why, if *a* is *b*, or if *a* is the same something or other as *b* (same horse, same tree, same planet, or whatever), then all different procedures of individuating *a* (provided they really do individuate *a*) must, if they yield any answer at all, yield the same answer with respect to *a*'s coincidence with *b*. This is to say in the timeless idiom

$$((\exists f)(a \overline{\underset{f}{=}} b)) \supset ((g)(g(a) \supset a \overline{\underset{g}{=}} b));$$

and that is to say **R** is false.

---

to believe, what is false, that '*a* = *b*' or '*a* is *b*' is an *incomplete assertion*. It is no more incomplete than $(\exists f)(a \overline{\underset{f}{=}} b)$, which is logically equivalent on my view to '*a* = *b*', is incomplete. It is no more incomplete than '*a* met *someone* here yesterday' is incomplete. Still less is it flawed in any way.

4. I shall call an individuative or sortal concept that adequately answers the question 'same *what*?' for an identity-statement *s*, a covering concept for *s*, and reserve the letters f and g to represent such sortal concepts. In the case of an identity '*a* = *b*' supplemented, as any fair discussion of **R** will evidently require, with covering-concept f, I shall write '*a* $\overline{\underset{f}{=}}$ *b*'. Instantiations of the ordinary predicate letters $\phi, \psi \ldots$ will embrace both sortal predicates and non-sortal predicates. On the interpretation of 'f' and 'g', see also *Preamble*, section 4.

To show this in detail will require the extension to '$\overline{\underset{f}{=}}$' of the formal properties that logicians associate with '$=$'. First, the strong reflexivity of *same* (dyadic identity)

$$(x)(x = x),$$

has as its *same* f counterpart the weak reflexivity property

$$(x)(fx \supset (x \overset{=}{\underset{f}{}} x)).$$

The congruence of sameness, affirmed by a principle usually known as Leibniz's Law or the Indiscernibility of Identicals, viz.

$$(x)(y)((x = y) \supset (\phi x \equiv \phi y)).[5]$$

has as its *same* f counterpart a property which may be stated in any or all of the following schemata:

$$(x)(y)(x \overset{=}{\underset{f}{}} y) \supset (\phi x \equiv \phi y))$$

$$(x)(y)((\exists f)(x \overset{=}{\underset{f}{}} y) \supset (\phi x \equiv \phi y))$$

$$(x)(y)(f)((x \overset{=}{\underset{f}{}} y) \supset (\phi x \equiv \phi y)).$$

The direct way of demonstrating the incompatibility of these two properties of identity with **R**, which says that for some a, b, f and g

$$(a \overset{=}{\underset{f}{}} b) \ \& \ (a \overset{\neq}{\underset{g}{}} b) \ \& \ (g(a)),$$

is to take the ϕ in the schema[6]

(1) $(a \overset{=}{\underset{f}{}} b) \supset (\phi a \equiv \phi b)$

as including among its substituends the predicable '$a \overset{=}{\underset{g}{}} x$'.

5. Given reflexivity, this schema is derivable from $(x) (y) (x = y \supset (\phi x \supset \phi y))$. See W. V. Quine, *Set Theory and Its Logic* (Belknap, Cambridge Mass. 1964) pp. 12–3.

6. See *Identity and Spatio-Temporal Continuity*, pp. 3–4. For similar derivations see John Perry 'The Same F'. *Philosophical Review* LXXX, 1970, p. 186; Leslie Stevenson, 'Relative Identity and Leibniz's Law', *Philosophical Quarterly*, April 1972, p. 155. Stevenson has worked out a formalized framework in which this and other claims can be evaluated in 'A Formal Theory of Sortal Quantification', *Notre Dame Journal of Formal Logic*, vol. XVI, no. 2, April 1975.

Then the premiss

(2) $(a\overset{=}{_f}b)$ & $(g(a))$

can quickly be made to contradict the supposition that $(a\overset{\neq}{_g}b)$. For (2)
yields

(3) $(a\overset{=}{_f}b)$.

Taking (1) with the predicable '$a\overset{=}{_g}x$', we get

(4) $(a\overset{=}{_f}b) \supset ((a\overset{=}{_g}a) \equiv (a\overset{=}{_g}b))$.

But then, by *modus ponens* and (3), we can detach the consequent of
(4) to get

(5) $(a\overset{=}{_g}a) \equiv (a\overset{=}{_g}b)$.

But by the reflexivity of '$\overset{=}{_g}$'

(6) $(g(a)) \supset (a\overset{=}{_g}a)$.

And so by the second limb of (2)

(7) $(a\overset{=}{_g}a)$.

Hence, by *modus ponens* with (7) and (5),

(8) $(a\overset{=}{_g}b)$.

But this shows that with $(a\overset{=}{_f}b)$ & $g(a)$ we can disprove $(a\overset{\neq}{_g}b)$.

Provided we have Leibniz's Law then, and provided that 'is the
same f as' is as Leibnizian as ' = ', we can disprove any purported
instance of **R**.[7] The only question is by what right we suppose that we
have either of these things.

7. Indeed, together with reflexivity, Leibniz's Law entails all the other properties. See
Quine, *Set Theory and Its Logic*, loc. cit. (n. 5 above). Nevertheless, for reasons that
Quine gives (ibidem, pp. 13–5, compare *From A Logical Point of View* Harvard, 1953,
pp. 70f., 117f.) and Geach has elaborated and kindly taken the trouble to impress upon
me, neither a relation R's satisfying the schema $(xRy) \supset (\phi x \equiv \phi y)$ nor its satisfying the
schema $\phi y \equiv (\exists x) (xRy \& \phi x)$ completely ties that relation down within a first order
formal system to what we normally intend by identity. This does not weaken the claim
that we need *at least* Leibniz's Law to mark off and elucidate what is peculiar to
identity. We do. Cf. Frege's remark in his review of Husserl, page 80 in Geach and
Black's *Translations from the Philosophical Writings of Gottlob Frege* (Oxford, Blackwell, 1952): 'I agree . . . that Leibniz's explanation *eadem sunt quorum unum potest*

(i) The principle marks off what is peculiar to identity and differentiates it in a way in which transitivity, symmetry and reflexivity (all shared by *exact similarity, equality in pay,* etc.) do not.

(ii) How if *a* is *b* could there be something true of *the object a* which was untrue of *the object b*? After all, *they are the same object.* The counter-examples to Leibniz's Law are scarcely more impressive than the counter-examples to the Law of Non-Contradiction. There is really something rather extraordinary here in speaking of *counter-examples* at all. Concerning modal and intensional contexts it is still enough, I think, to cite Frege's arguments.[8] His arguments show, and (this is not always understood) they show *quite independently of this*

---

substitui alteri salva veritate does not deserve to be called a definition; my reasons, however, are different from Husserl's. Since any definition is an identity, identity itself cannot be defined. This explanation of Leibniz's could be called an axiom that brings out the nature of the relation of identity; as such it is fundamentally important.' We may fault Frege's doctrine of definition here, and we ought to note that the *eadem sunt* principle says more than the principle that I have called Leibniz's Law. But when construed as a contention about Leibniz's Law, Frege's contention seems compelling. (See also *Grundgesetze der Arithmetik*, Jena 1903, II Band, 245.)

The Indiscernibility of Identical was familiar to Aristotle (see *De Sophisticis Elenchis* 179a37). But I follow custom in calling it Leibniz's Law. It is not to be confused with the distinctively Leibnizian (and non-schematic) converse, the Identity of Indiscernibles (which I discuss in section 2 of the next Chapter). Leibniz's *eadem sunt* principle presumably entails both Leibniz's Law *and* the Identity of Indiscernibles.

It may be asked what protects the schematic Leibniz's Law from illegitimate replacements for 'ϕ'. I follow Quine in holding that intensional replacements are excluded by 'the incoherence of bound variables in any but referential position' (see *Journal of Philosophy*, LXIV, 1972, p. 490). Quine writes 'This version of the principle of identity is a little broader than the version in terms of properties, since the open sentence represented by 'ϕx' can sometimes exceed the range of properties, for reasons unrelated to substitutivity and related rather to Russell's paradox'. By 'the version in terms of properties', Quine means the non-schematic second level principle that if x is y then every property of x is a property of y, which is defended in the 1971 article of Cartwright cited at note 8 below and frequently invoked in this book.

Quine's characterization of the substitutivity schema suffices in my opinion to answer questions about paradox that Geach has seen as counting against the congruence conception of identity. (See *Review of Metaphysics*, articles cited at n. 1.) But it would be a pity if this advantage of the schema led to an undervaluation of the properties formulation. Even though Russell's paradox will qualify all attempts to define 'property' in such a way that the reach of some second level principle matches that of the substitutivity schema, propertihood is certainly sufficient for Leibnizian purposes. And this can motivate us to search for an autonomous or metaphysical reason for regarding a certain expression as determining a genuine property, and as such a respect of indiscernibility.

8. In 'On Sense and Reference' reprinted in Geach and Black's *Translations*. Frege's defence of Leibniz's Law has now been fortified in a way independent of his theory of direct and indirect sense and real and apparent reference by Richard Cartwright in Milton K. Munitz, ed., *Idéntity and Individuation,* New York University Press, 1971, p. 119.

issue, that in many intentional contexts the real and apparent references of expressions both do not coincide, and need not have been expected to coincide.

(iii) If Leibniz's Law is dropped, or if classical identity is dropped in favour of some allegedly un-Leibnizian relative identity, then we need some formal principle or other, and one of at least comparable universality, to justify the valid instances of the intersubstitution of identicals. The instability, indeterminacy or arbitrariness of all extant emendations or relativizations of Leibniz's Law constitutes an important part of the case for a pure congruence principle such as Leibniz's.

(iv) Suppose there were terms t_1 and t_2 both designating z, and suppose there were a context $\phi(\ \ )$ such that the result of supplying t_1 to it was true and the result of supplying t_2 to it was false. What should we say if it were suggested that the open sentence $\phi(x)$ determined a property Q? Following Richard Cartwright, we should ask: How can z both have and lack the property Q? The question is unanswerable. If t_1 and t_2 both designate z, then the bearer of each, that is the entity z, simply cannot both have and lack Q. It is on pain of contradiction that we shall deny that every property of the bearer of t_1 is a property of the bearer of t_2, and on pain of the same contradiction that we shall withhold special treatment (Frege's or that of some modern replacement for his theory) from the contexts $\phi(\ \ )$ and *not* $\phi(\ \ )$. The **R**-theorist should take note that this argument can be stated, as it is stated here, without showing any special favour between '$=$' and '$\overset{=}{f}$'. It supports Leibniz's Law for both of these relations. To counter it, the **R**-theorist will have to uncover much more complexity than appears to be present in the innocuous locution 't_1 designates z and t_2 designates z'.

These four points do not constitute a proof that there is no coherent or non-self-contradictory position to be occupied by someone who distinguishes Leibnizian identity from relative identity, makes us a present of the former, but refuses to affirm the Indiscernibility of Relative Identicals (refuses to affirm even the congruence of *same* f *as* with respect to the extensional predicates of English). But this position faces two questions.

(a) Why is it impossible (as the discussion of example (λ) in section 7 below will suggest) to discover any stable or reasonable recipe for the modification of the Indiscernibility of ('$=$') Identicals that will serve as the principle of f-Indiscernibility of f-Identicals?[9]

9. See *Longer Note* 1.09.

(b) What reason is there, in view of the absence of any such principle for *same f as*, to suppose that relative identity is central to the individuation of particulars? Surely the corresponding ontology would have to be an ontology of relative existents. But this is not our ontology. (See Chapter Two, footnote 13.)

Without the backing of some however restrictive principle of congruence, *is the same f as* could not, I think, be as central to the problem of individuation as it seems to be (or as central as Chapter Two will argue that it must be). The final test of a theory of relative identity is not its internal coherence, but how it subserves a total theory of the individuation and existence of particulars. That is the *locus*, I should claim, of the final decision between the absolute theory of *same* and *same f* advanced in this book and a relative theory.

3. *Five ways for it to be false that* $a\stackrel{=}{_g}b$

The previous section showed why we should not expect to find any true sentences that entail the relativity of sameness. Given that we shall nevertheless have to examine some purported examples of $(a\stackrel{=}{_f}b)$ & $(a\stackrel{\neq}{_g}b)$ & $(g(a) \vee g(b))$ it will be as well to provide a routine analysis of all the ways in which it is possible for *not* $(a\stackrel{=}{_g}b)$ to hold. There are five types of case, though only three of these will provide anything approximating to interesting ways for **R** to appear to be exemplified.

(1) g may simply be the *wrong* covering concept for both *a* and *b* where nevertheless $a = b$. The evening star is the *same planet* but not the *same star* as the morning star. For Venus is not a star. This is not a case of

$$((a\stackrel{=}{_f}b) \, \& \, (a\stackrel{\neq}{_g}b)) \, \& \, (g(a) \vee g(b)).$$

(2) Venus is not *the same star* as Mars nor the same anything as Mars. For in this case (f) $(a\stackrel{\neq}{_f}b)$. Again this is irrelevant, because we do not have what is needed for the relativization thesis.

(3) We may seem to get nearer to what is required with the case where John Doe, the boy whom they thought a dunce at school, is the *same human being* as Sir John Doe, the Lord Mayor of London, but not the *same boy* (for the Lord Mayor is not a boy) nor the *same mayor* or *ex-cabinet minister* or *father of five marriageable daughters*. (For the boy did not attain office or beget children when a boy.) Yet surely, it may be said, *boy, dunce, mayor, ex-cabinet minister, father of five marriageable daughters*, are all sortal words and all make per-

fectly good covering concepts. One can count and identify such things, and so on. So this gives the appearance of a case where we have

$$(a\overset{=}{_f}b) \ \& \ (a\overset{\neq}{_g}b) \ \& \ (ga \lor gb) \ \& \ (-gb),$$

a case that is where a cuts out, as it were, under a sortal-concept g (e.g. *boy*) but can persist under another sortal-concept f (e.g. *human being*).

I submit that this case is not what the relativist is looking for. All it in fact shows is, first, the necessity for care about tenses, both in the interpretation of the formula $(a\overset{\neq}{_g}b)$ or $(a\overset{=}{_g}b)$ and in the interpretation of Leibniz's Law; and, second, the possibility of an interesting and highly important distinction within the class of sortal predicates.

If John Doe is still a boy then John Doe, the boy, *will* one day be a cabinet-minister and later the Lord Mayor of London, and he *will* beget five children. If John Doe is no longer a boy, then John Doe the boy (or Sir John Doe, when he was a boy) *was going to be* and *was going to do* these things. We only thought we had a case of **R** because we confused the timeless and the tensed way of speaking within one utterance. If 'g(Sir John Doe)' be a tensed statement, it should be read as saying that Sir John *was* a boy and it is true. If it is a tenseless statement, then it says of Sir John Doe that he is, was or will be a boy, or that at some time or other he timelessly is a boy. This again is true. If we take tenses seriously, it is impossible to say 'Sir John Doe *is* the same boy as John Doe', since it is false that Sir John Doe is now a boy. But it is true and perfectly unproblematic that Sir John Doe *was* the same boy as John Doe (was). It is precisely for this reason that Sir John Doe is not now identified or singled out under the temporally restricted sortal *boy*. From all this it follows that '$-(a\overset{=}{_g}b)$', properly read, is not true. We still do not have what the relativist was looking for.

The second matter that type-(3) cases bring to our attention is this. They underline the need to distinguish between sortal concepts that present-tensedly apply to an individual x at every moment throughout x's existence, e.g. *human being,* and those that do not, e.g. *boy,* or *cabinet minister*. It is the former (let us label them, without prejudice, *substance-concepts*) that give the privileged and (unless context makes it otherwise) the most fundamental kind of answer to the question 'what is x?'. It is the latter (one might call them *phased-sortals*) which, if we are not careful about tenses, give a false impression that a can be the same f as b but not the same g as b. In fact they do not conflict at all with what is to be proved: that for all x and all y, every concept that adequately individuates x for any stretch of its existence yields the same answer, either directly or via the principle of individuation for the predicate it restricts, as every other genuinely individuating concept for x or y to the question whether x coincides with y or not.

The first appearance of the phased-sortal is very likely the best moment to inveigh against a misunderstanding of identity which has culminated in attempts to show that the only true identity is the 'identity at a time' of one and the same phase or thing-moment of a thing, 'identity through time' being held by those in the grip of this conception to connote some different relation that holds between the different phases or thing-moments out of which individual continuants are supposed to be combined or concatenated.[10]

Whatever the merits of this idea as a programme for linguistic reform (and it is dubious that those drawn to it have always appreciated the scale of the reorganization that they are envisaging), there is no serious prospect that this view of the identity relation can do justice to any of the actual questions of continuity and persistence that perplex our habitual modes of thought about identity and difference. What these questions need is not replacement by other questions given in terms of phases of things or thing-moments, or in an alien four-dimensional mode.[11] What they want from philosophy is answers given in language that speaks as simply and directly as natural languages speak of proper three-dimensional continuants—things with spatial parts and no temporal parts, which are conceptualized in our experience as occupying space but not time, and as persisting whole *through* time.[12] Unlike sets

---

10. Cf. Hume, *Treatise of Human Nature,* bk 1, § 6: 'We have a distinct idea of an object that remains invariable and uninterrupted through a supposed variation of time; and this idea we call that of identity or sameness. We have also a distinct idea of several different objects existing in succession, and connected together by a close relation; and this to an accurate view affords as perfect a notion of diversity as if there were no manner of relation among the objects.' See also *Longer Note* 1.10.

11. See *Longer Note* 1.11. Against a related but distinct proposal, see Chapter Two footnote 16.

12. It is well worth remarking that by a transposition we arrive here at the everyday conception of event. An event takes time, and will admit the question 'How long did it last?' only in the sense 'How long did it take?'. An event does not persist in the way a continuant does—that is *through* time, gaining and losing new parts. A continuant has spatial parts, and to find the whole continuant you have only to explore its boundary at a time. An event has temporal parts, and to find the whole event you must trace it through its historical beginning to its historical end. An event does not have spatial parts in any way that is to be compared with (or understood by reference to) its relation to its *temporal* parts.

At least in the light of this conception of the differences of events and continuants, there appears to be a terrible absurdity in such claims as 'a material object is just a long event'. *Vide* Goodman (*op. cit.,* in footnote 22) and C. D. Broad in *Scientific Thought* (p. 54):

We usually call a flash of lightning or a motor accident an event, and refuse to apply this name to the history of the cliffs of Dover. Now the only relevant

or aggregates of anything, continuants can gain and lose proper parts. The terms of the identity questions we are concerned with in this book stand for these continuants themselves, John Doe, say, not for phase-thick laminations of their four dimensional counterparts, John Doe-when-a-boy, or for infinitesimally thin time-slices of these held fast between perceptual impressions, John Doe-there-then. And, by the same token, the phased sortals like 'boy' or 'old man' that we encounter in English never denote either 'phases' of entities or (if that were different) the entities themselves frozen at an instant. They denote the changeable changing continuants themselves, the things that are *in* these phases. No faithful elucidation of identity judgements will tamper with this.

Experience proves that at this point there is a choice between tedious repetition and scarcely prevailing against a deep seated tendency of the human mind towards confusion.[13] In the equivalence *x is a boy at t ≡ x is a male human being who has not at t reached maturity*, we have the substance term 'human being', and two qualifications of it which determine proper *subsets* of the class of human beings. I have followed Geach in calling these qualifications 'restrictions' of the concept *human being*. It follows that, unlike

---

difference between the flash and the cliffs is that the former lasts for a short time and the latter for a long time. And the only relevant difference between the accident and the cliffs is that if successive slices, each of one second long, be cut in the histories of both, the contents of a pair of adjacent slices may be very different in the first case and will be very similar in the second case. Such merely quantitative differences as these give no good ground for calling one bit of history an event and refusing to call another bit of history by the same name.

This will not do. *Material object* and *event* are in some sense *duals*. It has recently come to seem more and more important in philosophy to understand the notion of an event (cf. Donald Davidson, 'Causal Relations', *Journal of Philosophy* LXIV, 1967). A fair start can be made on these questions if we take note of all the hints of analogy and disanalogy we get from the unreformed language of things and events.

13. It is a profound and important question what underlies this *nisus* towards disorder. That it is not provincial to any particular language or culture is attested by the confusion, misrepresentation and misquotation to which Cratylus and others subjected the gnomically simple insights of Heraclitus, a thinker as innocent of the confusion of 'numerical' and 'qualitative' sameness as he was of any desire to equate *opposition* and *contradiction*. Robert Coburn has given an able account of some of the sources of confusion. (See 'The Persistence of Bodies', *American Philosophical Quarterly* vol. 13, 1976.) For another source, scrutinize the quotation from Hume at footnote 10. The capacity to make inner images is as difficult to control as it is indispensable in most human thinking. Perhaps it will even explain the folly Russell describes in 'The Philosophy of Logical Atomism' (*Logic and Knowledge*, p. 247) when he writes:

Identity is a rather puzzling thing at first sight. When you say 'Scott is the author of *Waverley*', you are half-tempted to think there are two people, one of whom is Scott and the other the author of *Waverley*, and they happen to be the same. That is obviously absurd, but that is the sort of way one is always tempted to deal with identity.

'boyhood', 'boy' cannot denote any phase of a human being. Nor can it stand for a stage of one. No human being is any stage of a human being, or an 18-year-old cross-section of a larger 70-year-long space-time worm. Suppose some boy grows up and lives seventy years. If that is how it is, then there is only one answer to the question 'How long did that boy persist in being?'— namely seventy years. He lived seventy years. He did not live seventy years as a boy, but when he grew up that was not the passing away of anything, not even of a boy.

Phased predicates are a special sort of restriction of substance predicates. If there were need, further refinements could be introduced at this point, e.g. between predicates like 'infant', 'adult', 'pupa', 'tadpole', which every member of the extension of the substance term that they restrict *must* in due course satisfy if only it lives so long, and predicates like 'conscript', 'alcoholic', 'captive', 'fugitive', 'fisherman', of which this does not hold. This distinction, like certain others that are there to be made, is not without interest. But we shall not need these refinements to dispose of type-(3) cases represented as cases of **R**.

The point we have now reached is the fourth and fifth types of would-be **R** specimen. Here at last we shall find cases with a real semblance of plausibility.

(4) is the variant where, in the timeless idiom,

$$(a \overset{=}{_f} b) \& (a \overset{\neq}{_g} b) \& (g(a) \text{ v } g(b)) \& (g(a) \& -g(b)).$$

(5) is the type of case where, allegedly,

$$(a \overset{=}{_f} b) \& (a \overset{\neq}{_g} b) \& (g(a) \text{ v } g(b)) \& (g(a) \& g(b)).$$

We need some examples which might be said by an **R**-theorist to be examples of type (4), and then some for type (5).

4. *Possible examples of type-*(4) *relativity*

(α) I might say to someone 'that heap of fragments there is the jug you saw the last time you came to this house'. They could not be *the same jug* but they might be *the same collection of material bits*.

(β) The visitor might be a person of tiresome ingenuity and cement the pieces of the jug together to make not a jug but, say, a coffee pot of a quite different shape from the original jug's. It might then be said that 'the jug is the coffee pot' is true with covering-concept *same collection of material bits* and false with covering-concept *same utensil*.

(γ) Perhaps the best and least strained example of type (4) is one of a kind which a champion of the relativization thesis that is given in P. T. Geach's *Reference and Generality* might describe in the following way:

'Linsky asked in his review of *Reference and Generality*[14] why "Cleopatra's Needle" could not correspond in use to "the same landmark" rather than to "the same (lump of) stone". And of course it could. For all one knows, "Cleopatra's Needle" in some people's use does work this way. In that case, if the stone obelisk brought from Alexandria to London in 1877–78 is eroded by the atmosphere, and is continuously repaired with concrete, so that in the end none of the original stone is left, then we shall have to say , "The same landmark, namely Cleopatra's Needle, was stone and is concrete." But now, whereas it would be true that Cleopatra's Needle in 1984 is the same *landmark* as Cleopatra's Needle in 1900, it would be false that Cleopatra's Needle in 1984 is the same *stone* as Cleopatra's Needle in 1900—or, indeed, the same stone as anything. For it wouldn't be a stone in 1984. This gives a case where Cleopatra's Needle is in 1900 both an f and a g, both a stone and a landmark, and goes on being the same f but doesn't go on being the same g.

'To take another case, during the Festival of Britain the stone in Meriden, inscribed to show that it marks the reputed centre of England, was removed from Meriden to London to be put on show. Such a performance is well within the limits of human folly. Well, during transport it will have remained the same stone but not the same landmark; it is questionable if after its return to Meriden it will be that landmark again—indeed old villagers are alleged to say that it is now some yards off its old site.'

These cases, (α) (β) (γ) seem to qualify, if they qualify at all, as cases of type (4), though for one or two of them type-(3) analyses might also be suggested.

5. *Some cases that might be alleged to be of type* (5)

(δ) An argument in Geach's *Reference and Generality*, page 151, might prompt the following suggestion. Whatever is a river is water. Suppose I moor my vessel at the banks of Scamander when that river

14. *Mind* LXXIII, Oct. 1964.

is in full torrent. The next day, the river on which my vessel is now moored is the *same river* as the river on which I moored it yesterday. But even though rivers are water the river is not the *same water*. The water in which I moored it is now part of the Aegean.

(ε) John Doe the boy is the *same human being* as Sir John Doe the Lord Mayor, but not the *same collection of cells* as Sir John Doe.[15]

(ζ) '. . . it may be said, without breach of the propriety of language, that such a church, which was formerly of brick, fell to ruin, and that the parish rebuilt the same church of freestone, and according to modern architecture. Here neither the form nor the materials are the same, nor is there anything in common to the two [*sic*] objects but their relation to the inhabitants of the parish; and yet this alone is sufficient to make us denominate them the same.'[16] So we may say of Hume's church that the present church is the same *church* as the old parish church but not the same *building* or the same *stonework* as the old parish church.

(η) At Paddington Railway Station I point to the Cornish Riviera Express and say: 'That is the same train as the train on which the Directors of the Great Western Railway travelled to Plymouth in 1911.' *Same train,* yes, it may be said, but not *the same collection of coaches and locomotive.*

(θ) A petitioner asks to see the same official as she saw last time. The man she sees is the *same official* but not the *same man*. (Cf. Geach, *op. cit.,* p. 157.)

(ι) The Lord Mayor is *not the same official* as the Managing Director of Gnome Road Engineering Ltd (indeed they often write one another letters) but he is *one and the same man*.

(κ) Dr Jekyll and Mr Hyde were the *same man* but not the *same person* or *personality*. (Cf. Locke, *Essay,* II, XXVIII, 9 and 23.)

(λ) 'There is but one living and true God . . . and in unity of this Godhead there be three Persons of one substance, power, and eternity; the Father, the Son, and the Holy Ghost.' (Article I of the XXXIX Articles.) This is to say that the Father, Son and Holy Ghost are the *same God* but not the *same person*.[17]

---

15. Cf. Hobbes, *De Corpore* ch. 11, § 7: 'It is one thing to ask, concerning Socrates, whether he be the same man and another to ask whether he be the same body; for his body, when he is old, cannot be the same as it was when he was an infant, by reason of the difference of magnitude; yet nevertheless he may be the same man.'

16. Hume, *Treatise* 1.4 (p. 244 in the Everyman edition).

17. A collection of the writings of the Church fathers on this problem is to be found at pp. 33–7, 45ff., 54ff., 58ff. of *Documents of the Christian Church,* selected and edited by Henry Bettenson, Oxford, 1963.

Some of these examples are more convincing than others, but I do not think that any of the examples (α)–(κ) is sufficiently secure to provide an independent argument for the logical possibility of (λ), the most difficult case. I shall argue that all the perspicuous cases repose on ambiguities of reference or logical form, and that none of them shows a way for relations like 'is the same horse as', 'is the same river as' (at least in their normal usage, and in the usage that ties them to questions of identity and existence) to escape from the congruence requirement. Any reader who is prepared to take this on trust, or can quickly satisfy himself of it, should skip now to section 9 of this chapter.

6. *Discussion of type-*(4) *cases*

(α) and (β) hang together. For if the jug is the same collection of bits as the heap of fragments and the heap of fragments is the same collection of bits as the coffee pot, then, by transitivity, the jug must be the same collection of bits as the coffee pot. Either both or neither, then, is a true identity-statement. The difficulty is that if the jug is the same collection of material parts, bits of china clay, as the coffee pot, that is if they are one and the same collection of china-bits, then their life-histories and durations must be the same. But the coffee pot *will* be fabricated or assembled at t_3 by my ingenious friend and exist only from then on. The jug won't then exist any more.

(α) will only be what is required as a case of type (4) if 'that heap is the jug you saw last time' comes to something more than 'the matter you see there is the same matter as the matter of the jug you saw when you came here last time'. Similarly (β) must not simply boil down to the unexceptionable claim that the jug and coffee pot are made of the same matter. Otherwise it is no longer obvious that we have the sort of type-(4) identity-statement the relativist required. To get that, the 'is' in 'is the same collection of china bits' of (α) and $\beta)$ must mean '$=$' and we must take *collection of china-bits* as a straightforward covering-concept. It must not be comparable to the 'is' in 'The soufflé you are eating is simply eggs and milk' or the 'is' of 'The portico is wood and stucco'. I shall call the latter the 'is' of *constitution*, contrast it with the 'is' of identity, and shall attempt to prove that it is precisely this constitutive 'is' that we have in (α) and (β). In which case 'is the same collection' means 'is constituted from the same collection'.

Suppose, with (α), that the jug is straightforwardly the same collection of china-bits as the heap of fragments. Then if this is a type-(4) identity-statement we are entitled to infer that the jug is (predicatively) a collection of china-bits. (If Hesperus is the same planet as Phosphorus then Hesperus is a planet.) But then there must be some collection of china-bits with which the jug is identical. (If you doubt the principle linking identity and predication, that if x is ϕ then there must be some ϕ-thing with which x is identical,[18] then consider the inference: if Hesperus is a planet then there is some planet with which Hesperus is identical.) Suppose there be some such collection. Then, again, we have trouble from the principle that if a and b are identical then they must have the same life history. Suppose I destroy the jug. Do I then destroy the collection? Either I do or I don't. If I do then both (α) and (β) fail of truth with covering concept *collection of china-bits* and fail as type-(4) examples. If I don't thus destroy the collection then it cannot be true of the jug that it *predicatively* is a collection of china-bits. But nevertheless it is *true* that the jug is a collection of china-bits. That is to say that it is china-clay. Therefore it must be true but not straightforwardly *predicatively* true. I suggest that it is true in the sense that the jug is *made of* china-clay or *constituted of* a collection of china-bits.[19] *This* is what is predicatively true of the jug. But this argument requires two supplementary remarks, one remark on the behaviour of 'same' in (α) and (β) with the gloss *same collection*, the other remark on the sense of 'collection'.

The argument for the non-identity of jug and collection does not rely on a special or unfair construal of the term 'collection'. In case that is not clear I had better show it. The possible construals seem to be three in number. 'ϕ (A)' where A is in some sense or other a collection can presumably mean either (i) that class A is ϕ or, (ii) that each of the As is ϕ, or (iii) that a *physical aggregate* A is ϕ.

Sense (i) cannot be what we are really looking for, even though skilful and opportunistic reinterpretations of ϕ might hold a set-theoretical interpretation of the 'A' in 'ϕ(A)' on the rails for an indefinitely long time. In the end the only way in which one could explain breaking or scattering a set-theoretical entity would be parasitic on the way one explained what one had to do to a physical configuration to break or scatter it. At root what we are interested in is a sense of collection or manifold for which there can be no

18. A principle no less true for having prompted false theories of predication, e.g. Antisthenes' identity-theory. Cf. Aristotle, *Metaphysics* 1024^{b32}; Hobbes, *De Corpore* ch. 3, § 2. It implies no such absurdity. The principle is denied by Noonan at *Mind* 1976, p. 572. Cf. also p. 573, where Noonan claims something can *be* a man by constituting that man, *but be not identical with that man*: 'What constitutes a man is not identical with *that* man, but on my account it is identical with something which *is* a man, namely itself.'

19. I am not saying that the possibility of this paraphrase by itself forces us to postulate this distinct sense of 'is'. I am saying that the independent plausibility of this paraphrase, *plus* the plausibility of Leibniz's Law which would otherwise have to be amended or abandoned, *plus* the difficulties of amending Leibniz's Law or finding any f-restricted version of this principle for *same* f that stands in the right connexion to what it is for an f thing to exist, forces us to postulate this distinct sense of 'is'.

For important confirmation of the *Identity and Spatio-Temporal Continuity* hypothesis that this distinct sense of 'is' needs to be postulated see the article by Tyler Burge cited at footnote 12 of Chapter Two.

empty or null collection,[20] and for which it holds that 'if we take the German Army as our manifold and an infantry regiment as a domain within it, it is all one whether we choose to regard as elements within it the battalions, the companies, or the single soldiers'.[21] Notoriously this is not true of sets.

Sense (ii) of collection is not what we are looking for either. If I repair or destroy an item, I do not repair or destroy each part of it. (Since each part of a part is a part this would be difficult.) Nor in any non-Anaxagorean universe do we wish 'Jug (A)' to mean each of the As is a jug.

Sense (iii) suggests the definition of *sum* or *fusion* in Leśniewski's mereology.[22] An individual X would be a Leśniewskian *sum of [all elements* of the class *parts of the] jug* J if all [elements of the class] *parts of* J were parts of X and if no part of X were disjoint from all parts of J.[23] This would certainly seem to be the sort of thing that we are looking for, because by this method (we are told) all collections of parts of the jug, however specified (whether as china-clay bits or as molecules, or as atoms), and all collections of collections of parts of the jug, etc., are intended to define and exhaust one and the same Leśniewskian whole or sum, X, of the jug. If 'collection' is defined in this way, however, and *if* mereology is grafted straight onto that pre-existing scheme of three-dimensional persisting things that we are operating (and anybody who wanted to obtain our type-(4) or type-(5) contrasts would have to be willing to operate), then perhaps the jug turns out *not* to be the same collection, in this sense of 'collection', as the coffee-pot in (α) and (β). For if X=J then among the parts of X is J itself. For everything is part of itself. So if J is broken at t_2 and there is no such jug as J after t_2, then it looks as if X does not survive t_2 either.[24]

In fact the problems that would arise in adding mereology to a logical system already possessed of a concept of identity defined for three-dimensional continuants have hardly been studied at all, because the adherents of mereology have almost always wished to operate a four-dimensional

20. 'If we burn down all the trees of a wood we thereby burn down the wood. Thus [in the concrete sense of class] there can be no empty class.' Frege's review of Schroeder's *Algebra der Logik* in Geach and Black's *Translations,* p. 89.

21. *Ibid.,* p. 87.

22. For a description of mereology (the calculus of individuals) see A. Tarski, 'Foundation of Geometry of Solids' in *Logic Semantics and Metamathematics,* Oxford, 1956, p. 24; or Nelson Goodman's *Structure of Appearance,* Harvard, Cambridge, Mass., 1951, ch. 2. See also J. H. Woodger *The Axiomatic Method in Biology,* Cambridge, 1937, ch. III, § 1, and appendix E (by Tarski), p. 161.

23. The definition of 'Y is disjoint from Z' is 'no individual W is a part both of Y and Z'. The reference to classes in the definition of *sum of elements* is eliminable (as is indicated by the square bracketing). The 'part of' relation is transitive in mereology.

24. It is pointless to try to counter this by redefining the Leśniewskian whole of J without including J as part of J. One cannot destroy the *non-proper* part of J without affecting the *proper* parts of J and doing something just as drastic to them as to J. For to shatter J, or even break it into two, is to shatter the indefinite, even potentially infinite, number of proper parts of it that lie across the break. This may amount to the destruction of these parts. For Mr Risto Pitkänen's objections to this argument (*Mind* 1976) see *Longer Note* 1.24.

scheme which (as I have already complained), reduces everyday continuants to temporal series of slices, or 'thing-moments', of spatio-temporal regions of the space-time continuum,[25] and have usually advocated an implausible semantic distinction between identity or difference *at* a time and identity or difference *through* time. For the former concept of identity, they say that '$x=y$' can be defined mereologically by the condition that x is a part of y and y is a part of x; whereas for spatio-temporal continuity (or what is sometimes called *genidentity*) these definitions have to be supplanted or supplemented by special conditions of a quite different character. What matters here, in a discussion of (α) and (β), is that however these extra conditions be stated, whatever alternatives there may be to Leśniewski's general method of defining 'concrete collection', and however three-dimensional wholes are accommodated, there remains the same fundamental dilemma. Either 'concrete collection' is defined in such a way that concrete collection X has the same principle of individuation as the jug, or it is not so defined. If it is not, then the life-histories principle debars X from identity with the jug and the type-(4) example disappears.[26] But if X does have the same principle of individuation as the jug, then again, for a different reason, we don't have a type-(4) example. For under this option the jug then isn't the same concrete collection as the coffee pot. What is more, the chances are that the whole project of equating thing and matter will then have degenerated into triviality. If X is to be defined so as to be no more and no less tolerant of damage, replacement of parts, etc., than the jug then we shall have to help ourselves to the everyday continuant concept *jug* so as to secure the right configuration and persistence-conditions for X. But this is to ascend from the level of bits of things to the level of something whole, structured, and jug-like, namely a jug. The jug is *constituted of* certain matter and identical only with a certain *whole* or *continuant* at present constituted in a certain way out of that matter. That is to say with the jug. Unless the project is thus trivialized and concrete collection is so defined, the true statement that the jug or the coffee pot *is* X must not be allowed by anybody who accepts the life-histories principle to have the standard consequence of predicative 'is' that it is *identical* with X. The 'is' must mean 'is constituted of', and *collection of parts* will not function standardly as a normal covering concept in either (α) or (β).

25. See Carnap's *Introduction to Symbolic Logic and Its Applications*, New York, Dover edition, 1958, p. 157ff., 198, 213f.
26. Still a doubt may persist. Isn't the life-histories principle too strong? Might not the jug be identical with a stretch of some Leśniewskian whole X for such time as no part of the jug is broken or replaced? But quite apart from the support we have adduced for the strict life-histories principle, this 'temporary identity' is surely a very peculiar sort of identity. We surely cannot give a sense to the supposition that Hesperus might be the same planet as Phosphorus for a bit and then stop being Phosphorus. But then the relation between the jug and the redefined whole X looks as if it cannot be the same sort of relation as that between Hesperus and Phosphorus. The conclusion for which I am arguing is of course just this, that they are related by the one being composed or constituted of the other, not by identity.

Since 'the jug is the heap of fragments' and 'the jug was the same china-clay as the coffee pot' both boil down to identity of *matter*, the supplementary remark about 'the same' that was promised on page 31 is simply this, that 'the same' can do appropriate duty with this constitutive 'is' just as readily as it can do duty with 'is' in the sense of ' = ', where it yields so called numerical identity ('is the *same substance* or *continuant* as'). So much for (α) and (β).

Example (γ) also requires considerable unpacking, but I think its power to convince is quite deceptive. We may begin by asking what is *meant* by 'Cleopatra's Needle'—what it is that someone points to when he points to Cleopatra's Needle. There is here a special difficulty that has to be faced by a consistent defender of the position Geach took up in *Reference and Generality*. To keep (γ) in play at all as a type-(4) example, the defender will have to claim that *landmark* and *stone* give different principles of identity. But by the theory of proper names defended in *Reference and Generality*, the sense of a proper name is given by the principle of identity built into the general term associated with it. It seems to follow that if 'Cleopatra's Needle' had two equally good but different 'nominal essences' then it ought to be ambiguous. In which case (γ) should not surprise or impress us any more than any other startling paradox arrived at by equivocation.

Rather than object in general to this theory of proper names,[27] let us simply examine the different specifications one might give of the meaning of 'Cleopatra's Needle'. What is Cleopatra's Needle? What substance is it? Is it a stone? If a stone is what it (substantially and predicatively) is, then surely when that stone is rotted away completely Cleopatra's Needle is rotted away completely. For they are one and the same stone. Cleopatra's Needle, the stone, is not then the same *anything* as anything which exists in 1984. For if that stone, Cleopatra's Needle, no longer exists in 1984 then it is not the same landmark then as anything in 1984, even though something different may have come to fulfil the same role as it did.

But perhaps the fact the stone has completely rotted away by 1970 does not imply that there is no longer any such thing as Cleopatra's Needle. *Stone* is not then the sense-giving sortal. It may be that *monument* or *monument suitable for use as a landmark* is what Cleopatra's Needle substantially is. And perhaps monuments can be completely refashioned and still persist. But then 'Cleopatra's Needle in 1984 is not the same stone as Cleopatra's Needle in 1900' need only mean that Cleopatra's Needle is not made of the same material as it was in 1900. The dates surely qualify the verb in any case. Cleopatra's Needle is not constituted in 1984 of the same material as Cleopatra's Needle was constituted of in 1900. Once its matter was a (piece of) stone, now its matter is concrete. In that case the words 'the same' are serving in (γ), with the versatility already remarked upon in connexion with (α) and (β), to indicate that you can't say about the *material* of Cleopatra's Needle in 1984 what you could have said in 1900. (A type-(3) analysis may be possible too.)

---

27. Which could be defended against Linsky all the more effectively if my general thesis were correct.

These are not all the possibilities. One might think *landmark* was what gave 'Cleopatra's Needle' its sense. But there is something rather peculiar about treating 'landmark' as an ordinary substance-concept suitable for giving a proper name a sense. It is really more like a title conferred on an object when it secures a certain position of a certain conspicuousness, almost like 'chairman' or 'official' or 'president' or 'sovereign'; in which case, in one use, it is a qualification of a sortal and will presuppose some underlying sortal that says what *sort* of object. This takes us back to the alternatives already mentioned. There does, however, exist the possibility of another use, which one might call a *titular* use, of the phrase 'same landmark'. According to this, for x to be the same landmark as y, x has simply to mark the same spot as y did.[28] But in this use, *something else,* something non-identical with the obelisk and distinct under every genuine covering-concept, can succeed it as the same landmark. It must be this view of 'landmark' that (γ)'s defender exploits in suggesting that the Meriden stone ceases to be the same landmark when it is transported to London. 'Cleopatra's Needle' then turns out not to be an ordinary proper name at all but to be an abbreviation for the description 'whatever suitable object of suitable dignity conspicuously marks such and such a spot on the Embankment in London'.

The effectiveness of this critique of example (γ) does not depend on there being a hard and fast or canonically correct answer to the question 'what is Cleopatra's Needle?'. The example may owe a specious plausibility precisely to the fact that 'Cleopatra's Needle' can sustain an ambiguous poise between these and perhaps yet other incompatible interpretations.

With this the alleged cases of (4) are concluded. It begins to appear why there simply cannot be cases of type (4). Where $(\exists f)(a \overline{=}_f b)$ and allegedly $(\exists g)(a \neq_g b)$ and $g(a) \lor g(b)$, either g is a substantial sortal or it is not. If it is not substantial then it will always need to be proved that we have more than a type-(3) case or a case of constitutive 'is'. If it is a substantial sortal then either a or b has to be a g without the other being a g. But this violates Leibniz's Law.

7. *Discussion of type-(5) cases and some attempted amendments of Leibniz's Law*

The identity-interpretation of (δ) and Leibniz's Law are incompatible. Unlike the water, the river on which I moored my boat yesterday is not a part of the Aegean. Rivers are indeed water but this means that water goes to make them up. 'Same water' is not therefore a covering concept for an identity statement identifying a river with something.

28. If this use exists and extends to 'sovereign' then all that is required for Queen Elizabeth II to be the same sovereign as Queen Elizabeth I is that she should rule the same country. And perhaps 'The same sovereign was a man, is now a woman' need not signify that anybody has changed sex (unless 'anybody' be thought of as adapted to perform precisely the same trick as 'sovereign'). Queen Elizabeth succeeded a man.

(ε) is fairly easily unmasked. If 'collection of cells' will do as covering concept, and if 'is a collection of cells' doesn't merely mean 'is made up of cells', then John Doe must be identical with some definite collection of cells, and this will have to share all properties of John Doe. *What* collection of cells? Suppose we make 'collection of cells' mean 'such and such aggregate' (with fixed constituents). But then one aggregate is succeeded by another. John Doe is not similarly succeeded. One aggregate is dissipated. John Doe isn't. But then 'John Doe is such and such collection of cells' has to have the constitutive interpretation. (Compare (α) and (β).) Suppose we make 'collection of cells' mean 'composite with a succession of constituents through time'. Then we no longer have an example of type (5) at all, i.e. change of truth-grounds by change of covering concept. For in this sense man and boy are the same collection of cells.

(ζ) resembles (γ) in a certain specious exploitation of ambiguities. The example has intrinsic interest, but, because the analysis is intricate and partly predictable, I relegate the discussion to a note.[29]

In (η) the appearance of a type-(5) case relies entirely on the failure to say what is meant by 'Cornish Riviera Express'. Once this is specified, all semblance of support for **R** disappears. Manifestly, to admit the possibility of an express surviving its present coaches and locomotive is to admit its non-identity with these. But then *collection of coaches and locomotive* is a non-starter for straightforward covering concept, and we have a constitutive 'is'. (Alternatively, perhaps we have a titular use of 'same train' or 'same express'.)

(θ) is equally easily exposed. Suppose official *a* is succeeded by official *b*. The petitioner therefore sees *b* on her second visit. She doesn't see the same office-holder but the holder of the same office, *whoever he is*. '*a* is the same official as *b*' doesn't ascribe 'numerical identity' to *a* and *b* at all. It *predicates* something of them in common, holding a certain office. In *the same*'s extensive repertoire this is one of the better known roles. (Cf. *landmark*, and example (γ).)

(ι) also exploits an ambiguity. Under one interpretation it is simply false that the Lord Mayor is not the same official as the Managing Director of Gnome Road Engineering. John Doe, that tireless official, is both Lord Mayor and Managing Director. So the Lord Mayor is the same official as the Managing Director. The interpretation that makes the first part of (ι) true concerns *what it is to be Lord Mayor* and *what it is to be Managing Director of Gnome Road Engineering*. These Frege would have called concepts. And what (ι) then says is that to satisfy the one concept, hold the one office, is not to satisfy the other, hold the other office. To add 'they often write one another letters' is to make a zeugma. For now 'they' must be understood as 'the man who satisfies this concept and the man who satisfies that concept'. And it is in this sense (in which they are the same official) that 'they' are the same man.

(κ) touches on large issues to which we shall return in Chapter Six.

29. See *Longer Note* 1.29.

Certainly neither *human being* nor *homo sapiens* is synonymous with *person*, but this does not prove the point. And the difficulty is this. If, as (κ) says, Mr Hyde and Dr Jekyll are the same man, then, if Mr Hyde visited Tilbury Docks at 9.30 p.m. on 18 December 1887, then Dr Jekyll did so too, and did whatever Mr Hyde did. Now Dr Jekyll the man is a person and he did these things at Tilbury Docks. But then is he not the person who did these things at the docks? How then can he be a different person from Mr Hyde? The only way to make (κ) even come out true is to give it a rather odd and implausible interpretation, and interpret it to mean that to satisfy the concept *person who is ϕ* is not necessarily to satisfy the concept *person who is ψ*. To have these personal characteristics is not necessarily to have those personal characteristics. Contingently, though, to satisfy the one concept was (in R. L. Stevenson's story) to satisfy the other. 'Dr Jekyll' and 'Mr Hyde' have then to be read twice over in (κ) to make it come out true, first as standing each for a man (this individual is the same man as that individual), the second time as standing for a certain kind of character or personality. (These personalities, not these men, are different.) But this ruins the prospects of seeing it as a case of **R**; and the example really represents an implausible attempt to postulate philosophically defined schizophrenia without going the whole way and postulating two men sharing one body, each taking his turn to control it.

This brings me to (λ), and to what is now overdue, a re-examination of Leibniz's Law. I cannot hope to exhaust all the theological implications or examine every possible formulation, but the plain difficulty is that if the Son who was God was crucified and was the same God as the Father then, according to Leibniz's Law unamended, the Father was crucified. I believe this involves one in the heresy of *patripassionism*. What is more, one application of Leibniz's Law is as good as any other. If the Fathers of the Church had allowed the Patripassiani their way, then the three Persons, Father, Son and Holy Ghost, would have been in danger of collapsing into one another. For, in exactly the same way, all the predicates of Christ that applied uniquely to him or applied to him at a time and place will have applied to the Father and Holy Ghost; and one would not need the full dress Identity of Indiscernibles

$$((\phi)\,(\phi(a)\equiv\phi(b)))\supset(a=b),$$

where ϕ is restricted to genuine predicates,[30] but only the obviously true principle that results from lifting all restrictions on the range of ϕ and admitting impure predicates with imbedded proper names, in order to prove heretically that Son, Father and Holy Ghost coincided at a place and time under the concept *person* as well as coinciding, presumably in some other way, under the concept *God*.

The difficulty for the relevant formulations of the doctrines of the Trinity

---

30. See Chapter Two, section 2, for the Identity of Indiscernibles.

and Incarnation, and for all purported cases of type (5), is this. The truth that we shall find in thesis **D** may seem to constitute a philosophical motive for enriching the predicate calculus by the addition of sortal and substantial-sortal variables, and for restating the familiar laws in a restricted form. Transitivity would be restated and restricted as

(f) $(x)(y)(z)((x \stackrel{=}{_f} y \ \& \ y \stackrel{=}{_f} z) \supset (x \stackrel{=}{_f} z))$,

and similarly symmetry and reflexivity. But the whole project turns out to be pointless, and cases of type (5) turn out to be impossible, if the resulting calculus collapses into the unrestricted calculus. Yet this is precisely what happens if Leibniz's Law remains in its familiar form.

For an upholder of (λ) one proper recourse here is to try to break the linkage on which I have relied in this and previous arguments between '$x = y$', conceived as I follow Leibniz in conceiving it,[31] and '$x \stackrel{=}{_f} y$'; and then to weaken or restrict the congruence that is to be expected of the f-relativized (he will say non-Leibnizian) identity of x and y. The question then becomes: What is the connexion between *the same* and *the same f* relations? If there were some access to the sameness of things that was perfectly independent of x and y's being the same *something or other,* and if (contrary to the view put forward in section 6 of Chapter Two) our notion of tensed existence did not need absolute identity, then the connexion of the two relations could be allowed to be fairly remote and obscure, or '$x = y$' could be dispensed with. But in fact both relations are needed, and the **R** theorist has to redescribe the connexion between '$x = y$' and '$x \stackrel{=}{_f} y$' with great care. He must make provision (I hold) for an however circuitous progress from $x \stackrel{=}{_f} y$, and from favourable x, y and f satisfying whatever extra conditions he may lay down, to inter-substitutability. There must be *some* condition under which we have the interdeducibility of y's having a genuine property and x's having that property.

The relativist might begin by replacing my equivalence

† $x = y \equiv (\exists f)(x \stackrel{=}{_f} y)$

by a more demanding condition,

†† $x = y \equiv (\forall f)((fx \lor fy) \supset (x \stackrel{=}{_f} y))$.

The classical and relative theories could then be put together to give the derivative principle

LL.I: $(\forall f)((fx \lor fy) \supset (x \stackrel{=}{_f} y)) \supset (\forall \phi)(\phi x \equiv \phi y)$.

The only difficulty that remains is to find an account of what it takes for a and

31. See the end of section 2, especially (iv).

b to count as f-identical for *every* sortal concept f such that a or b lies within the extension of f. What does this amount to? It seems that the very least we shall require is more information about the case of the *restricted* congruence that results from the g-identity, for *some one* sortal concept g, of x and y. No stable formulation of restricted congruence is available, however. Nor, I suspect, will it ever be given.[33]

There are relativists who will react to this by denying that we need any general principles at all, over and above the requirement that '$x \underset{f}{=} y$' be an equivalence relation. (And why should this not be weakened too, now that relative and classical identity have come adrift?) This need not be the reaction of despair, or tantamount to the disappointing suggestion of a complete divorce between '$x = y$' and '$x \underset{f}{=} y$'. If it is neither of these things though, then it must represent some faith in other expedients.

A method of dispensing with Leibniz's Law for '$x \underset{f}{=} y$' that I once had occasion to explore with the help of Wilfrid Hodges was to make do with this property of '$\underset{f}{=}$',

LL.II: $(a \underset{f}{=} b) \supset (\phi)[(x)(x \underset{f}{=} a \supset \phi x) \equiv (y)(y \underset{f}{=} b \supset \phi y)]$.

The principle is unquestionable on any view. Suppose we know that

(1) Cicero $\underset{\text{man}}{=}$ Tully

and that

(2) ϕ (Cicero) (e.g. Denounced Catiline (Cicero)).

Then by *modus ponens* and universal instantiation it follows that

(3) (x) $(x \underset{\text{man}}{=} \text{Cicero} \supset \phi(x)) \equiv (y)$ $(y \underset{\text{man}}{=} \text{Tully} \supset \phi(y))$.

But to get anything more interesting than (3) we need something that cannot be regarded as guaranteed when unrestricted Leibniz's Law is withdrawn, namely,

(4) (x) $(x \underset{\text{man}}{=} \text{Cicero} \supset x$ denounced Catiline).

In the presence of (4), we can deduce

(5) Tully denounced Catiline.

But where do we obtain (4) from? On what, rather, does the *relativist* take the question of the truth or falsity of (4) to depend? And what, in the absence of

---

33. Griffin has tried to describe this restricted congruence. I believe that his attempt is unsuccessful. See *Longer Note* 1.09.

any congruence principle for '$x \bar{\bar{f}} y$', does he take to ground the truth of propositions that link particulars and attributes in the way in which (4) links *man*, Cicero and *denounced*? Why is there no similar true proposition leading to a similar deduction with the subjects The Father and The Son, the sortal predicate *is God*, and the predicate *was crucified at such and such a time and place*? The answer must be that the connexion that holds between *man*, Cicero, Tully and *denounced* and makes (4) true does not hold between *God*, the Father, The Son, and *crucified at such and such a time and place*. It might be said, as Hodges put it, that *crucified* does not *transfer over* the concept God. But now one wants to ask, why not? There must be some principle of some sort to be found here from which one could gain an idea of what counts as a consideration for or against such claims as (4).

These questions become more immediately important for present purposes—among which I do not here number attempting to refute (λ) under all interpretations, only refuting it as an identity-statement with some independent leverage in the larger logical dispute—if we ask how the predicate *God who was crucified* can fail to transfer over the concept *God*. Yet surely if Christ is God and was crucified then he is God who was crucified. He cannot be a different God who was crucified from the Father.

An obvious way to block the last inference to 'Christ is (the) God who was crucified', and a way that has attracted some thinkers, is to deny that it was *qua God* that Christ had a body or was crucified.[34] But if this escape is used then there is a simpler relativization of Leibniz's Law which promises to provide both the restricted congruence and the adjudication that we have wanted for sentences like (4):

LL.III: $(a \bar{\bar{f}} b) \supset (\phi(a)$ as an f $\equiv \phi(b)$ as an f).

It is not necessary to inquire how, on any view resting on the non-transferability of *crucified* with respect to *God*, it would be possible for Christ the God to be the same anything as Christ the person that was crucified, or to try to devise clever questions about the complex predicate 'was, *qua* God incarnated, *qua* person crucified'. What matters are the general difficulties in making the required sort of sense of *qua* or *as*.

34. This will lead to a division of predicates similar to one which Hodges pointed out to me that Pope Leo made in his *Tome* of 449. 'Deus per id quod omnia per ipsum facta sunt et sine ipso factum est nihil; homo per id quod factus est ex muliere, factus sub lege . . . esurire, sitire, lassescere atque dormire evidenter humanum est.' See also Griffin, *op. cit.*, pp. 140–1, and a passage of Leibniz that I will give away with a packet of tea to anyone who can make room for it in a general theory of *qua* or in a usable non-arbitrary relativization of Leibniz's Law:

Peter and the apostle who denied Christ are the same, and one term can be substituted in place of the other, except when I consider this manner of conceiving itself, which some call reflexive; e.g. when I say Peter, *inasmuch* as he was the apostle who denied Christ, sinned, Peter cannot be substituted. One cannot say that Peter, inasmuch as he was Peter, sinned.

See p. 475 in F. Schmidt, *Gottfried Wilhelm Leibniz: Fragmente zur Logik*, Berlin, 1960.

In considering LL.III we are to suppose that LL.I, LL.II and LL.III are all available, and that Leibnizian identity is reached through relative identity. We are to suppose that LL.III is our only account of how a sortal concept f and a property F must be related if F is to transfer from a to b where $a =_f b$.

Now there are undoubtedly places where *qua* or *as* or similar devices occur essentially, and where an individual has to be characterized (ϕa as an f) and (not-ϕa as a g). But I shall submit that this is a circumscribed and special phenomenon.

(1) It may arise with what have been called *attributive* adjectives such as *big, small, tall, short, real, good, bad*. Thus a ship can be big for a destroyer and small for a cruiser, a man tall for a Japanese but short compared with most Americans, a wooden duck a real decoy duck but not a real duck, a witticism a good joke but not a good thing to say at that particular moment.

(2) There can be reference via *qua* or *as* to a role that a thing or a man plays: As a general he was obliged to be present at the Court Martial, as the best marksman in the regiment not; Sir John Doe sent the letter as Managing Director (i.e. in the course of his duties for Gnome Engineering), not as Lord Mayor.

(3) *Oratio obliqua* and straightforward referential opacity can also take cover under *as* or *qua*: x sent the letter to Sir John Doe as Lord Mayor not as Managing Director (i.e. x *addressed* or *directed* the letter 'The Lord Mayor'); Philip, who does not know that Cicero is Tully, may believe Cicero, as Cicero but not as Tully, (or believe Tully, as Cicero but not as Tully) to have denounced Catiline (i.e. think of him under this name rather than that).

What the present proposal seeks to do, however, is to generalize this phenomenon, without doing anything to show us how to find a '*qua* f' for every ϕ, or how to decide the applicability, meaning and satisfaction conditions of every such composite predicate. At greater length a rather more exhaustive and exact typology of *qua* and its congeners could have been devised, but what is certain is that *qua* is not ubiquitous in its operation to produce these or comparable effects.[35] Not every adjective has an attributive use. Individuals are many things (satisfy many predicates) otherwise than by virtue of playing some role or other. Referential opacity is not to be found absolutely everywhere. Moreover it is certain that *qua* does not always produce a single kind of effect for which a unitary rule of the proposed kind could be laid down. Consider the difference that, with certain precautions, '*qua* f' is detachable *salva veritate* from affirmative 'ϕ *qua* f' in kinds (2) and (3), and not so removable in kind (1). And why, one wonders, should one be

35. I owe reference to an example which falls outside these three kinds to Professors Geach and Anscombe. See Aristotle *Physics* III.3, 202[b]. Consider the road from Athens to Thebes. It is the same road as the road Thebes to Athens. But the road Athens–Thebes is uphill and the road Thebes–Athens is downhill. My objection to allowing this example (*qua* Athens–Thebes uphill, *qua* Thebes–Athens downhill) is that either 'road' means an actual feature of the landscape, in which case 'uphill' collects a term giving the direction, and there is a simple relational predicate true of that road; or else it means 'journey by road', in which case there is no identity.

content with one *qua* f once one has got started? If Jesus Christ could teach the doctors at the age of twelve, then he was by that age good *qua* scholar, that is to say a good scholar. This he was *qua* man. This he was perhaps *qua* person, not *qua* God. . . . How in general do we know when we have enough *quas*? And, when we know that we have, why shouldn't we transfer the whole compound predicate ((φ *qua* f) *qua* g) . . .? It is clear that we can do this. It is difficult to see that there is any rationale for it which is not the rationale for the unrestricted Leibniz's Law.

8. *A mathematical example supposedly of type* (5)

This book is not directly concerned with abstract entities but since the arguments that have been used against examples (α)–(λ) have been formal arguments, they ought, if they are good arguments, to work equally well against purported **R**-examples of a mathematical or logical character.

(μ) Suppose we have a relation R that holds only between *a* and *b* and between *c* and *d*. Then the relation R in extension may be said to be the set $\{\langle a,b \rangle, \langle c,d \rangle\}$, i.e. the set whose members are the ordered pairs $\langle a,b \rangle$ and $\langle c,d \rangle$. Now there are a number of different and equally allowable definitions of an ordered pair. For example, $\langle x,y \rangle$ can be defined either as $\{\{x\}, \{x,y\}\}$ or as $\{\{x\}, \{\wedge, y\}\}$. One might then say (from the *extrasystematic* point of view) that the set S, namely $\{\{\{a\}, \{\wedge, b\}\}, \{\{c\}, \{\wedge, d\}\}\}$, was *the same relation as* set S', namely $\{\{\{a\}, \{a, b\}\}, \{\{c\}, \{c,d\}\}\}$. But it is certainly not *the same set* as S'.

As usual the objection to accepting this apparent type (5) example at its face-value is Leibniz's Law. If S = S' under the concept *relation* then whatever is true of S is true of S' and *vice versa*. But S has $\{\{a\} \{\wedge, b\}\}$ as a member and S' does not.

Notice that any project of saving (μ) by some amendment or relativization of Leibniz's Law plus some doctrine or other of categories is manifestly hopeless. Suppose we say that we can only expect what is true of S *qua relation* to be true of S'. Well, either relations are or they are not sets.[36] If they are sets then the plea is absurd, R is a set like S and S' and we still have the violation of Leibniz's Law. If they are not sets, however, then the true statement 'set S is the same relation as S'' must not be allowed to have the consequence that S or S' (predicatively) is a relation. We must only allow, when we are looking at this question extra-systematically, that it *represents* a relation. But to block this consequence is to withdraw (μ) as a genuine case of type (5). If we want a reduction of relations of degree *n* which strictly equates

---

36.
'Different things cannot be made to coincide by abstraction, and to regard them as the same is simply a mistake. If abstracting from the difference between my house and my neighbour's, I were to regard both houses as mine, the defect of my abstraction would soon be made clear.' (Frege, *Grundgesetze der Arithmetik*, §99.)

them with something then we shall have to isolate and utilize what it is that all mathematically satisfactory definitions of ordered *n*-tuples have in common.

If we do block the unwelcome consequences of (μ) (rather than vainly try to settle which is 'the right definition' of ordered pair) then what sort of 'is' do we have in (μ)? Presumably it is analogous to the 'is' of 'Irving is Hamlet' or the 'be' of 'that piece of sugar can be your queen [at chess] while I glue the head of the queen back on'. It may be that the 'identifications' of the reduction of arithmetic to set-theory have to be similarly explained, in terms of realization or representation.[37]

9. *Conclusion concerning the Relativity of Identity, Thesis* **R**

It may be helpful to conclude with some general remarks about the defects we have discovered in purported type-(4) and type-(5) instances of **R**. Almost all of the readings of these that have given **R** the semblance of support have depended on ignoring one of two things:

(i) the definite but limited ambiguity of 'is' (for which we have given some collateral evidence, almost all of it dependent at closer or further remove on Leibniz's Law), most particularly the '*x* is constituted of *y*' reading of '*x* is *y*';

(ii) the deceptive designation of certain referring expressions. ('By "that Hermes" do you mean "that statue of Hermes" or "the matter of that statue of Hermes", or what exactly?' Again, it is only in the presence of Leibniz's Law that such questions have any point.)

In the case of some putative examples of **R** it is hard to say which is the dominant confusion. Other people's appreciation of certain cases may differ from my own. But prolonged experimentation has led me to believe that, although there is overlap in the **R**-candidates they disqualify, no one of these diagnoses will account for everything that is going on in the full corpus of apparent examples. Neither diagnosis is dispensable.

The need we have found for the second diagnosis is particularly interesting. At § 46 of *The Foundations of Arithmetic,* Frege wrote (in J. L. Austin's translation, my italics):

While looking at *one and the same external phenomenon* [derselben äussern Erscheinung] I can say with equal truth both 'It is a copse' and 'It is five trees', or both 'Here are four companies' and 'Here are 500 men'. Now what changes here from one judgement to the other is neither

37. For 'theoretical identification', see Putnam's essay in Sidney Hook, ed., *Dimensions of Mind,* New York, 1960, p. 155. For set-theory and arithmetic see Paul Benacerraf's 'What Numbers Couldn't Be', *Philosophical Review* XXIV, Jan. 1965.

any individual object, nor the whole, the agglomeration of them, but rather my terminology. But that is itself only a sign that one concept has been substituted for another. (Cf. §§ 25–7.)

What is true and unshakeable here is the justly celebrated insight of Frege for which he is preparing to argue in this passage—that numbers attach to the concepts under which objects fall and not to the objects themselves. But for any good thesis there exist both good arguments and bad arguments; and there is at least one bad argument here *if* Frege really meant to suggest that, holding my gaze constant upon one external phenomenon,[38] I can subsume the very same something first under the concept *copse* then under the concept *trees,* and do this assigning to the first concept the cardinal number one and to the second concept the number five. Obviously a copse *is* trees. But the copse itself is not identical with any tree *or* with any aggregate of trees. (The copse tolerates replacement of all its trees, for instance, but neither the aggregate nor the class comprising the present trees in the copse can survive such replacement.) There is no real prospect of this 'this' (the 'dies' in 'dies ist eine Baumgruppe' and 'dies sind fünf Bäume') having constant reference, even though the stuff (wood) that makes up the this both makes up a copse and makes up five trees.[39] What interests Frege of course is that, according to which of these choices we make, we either arrive at a concept with the number one or arrive at a concept with the number five. What interests me, however, is that, if we are concerned with the reference of 'this' or of any other designation whatever—concerned that is about what object it designates—then we have to take care to discover whether the term stands for a copse or for a class or aggregate of trees. These are not the same thing.

38. Is the *Erscheinung* a sort of internal accusative of *ansehen,* or the whole visual field of the seeing, or the *object seen*?—and, if the last, why suppose there is one and only one such object?

39. See 'On Being in the Same Place at the Same Time', *op. cit.,* preface (1). When Socrates claims in the *Parmenides* that he is one man and many parts, right and left parts, back and front parts, upper and lower parts, all different (enumerated at 129[e], cf. *Philebus* 14[d]), Plato seems to say that *Socrates himself* partakes both of one and of many. Of course Frege could not say such a thing. And, if we credit him with following through consistently the idea that 'to use the symbol *a* to signify an object, we must have a criterion for deciding in all cases whether *b* is the same as *a*' (§ 62), then we shall deny that he is in any way suggesting at § 46 that the 'dies' has constant reference. His sole interest is in the shift of concept. ('Neither any individual object' is intended perhaps to dismiss the *whole question* of objects.)

Upon those who step into the same rivers different and again different waters flow. The waters scatter and gather, come together and flow away, approach and depart. (Heraclitus, Diels fragments 12, 91, text and translation after Kirk, *Cosmic Fragments,* Cambridge, 1954, pp. 367–84.)

In the state of living creatures, their identity depends not on a mass of the same particles, but on something else. For in them the variation of great parcels of matter alters not the identity: an oak growing from a plant to a great tree and then lopped, is still the same oak; and a colt grown up to a horse, sometimes fat, sometimes lean, is all the while the same horse. (John Locke, *Essay Concerning Human Understanding* II, xxvii, 3.)

All constituents of living matter, whether functional or structural, of simple or complex constitution, are in a steady state of rapid flux. (Rudolf Schoenheimer, *The Dynamic State of Body Constituents,* Cambridge, Mass., Harvard, 1942.)

CHAPTER TWO

Outline of a Theory
of Individuation

1. Proposition **D** and the rationale of the 'same what?' question

If identity were sortal-relative and sortal-relative because **R** (=the Relativity of Identity) held, then that might be thought to support **D** (=the thesis of the Sortal Dependency of Identity). For **D** is a thesis that certain champions of **R** have mistakenly wished to equate with a kind of obverse of **R**. This obverse is the doctrine that, on pain of indefiniteness, every identity statement stands in radical need of an answer to the question *same what?*[1] But in fact **R** is false, and can lend no support to anything; and there has been no temptation at all to claim that there is some semantical indeterminacy in the plain '*a* is *b*' locution. Still less then has there been temptation to claim that there is an incompleteness such that an identity sentence '*a* is *b*' might be true when glossed with one sortal concept truly applicable to *a* and false when glossed with another.

When **D** is clearly dissociated from **R** it will make two claims. The first is that, if *a* is the same as *b*, then it must also hold that *a* is the same *something* as *b*. This claim belongs in the object language, the object language being ordinary English, which admits the locutions 'same what', 'same something', as well as predicates such as 'the same

---

1. Some but not all champions of **R** have taken this view. Griffin for instance, rather than insist '$a=b$' must be incomplete or indeterminate, sees absolute Leibnizian identity, not as incoherent, but as a determinate, extremely strong relation, and the limiting case of a weaker relative relation which is not Leibnizian.

'$a=b$' is treated in this book, as it was in *Identity and Spatio-Temporal Continuity*, as a congruence relation and as logically equivalent (guaranteed the same truth value as) '$(\exists f)\,(a\overset{=}{_f}b)$'. This entails that there are two reasons why there has never been any temptation to ascribe to '$a=b$' any semantic indeterminacy or indefiniteness. First $(\exists f)\,(a\overset{=}{_f}b)$, which is equivalent to '$a=b$', is closed and semantically determinate. ('a is the same something as b' has the same status.) No variable is free. Second, being Leibnizian, '$(\exists f)\,(a\overset{=}{_f}b)$' and '$a=b$' are both determinate in the further sense of excluding $(\exists g)\,(ga\ \&\ a\overset{\neq}{_g}b)$.

donkey', 'the same tree'[2]; and the two-place relation x *is the same something as* y, like all the sortally definite two-place relations subordinate to it (e.g. x *is the same tree as* y, x *is the same donkey as* . . .), is here absolute and subject to Leibniz's Law. The second claim comprised by **D** (**D** as dissociated from **R**, that is) is that the *elucidation* of the identity '$a = b$' depends on the kind of thing that a and b are.

Consolidating all this we have a threefold doctrine:

D: $a = b$ if and only if there exists a sortal concept f such that
(1) a and b belong to a kind which is the extension of f;
(2)   to say that x falls under f—or that x is an f—is to say what x is (in the sense Aristotle isolated);
(3) a is the same f as b; or a coincides with b under f, i.e. coincides with b in the manner of coincidence required for members of f, . . .

Note that, if this thesis of Sortal Dependency is true, then, although the statement that $a = b$ will always entail that there is an f such that $a =_{f} b$, it will not specify what the sortal concept is. Nor need the man who says or knows that a is b know which concept it is. (If he knows on authority that a is b, for instance, he may have no idea what a or b is.) All that a man who says that a is b commits himself to is that a and b are the same *something*—a self-sufficient and self-standing claim.

But why dwell so particularly upon **D** if the three-place predicable 'x is the same f as y' will always be Leibnizian? Why is this attenuated version of **D** worth salvaging from the wreckage of **R**?

However vacuous **D** may seem, and however gratuitous the obsession with it should at first appear, the object of this chapter is to argue that, if we do not salvage so much, then we can scarcely understand the nature of sortal concepts for continuants. If all systematic understanding of the point that is at issue in questions of continuant identity is not to escape us, then no matter what its form or derivation should be, the English form 'x is the same . . . as y' requires to be

2. 'a is the same something as b' gives the appearance of a second level quantification over sortal concepts. But I think its availability in English is far more important than the question of its final analysis (e.g. how what appears as quantification over concepts is to be brought into the right relation with first level predication, and whether a substitutional account would be most appropriate). I claim that the theses of Chapters Two and Three permit me to leave undecided (are insensitive to the resolution of) the question whether 'x is the same something as y' has the same form as its logical equivalent $(\exists f)\,(x =_{f} y)$. (Logical equivalence amounts only to their being logically guaranteed the same *truth*-value.) For more discussion see *Longer Notes* 0.02, 0.03, 0.04. All claims in Chapters Two and Three are indifferent between options (i) and (ii) and (iii) of *Preamble*, section 6, and can be transposed to that expression which is most natural for each.

taken at least as seriously as **D** takes it. But none of this will imply that there is never nothing at issue in questions of identity, or that no identity question is ever ill-defined, empty or trivial. It will only imply that, where an identity question is a substantive question and does have a point, **D** gives the general form by which, in the first instance, the point that is at issue may be elucidated. The claim made by **D** is that, where there is a point at issue, this depends in a systematic way upon what *a* and *b* are.

The merits and attractions of **D** may be brought out by considering the position of a philosopher who rejects the doctrine. So far as he is concerned the point at issue in questions of *a* and *b*'s identity or difference is independent of what *a* and *b* are except to the unremarkable extent that, in order to be the same, they will have to agree in respect of all the properties and relations they fall under, sortal properties themselves being among these properties. And it will be typical of the enemy of **D** to deny that there can be any better elucidation of identity than the condition of complete community of properties.

Against that position I shall suggest that, so far from being a correct philosophical account of identity or explicating what a substantive well-founded question of identity turns on, the relation of agreement in every property or relation must flow from identity itself; second, that this relation of agreement depends not merely epistemologically upon identity: and third, that identity is a primitive notion, transcending any philosophical reduction even of this kind. But I shall also try to show that the primitiveness of ' = ' in no way excludes discursive elucidation in terms that are collateral or coeval. Nor will it rule out the unfolding and articulation of the several ideas by whose possession we are able to apply 'the same' so confidently within any arbitrary kind of entities. Discursive elucidation of the notion is precisely the mission of **D**. Indeed it is the project of this book.

Suppose I ask: Is *a*, the man sitting on the left at the back of the restaurant, the same person as *b*, the boy who won the drawing prize at the school I was a pupil at in the year 1951? To answer this sort of question is surprisingly straightforward in practice, although it would be a complicated business to spell out the full justification of the method we employ. Roughly though, what organizes our actual method is the idea of a particular kind of continuous path in space and time which the man would have had to have followed in order to end up here in the restaurant; and the extraordinary unlikelihood (if the man himself were questioned and these dispositions investigated) of certain sorts of memory-dispositions existing in anyone or any-

thing that had not pursued that path. The alleged theoretical complications of personal identity as a special case are here irrelevant; and
the advantage of an example of this sort involving a remembering
entity is only that, among objects and their traits, an entity with this
or that memory is endowed with a conspicuously good distinguishing
mark. Once we have dispelled with its theoretically dispensable aid
any doubt that there is a path in space and time along which we could
have traced that schoolboy and found him to coincide in the fashion
of human being with the person at the back of the restaurant, the
identity is settled. And *then* we can say that, no matter what ϕ is
(provided it stands for a genuine property), and no matter whether
the entity's satisfying or not satisfying ϕ figured in our inquiry into
the spatio-temporal paths of a and b, ϕa if and only if ϕb. The
continuity in question here is not bare continuity, however. It is the
kind of continuity that is brought into consideration by what it is to
be a human being. (If *mutatis mutandis* we had been speaking of
democracies or republics for instance, or of proper spatio-temporal
continuants less tolerant of intermittent manifestation than these but
more tolerant of it than men, then a different conception of tracing
and a different allowance of gappiness would have operated.)

I am not urging here that our actual method, focused upon the
question of this *man*-path, gives us a risky but practically indispensable short cut to establishing each of the infinitely many instances of
the schema $\phi a \equiv \phi b$. Nor is it being urged that it happens there is no
other way of establishing them, though that is certainly a capital
consideration. It is being urged that to determine correctly the answer
to our continuity question about the traceability of things through
their life-histories *is* in a case of this sort to settle that $\phi a \equiv \phi b$: and
(the epistemological reflection of a criteriological point) that it is
impossible *even in theory* to conceive of a way independent of the
prior discovery that $a = b$ by which to establish that, for all ϕ, *no
matter what property ϕ is, $\phi a \equiv \phi b$*. For suppose one should leave the
identity open and renounce all elucidations of identity other than a
and b's complete community of properties. How would one then
think about the temporary properties enjoyed by an individual a
identified with respect to the past and the temporary properties
enjoyed by an individual b identified with respect to the present? 'For
all ϕ, $\phi a \equiv \phi b$', considered as an account of a and b's identity or what
it *is* for them to be identical, puts everything back to front.

The moral I draw is that our preferred recipe for the elucidation of
identities, if it is to capture what we mean by ' $=$ ', must do better than
$(\forall \phi)(\phi a \equiv \phi b)$. And in the case of an identity of *continuants*, the idea

of a traceable path or a life story is what any elucidation made by the preferred recipe must recapitulate if it is to catch hold of the use that we make of the identity-concept. It is this idea that the thesis of the Sortal Dependency of Identity or **D** brings into consideration in just those cases where the sortal concept in virtue of which *a* and *b* are the same something is the sortal concept for a kind of continuant, and one can ask 'what is it for an f to *persist*?'

So much for the general picture or programme, and so much for the part played within it by Proposition **D**. The programme is independent of any conception of the problem of identity that dismantles the concept and translates identity questions about persisting substances into questions about some allegedly determinate finer-grained continuity relation analytical of ' = ' and holding between items from among the contents of the world frozen at time *t* and items from among the contents of the world frozen at *t'*. There is no such relation, I claim (see *Identity and Spatio-Temporal Continuity*, p. 35); there is no such freezing (see Chapter One, section 3); and there is no prospect at all, I believe, of giving or explicating the terms of an identity sentence in a way that is not itself identity- and continuant-involving. **D** will not help one to do this, and nothing else will either.

The last contention will provoke the charge that the only thing that I have left for the philosophy of individuation to attempt will be circular. The charge is worth considering in a little detail, first as directed against the elucidations of particular identities for which **D** provides the recipe, then as directed against the recipe itself.

By the elucidation of identity that I advocate, one who knows what he is saying, and who agrees to amplify his assertion of a continuant-identity '*a* = *b*' for purposes of the elucidation of its truth grounds and the eventual adjudication of its truth-value, will first have to say what are the terms of the identity. He will have to explain that *a* is a continuant which . . . and *b* is a continuant which ———, and then expand each specification separately in a way sufficient to make determinate (with the help of the world) which continuant *a* is and which one *b* is, and what each is. Then some common sort f will have to be found that they both belong to. Finally there may be need of some explication of what it *is* for an f to persist. The first apparent circularity is that if the author of the statement '*a* is *b*' says what each item is in this way, then his amplification of the judgement already involves the general idea of continuant-identity. But I claim that there is no harm in this, and no circularity, provided that the question of the identity of continuant *a* in particular with continuant *b* in particular remain open. And this question *can* be left open. It can even be left open if a correct answer is, if correct, then necessarily correct.

The second apparent circularity is harder to see clearly, because it relates to the recipe itself. **D** may appear to direct us to explicate what f-*continuity* is. But how can it be that we understand the recipe itself, or grasp the notion of identity by its means if, as we have already insisted, there can exist no general account of what it is for an arbitrary individual *a* to coincide or not coincide with an arbitrary individual *b* nor any effective or usable account of what it is in general to make a mistake or avoid a mistake in tracing *a* and tracing *b* to see whether they coincide on some continuous spatio-temporal path. To trace *a* I must know what *a* is, we have said, as if that met the whole point. But what counts as knowing what *a* is in the Aristotelian sense? And what counts as a sortal concept for a continuant? The answer may appear to depend in part on the idea of a principle of continuity for *a*.

Here we are caught in a circle that would certainly be vicious if we thought we were bringing the concept of identity into being by means of other ideas better understood, or if we could not appeal both to some extant *a priori* understanding of the identity relation and to a going practice of the sortal articulation of individual continuants as *this* f or *that* g or whatever. Happily, though, we lack neither of these things (unless we want to sacrifice the first and offer up Leibniz's Law to some numen of confusion). And where the aim is only to enhance the understanding that we already have of sameness as ascribed to continuants, two points will suffice to meet the question of circularity.

In the first place the notion of continuity has no place in Proposition **D**. What we have there is a general notion or determinable, viz. *x is the same . . . as y,* and its only modestly technical alias, *x coincides under . . . with y.* In so far as the notion of continuity is imported at all, it is always some kind-specific continuity, and this is brought into consideration by some sortally specific relation (such as *x* is the *same donkey as y,* the *same house as y*) appropriate for the particular terms of the identity. As Leibniz points out: 'By itself continuity no more constitutes substance than does multitude or number. . . . *Something* is necessary to be numbered, repeated and continued' (Gerhardt II, 169).

Note in the second place that, within the recipe itself, merely determinable notions will *suffice,* provided that they are perspicuous or we can explain them by reference to what is perspicuous. Are 'sortal concept' and 'coincides' then perspicuous? It is true that neither is ordinary English and both need explication. But I submit that their meaning is fixed uniquely by the following schema:

(x) (y) (x coincides under sortal concept f with y just if $\ulcorner x$ falls under f$\urcorner$ says *what x is* and $\ulcorner x$ coincides under f with $y\urcorner$ implies that, for all ϕ, $\phi x \equiv \phi y$).

This schema requires some collateral understanding of the *what is it* question, of implication and of $(\forall\phi)$ $(\phi x \equiv \phi y)$. But all this is in fact available to us; and the schema vindicates both the fidelity and the unity of the conception of identity embodied by our method of elucidation. We need not deceive ourselves or exaggerate what has been accomplished, but now let us add to the third clause of **D**, and supplant the lacuna '. . .' that was left there with the words 'congruently, that is in such a way as to entail the Leibnizian community of what is true of *a* and true of *b*'.

The approach to identity just explained will rightly remind the reader of various doctrines of 'criteria of identity'. Some philosophers have used 'criterion' to mean 'way of telling' or 'conceptually determined way of telling'. Where they have meant this, there is a contrast with my theory. The Aristotelian *what is it* question does both less and more than provide what counts as evidence for or against an identity. It does less because it may not suggest any immediate tests at all. It does more because it provides that which *organizes* the tests or evidence, and that which has been wanted by whoever has asked for a criterion of identity in the sense that Frege did. That is an account of what *constitutes* identity. My approach here is a variant on Frege's and, if it differs in any important way, that is only in virtue of a pessimism (corresponding to a difference of subject-matter) that I feel about the prospects for analysis. Perhaps some who have followed Frege (*Foundations of Arithmetic*, § 62) in asking for the criterion of identity have wanted from such a criterion a breakdown of identity into materials that are singly independent of identity. But this was not necessary. Nor is the Fregean demand inextricably linked with the puritanism of those who have insistently required criteria of identity in fanatical pursuit of ontological parsimony. They have wanted to refute claims that this, that, or the other kind of entity exists. That is not my concern, however, and it was not Frege's.

The real and abiding interest of Frege's demand for the criterion of identity seems to me to be this: Wherever we suppose that entities of kind f exist we are committed to ascribing some point to typical identity questions about particular fs; and, in so far as identity is a puzzling or problematic relation, the first concern of the philosophy of any subject matter must be to enhance our powers of finding the elucidation (whether or not we use here the language of criteria) for its disputed identity questions. These explications or glossings may be as discursive and heterogeneous as we will from case to case, I hold, provided that they all originate from what we can recognize as a unitary understanding of *identical* and *the same*.

For a question to have a point is not yet for it to be a question that is decidable (either in the ordinary sense or in the technical sense of belonging to a question class such that there exists a method of deciding every question in that class). But, in an ordinary case where an identity-question is in fact decidable, we shall expect the particular criterion—or the account of what is at issue—appropriately extracted from the answer to the 'what is it?' question, to lead us back to what was intended by all the pre-Fregean philosophers (scholastics, rationalists and others) who have spoken and written of a *principium individuationis* or principle of individuation. It is my hope that, in the presence of **D**, we can reanimate these old doctrines in a way that is demonstrably independent of mythical conceptions of bare continuity; and that we can also find a way to bring to bear upon identity questions about fs all the empirical facts that we treat as amplifying Aristotelian identifications of the form *a is an f*. Indeed such principles of individuation, seen always as correlative with Aristotelian identifications of this form, provide the only explanation which can possibly measure up to the surprising determinacy of most of the identity questions that we encounter in real life.

To conclude these methodological preliminaries, I shall take the risk of stressing once more that I have not said that a criterion of identity or a principle of identity is itself to be the test or method of establishing identity. I have implied at most that any elucidations of identity that we formulate must be such there can in decidable cases *be* corresponding tests or methods (tests or methods being not necessarily tests or methods we can always use, or need always use—for we may find ourselves either badly placed or exceptionally well placed, with access to authority—when we try to confirm or refute an identity); and second that, if we can try to understand what *organizes* the tests or methods that we actually use, then it may be possible to see the way backwards from the tests we do use to the underlying point of these tests or methods; and that is the trail back to what the tests are tests of, and why they are tests, viz. the identity of the thing or things in question. In the case of continuants it is the special effectiveness of the 'what is it' question that it refers us to the ideas of the persistence and lifespan of an entity, and so makes manifest the connexion, which it was always evident that there must be, between the identity over time of such an entity and its persistence, between its persistence and its existence, and between its existence and its being the kind of thing it is.

2. The identity of indiscernibles

It is denied then that it is any confusion of epistemology with philosophical elucidation or analysis to require that 'for all ϕ, $\phi a \equiv \phi b$' should be the consequence and not the criterion of an identity judgement's being true. What is more, it will emerge in the course of the gradual elaboration of the consequences of **D** that there can really exist for a kind k a condition for '$=$' whose satisfaction by a and b belonging to k has the amiable property of entailing that, for all ϕ, $\phi a \equiv \phi b$. But, in the meanwhile, it may help to consolidate some of the claims issued already to enlarge for the length of one short section upon a principle that has been in the background for some time now. That is the Identity of Indiscernibles: by which I mean the principle which results from taking the converse of the first order principle that I called Leibniz's Law, and then transposing the schema into a second-order formula—the need to do this can scarcely be sufficiently emphasized—by prefixing to the antecedent $(\phi a \equiv \phi b)$ a second-level quantifier with scope confined to that antecedent. Thus the Identity of Indiscernibles is

$$[(\forall\phi)\,(\phi x \equiv \phi y)] \supset (x = y).$$

The shortcomings of this principle are intimately connected with the failings of community of attributes and relations as an elucidation of identity, and also with the failure of all reductive accounts of '$=$'.

Leibniz's own view of the principle may be made plain by quotation:

> There is no such thing as two individuals indiscernible from each other. An ingenious gentleman of my acquaintance, discoursing with me, in the presence of her Electoral Highness the Princess Sophia, in the garden of Herrenhausen; thought he could find two leaves perfectly alike. The Princess defied him to do it, and he ran all over the garden a long time to look for some; but it was to no purpose. Two drops of water, or milk, viewed with a microscope, will appear distinguishable from each other. (*Correspondence with Clarke*, p. 36 in the H. G. Alexander edn, Manchester, 1956.)

I have said that it is not possible for there to be two particulars that are similar in all respects—for example two eggs—for it is necessary that some things can be said about one of them that cannot be said about the other, else they could be substituted for one another and there would be no reason why they were not called one and the same. Moreover, if they have diverse predicates the concepts too, in which these predicates are contained, will differ. (Pp. 476–7 in F. Schmidt *Leibniz Fragmente zur Logik*, Berlin, 1960; cf. p. 9, Couturat, *Opuscules et fragments*.)

If we ask about the strength of the antecedent $(\forall\phi)\,(\phi x \equiv \phi y)$ in Leibniz's reading of his principle, then it is clear that it is as if he considers the principle to be protected from triviality by his excluding from the range of this variable 'ϕ' not only predicates compounded from '=' itself but also such predicates or relations as 'five miles S.W. of Big Ben'—indeed by his excluding all predicates presupposing place- time- or thing-individuation.

It is always necessary that beside the difference of time and place there be internal principles of distinction ... thus although time and place [external relations, that is] serve in distinguishing things, we do not easily distinguish them by themselves.... The essence of identity and diversity consists ... not in time and space. (*Nouveaux Essais* II, 27.1 and 3; cf. II, 1.2, and letter to De Volder, Gerhardt II, 250.)

By no means everyone who has wanted to defend the Identity of Indiscernibles has been prepared to follow Leibniz into his theories of relations, space and time. But, unless one is prepared to follow argument where argument leads and delimit the range of the variable 'ϕ' in something approximating to Leibniz's manner, the condition $(\forall\phi)\,(\phi x \equiv \phi y)$ is a trivial condition. With '=' and derivatives all included within the range of 'ϕ', it cannot parade either as an analytical explication or even as a good elucidation of identity. For the condition manifestly presupposes identity in such a way that any particular issue of identity will move round and round one small circle. Community of properties in this sense is at best, I assert, a consequence of identity.

On the other hand, if one gives the principle of the Identity of Indiscernibles the Leibnizian or more interesting interpretation, or if (as Leibniz did not) one envisages the principle being used, not merely for the refutation of identity claims, but for their positive or effective determination, then strange results follow. Wittgenstein noted at *Tractatus Logico-Philosophicus* 5.5302 that the Identity of Indiscernibles denies the logical possibility of a universe consisting only of two qualitatively indistinguishable spheres. But that is not all. On the purist view of the principle, which disqualifies as values of ϕ all properties with definitions that involve identity itself and scrupulously disqualifies all the other predicates whose exclusion is demanded by parity of reason (e.g. all monadic and polyadic properties that require definitions already presupposing place-, time- and thing-individuation), the principle may seem to exclude situations much more readily conceivable than the one Wittgenstein envisaged. Most notably it excludes the existence in this world (in my pocket, say) of a symmetrical object. Any such object is reduced to half of itself by the principle. And an object that is symmetrical about all planes which bisect it is precluded altogether from existence. For the top half of such an object would be identical with its bottom half, and the left side of the bottom half would be identical with the right side of the bottom half, and any residual eighth of the object would be identical with some ('other') residual eighth . . . We are eventually left with nothing but a geometrical point.[3]

3. *Proposition D further explicated and amplified: preliminaries*

The next step must be to bring the fundamental tenet **D** into a clearer relation with the notions of *principle of individuation* and *substance concept* (in the sense of Chapter One, section 3).

First, for purposes of contrast, a proposition will be proved that is far too weak to exhaust **D**'s proper content or elucidate the truthgrounds of statement of identity in the manner envisaged by doctrines of *principia individuationis*.

Suppose $a=b$. Then, since every entity is something, there must exist such a thing as a. In that case there must be some f that a belongs to. *Existent* is not a candidate to play the role of f here. For 'an existent' does not answer the question 'what is a?' A substantial or sortal predicate, on the other hand, is precisely the sort of predicate that answers this kind of question. Assembling these materials, then, we have

(i) $a=b$.
(ii) $(\exists f)(f(a))$.

3. It is worth remembering that one need not be an overt Leibnizian in order to claim that the notion of identity can be analysed without residue into the notion of community of all properties and relations. Consider Quine's position, on which see *Longer Note* 2.03.

Let f be some arbitrary sortal predicate such that f(a). By reflexivity or

(iii) $f(a) \supset a_{\bar{f}} a,$

we have

(iv) $a_{\bar{f}} a.$

By Leibniz's Law we have

$$a = b \supset ((a_{\bar{f}} a) \equiv (b_{\bar{f}} a)).$$

So by (i) and *modus ponens*,

(v) $(a_{\bar{f}} a) \equiv (b_{\bar{f}} a).$

By (iv) and *modus ponens*,

(vi) $b_{\bar{f}} a.$

So

(vii) $(\exists f) (a_{\bar{f}} b).$

Discharging (i), we then have

(viii) $a = b \supset (\exists f) (a_{\bar{f}} b).$

This is all right so far as it goes. Abstractly and schematically we see that, if this were all there was to it, then **D** would be a near tautology. Nothing is added to the results of Chapter One, and nothing new emerges about the point (or even about the ultimate acceptability) of locutions of the form '*a* is the same f as *b*'. But something more is needed if the interdependence of substance and identity is to be fully made out and the stringent conditions are to be discovered that their office under **D** imposes on all general terms purporting to be adequate to what *a* and *b* sortally or substantially are. We have to state and justify some stronger assertion than (viii).

Perhaps the most important and most general single feature of sortal predicates is that they are used not only to say what things are but also to cover identity-statements in the '*x* is the same f as *y*' form—a form available in every natural language about which I have been able to get reliable information. Naturally, I hold that this double function is no accident. It is one half of our immediate task to understand (remind ourselves) what fits them for this role and how the role itself is shaped by the formal character of the identity relation (most notably by its Leibnizian absoluteness). The second part of the task is only notionally separable. It is to discover what justifies the other mark of faith in a more than grammatical distinction between noun and adjective. This is the belief, which may be called the substance-assumption, that, for any identity-statement whatever, there is always to be discovered not merely what we have called in section 3 of Chapter One a phased-sortal concept but also a substance-concept appropriate to cover it; and that, no matter how disparate in respect of temporal and other identifications the two designations flanking the identity symbol may be, a phased or re-stricted sortal predicate covering a true identity sentence can always be supplanted *salva veritate* by a more comprehensive substance predicate, to yield an equally true affirmative identity-statement.

We shall find our way towards the formulation that we need if we remark first that it is enough for everything to be something, and for $a = b \supset \exists f(a \overline{\underline{f}} b)$ to hold, if for all times t at which a continuant a exists there is a g under which a falls at t; or more perspicuously

D(i): $(x)(t)[(x \text{ exists at } t) \supset (\exists g) (g(x) \text{ at } t)]$.

What this guarantees is only a *succession* of possibly different phased sortals for every continuant. It does not guarantee what the substance assumption envisaged, that there will be any preferred sortal-concept in a hierarchy of sortal concepts (or any set of preferred sortal-concepts in such a hierarchy) that a thing will fall under throughout its existence. If the idea of continuity is to elucidate the truth-condi-tions of identity statements in the manner envisaged by **D**, then what we really need is the stronger principle

D(ii): $(x)(\exists g)(t)[(x \text{ exists at } t) \supset (g(x) \text{ at } t)]$.

Here '*x*' ranges over three dimensional continuants, '*t*' ranges over times and the letters 'g', 'f' range over individuative or articulative concepts which 'divide their reference' and answer the question *what is x?*

4. *D(ii)* as the proper development of *D*

Suppose now that we raise again the question what renders identity questions about continuants so determinate as they are; and suppose (which is the present stage of the argument) that there is no better explanation to be had of this definiteness and determinacy than that what an entity is determines what shall count as the continuance and persistence of that entity, and that what determines the continuance and persistence of an entity determines what it is to *be* that entity. Then by this explanation, which is only a further elaboration of the *this such* conception of identity and individuation, it seems that an account of what *x* sortally is and the specification of the principle of individuation of *x* are two aspects of one and the same thing; and we can expect that, for every completely determinate continuant, there will be at least one sortal concept that it falls under and that determines a principle of persistence for it. But the denial of **R** then tells us that, if there are several such concepts, then *they cannot disagree in the persistence condition that they ascribe*.

This is the conception of identity and individuation to which, in the presence of Leibniz's Law, I claim that our actual notions and practices have committed us.

It may be objected against this general line of argument (to be developed here and in the next section) that an entity could have determinate persistence and identity conditions otherwise than by virtue of being what (in the Aristotelian sense) it is. My only counter to this objection is to ask to be shown how, and to point again to the inadequacy of the community of properties account of individuation. But of course this dialectical reply is on a par with most cases of the defence of an explanation. The explanation is not guaranteed against a competitor.

A would-be counterexample to what is claimed by **D**(ii) will further clarify its content. Consider the story of Lot and his wife, as given in *Genesis,* chapter 19:

17. . . . And it came to pass, when they had brought them forth abroad that [t]he [Lord] said [unto Lot]: Escape for thy life; look not behind thee, neither stay thou in all the plain. . . .
18. Then the Lord rained upon Sodom and upon Gomorrah brimstone and fire from the Lord out of heaven. . . .
20. But his wife looked back from behind him [Lot] and she became a pillar of salt.

Here the sceptic of **D**(ii) will claim that the story is a possible one and the champion of **D**(ii) must make a difficult choice. Either I trivialize **D**(ii) altogether by arbitrarily inventing a concept *woman-pillar*, which a thing satisfies by being first a woman and then a pillar of salt, or I must allow a real and substantial discontinuity (as judged by standards of the answer given here to the 'what is it?' question) between Lot's wife and the pillar of salt. Certainly there is no substantial sortal, if we avoid the trivializing alternative, suitable to cover the identity between Lot's wife and the forty foot pillar of salt that is still to be encountered even now on the Jebel Usdum near the Dead Sea. What I think that shows is that we *cannot* say that this pillar is the same as the wife of Lot. But the sceptic of **D**(ii) will say that there is no *cannot* to be had here. What is the matter with the narrative?

In order to avoid complications that are complications for everybody and to focus upon the cardinal point—which is the necessity I allege for *at least* one underlying substance-concept—the opponent of **D**(ii) might well allow that we should simply concentrate upon the change in Lot's wife's body. He could also fortify his objection and his counterexample to **D**(ii) by suggesting that we imagine that the change in question was continuous, so that at least at one stage in the process there was something that was a candidate to count both as a human body and as crystallizing into salt. Then there would not even be any violation of a plausible principle that is much weaker than **D**(ii) and might be called the *principle of sortal continuity*:

If an entity x survives from t to t', then there is some articulation of the time between t and t' into periods $P_1, P_2, \ldots P_n$ such that, for every period P_i, $(\exists f)$ $(f(x)$ throughout $P_i)$ & $(f(x)$ throughout the adjacent period $P_{i \pm 1})$.

The rationale for this principle is the necessity, which an opponent of **D**(ii) has no need to deny, to distinguish as sharply in principle as we do in practice distinguish between the persistence of a thing through change and its replacement by some quite other thing.[5]

5. Cf. Aristotle: 'Unqualified coming to be and passing away takes place when something as a whole changes from *this* to *that*. Some philosophers hold that all such change [coming to be and passing away] is mere alteration. But there is a difference. For in that which underlies change there are two factors, one relating to the *logos* of the subject [i.e. what it is], the other relating to the matter that is involved. When the change affects both of these, coming-to-be or passing-away will occur. But when the change is not in the *logos* but only in the qualities [i.e. in respect of categories other than substance], i.e. when the change is a change in accidents, there will be alteration.' (*De Generatione et Corruptione*, 317ᵃ²¹ ff.)Aristotle's is a potentially stronger claim (given

It must be clear that, from the pure resources of deduction (not excluding predicate calculus with identity), **D**(ii) cannot be proved. Nor can **D**. There is nothing in pure logic to force us into an ontology of changeable continuants (that is three-dimensional things, which, as I have claimed that we conceive them, have spatial parts and no temporal parts and endure *through* time). Logic alone cannot force us into any particular ontology. (First-order quantification theory does not even constrain the ' = '-predicate narrowly enough to force upon it an interpretation coincident with what we mean in English by 'same' or 'identical'.) The best that can be done for **D**(ii) is to show (by reasoning involving among other things Leibniz's Law and the rest of applied predicate logic) that the denial of **D**(ii) or the sacrifice of the substance assumption would entail the denial of truth or significance or possibly both to indefinitely many of our existing beliefs; and that these beliefs are fundamental to our actual individuative practices. Whoever wants to give these up may do so. When he has done that (not merely said that he will), we can take him as seriously as he takes himself.

5. *The argument for D(ii)*

D(i) claimed that in respect of everything that exists there is an answer, whether known or unknown, and whether expressible in an extant language or only in the extension of one, to the question what it is. The argument for **D**(ii) enters it as its first claim that to fulfil its office and constitute an answer to the *what is it* question, a genuinely sortal predicate must stand for a concept that implicitly or explicitly determines identity, persistence and existence conditions for members of its extension. The status of this controversial claim is not stipulation or *a priori* argument from the null class of premisses but observation (theory-laden observation, the theory being defeasible by a better if there be such), first of what we say and do with the *what is it* question and its variants, and, second, of what, in the context of

---

Leibniz's Law and the arguments that are shortly to be presented for **D**(ii)) than the principle of Sortal Continuity. But the power of both is attested by the lengths to which poets and story tellers will go, when concerned to pass off unqualified passing away as persistence-through-alteration, to give the however mendacious impression that the conditions for alteration are scrupulously respected. The trick is to describe the change as happening very gradually. See particularly Ovid, *Metamorphoses*. The metamorphoses of Proteus—see, e.g., Homer, *Odyssey* IV, 453–63—represent a special artistic problem, corresponding to a conceptual impossibility of really imposing dimensions. See Chapter Three, section 1.

singling things out, we require from these answers, and can in fact supply. The claim about sortal concepts stands or falls with such observation, with Leibniz's Law, which informs the theory that informs the observation, and with the success or failure of the total theory of individuation by which I seek to explain the determinacy of identity. It is not immune from replacement by some rival total theory that explains the determinacy of individuation equally well while dispensing with the idea of a principle of identity. It would also be vulnerable to a demonstration that determinacy was an illusion. That this determinacy is a fact and requires explanation is a premiss separate from Leibniz's Law and separate I suppose from what was announced as the first step. And strictly speaking the succeeding steps require three terminological preliminaries:

(i) A sortal predicate may be highly restricted in Geach's *Reference and Generality* sense and still meet all requirements on being sortal. Consider for instance *Anzac,* which I should call a contingent phased sortal predicate and shall gloss here as *human being who was of military age and sex between 1914–18 and a member of the Australia New Zealand Army Corps sent to fight in the Great War.* Here the principle of individuation is certainly present, but it is buried and must be disinterred from much that is irrelevant to it. (No Anzac ceased to exist just by virtue of his being released from the Corps, or by the demobilization of the Corps at the end of the War. For the ceasing to exist of an Anzac, i.e. a man who is or was an Anzac—as opposed to the ceasing to qualify for a count at *t* of persons who are Anzacs at *t*—, nothing more and nothing less is required than the man's death. It does not matter whether the demise was in the Dardanelles campaign or at a subsequent time.)

(ii) At the other extreme, one must note that a concept may be very general or virtually unrestricted and still qualify. Perhaps *animal* is such a concept. 'It is an animal' counts as a minimally satisfactory answer to the 'what is it?' question—however rudimentary and, for many contexts, unhelpful the answer may be when compared with that given by a species term. But D(ii) is unaffected by this general issue of specificity or generality, as it is by the question how closely highly generic concepts like *animal* (cf. *machine*) approximate to the status of concepts that are for these purposes inadmissible, e.g. *space-occupier, entity* and *substance.* In the case of these last, a principle of individuation will have to be supplied by reference to the particular *kind* of space-occupier, entity or substance to which the thing in question actually belongs. For a formal concept like *entity* or *substance* has no autonomous individuative force of its own, and must be variously supplemented, wherever it appears in contexts of identification, according to the kind of the individual in question. If supplementation yields all sorts of different principles of individuation according to the compliant and context, and if there are no restrictions on how it is filled out except for context-relative or merely categorial ones, then a concept is too 'high', too unspecific, to count as an answer to the question *what is x?* It is not a sortal concept in our sense, or a proper substituend for 'f' in **D**(ii).[6]

(iii) So much for very unspecific answers and non-answers to the question *what is x?* Note next that, among the more specific answers, there are many restricted sortal predicates whose status as such is not structurally or even etymologically manifest, e.g. boy, foal, cub, gaffer, *graus* (Greek for an old woman); and many whose precise status is not only structurally unmarked but has also to be discovered empirically, e.g. tadpole, caterpillar.[7] But in the end it will prove that all phased sortal concepts are either latently or manifestly restrictions of underlying more general sortal concepts. *Boy* is definable as *human being that is male and biologically immature,* and so on.

So much for terminological explanation. The argument can now go forward. And the next step is to spell out a distinction, already employed in this and the previous chapter, among sortal predicates both restricted and unrestricted. (The restricted/unrestricted distinction is *not* the same as the distinction now to be determined.) This is the distinction between predicates that are such that they apply at every moment of an entity's life-span—e.g. 'man', 'horse', 'tree'—and predicates which fail this test, e.g. 'boy'. (Cf. Chapter One, section 3.) According to whether '*x* is no longer f' entails '*x* is no longer', the concept that the predicate stands for is in my usage a *substance concept*. No argument is known to me for the conclusion that an individual can answer to only one substance concept; and the sense just defined for 'substance-concept', allows an individual to fall under several or many. It is not even obvious that, among the distinct substance-concepts that one individual may fall under, any single

6. This claim has the same status as the first claim of this section. *Material object* is now ruled out from sortal status, and so are other dummy substantives, but the discussion of **D**(ii) is not sensitive to particular decisions about the individuativeness of particular predicates. See also Chapter Four, section 7, following.

7. Nothing in the argument here is meant to depend upon a certain conceptual conservatism into which no philosophical inquiry into substance and identity should find itself forced, viz. the supposition that one can tell *a priori* for any given sortal, e.g. the sortal *tadpole* or *pupa,* whether or not it is a substance-sortal or merely a phased sortal. Room must be found for the empirical and surprising discovery that there is something which is first a tadpole and then a frog—let us designate what goes through the whole cycle, what becomes this and then turns into that, *batrachos*—or is first a pupa or chrysalis and then becomes a perfect insect. The ensuing argument leaves room for that, room which will be taken up in Chapter Three.

'Another type of linguistic shortcoming [in biology] is illustrated by the persistence of our tendency to identify *organisms* with *adults* . . . it is not just adults we classify when we classify organisms. . . . We can speak of the egg as the primordium of the future adult, but not of the future organism because it already is the organism'. J. H. Woodger 'On Biological Transformation' in Le Gros Clark and Medawar, eds, *Growth and Form, Essays for D'Arcy Thompson,* Oxford, 1945.

concept need be the 'highest'.[8] But **D**(ii) does not require this. Nor does it preclude the cross-classification of substances.[9] What it requires is only that for any individual there be at least one substance concept. And now the denial of **R** ensures that, if there are several such concepts, then they will all agree in the persistence condition that they ascribe to an individual lying within their extension. (Such a set of concepts may be called *sortally concordant*.) For it is excluded that some entity *a* might answer to both f and g, f and g being both substance concepts, and be the same f as *b* but not the same g as *b*.[10]

How could an entity escape this argument for **D**(ii)? It could escape only by lacking a principle of identity and persistence made fully determinate in the manner we have envisaged by a substance-concept or set of substance-concepts.[11] But it would be no great defect of the argument for **D**(ii) as I conceive it if it had the following as one of its premises: at least some identity and persistence questions about the substances we have experience of do have definite or discoverable answers; and, at least within the ontology of changeable Aristotelian continuants to which so many of these familiar things belong, there are, for instance, many things that have *definitely ceased to exist*.[12]

8. The highest or most general concept, if any single concept is *the* most general or highest, that is still individuative with respect to an individual *x* I shall call *x's ultimate sortal concept*. It is the sortal concept which is individuative of *x* and restricts no other sortal concept that is individuative of *x*. See *Longer Note* 2.08.

9. See *Longer Note* 2.09.

10. Nicholas Griffin has complained about this demonstration that it assumes that no two ultimate sortals can overlap. But the argument does not assume that. It implies it. See *Longer Note* 2.10.

11. See *Longer Note* 2.11.

12. This implies that there are no principles of conservation that apply to continuants as such: but to deny that there are such principles is not of course to deny that the *matter* of such continuants is subject to any and all such principles as physics can demonstrate. Nor is it to deny that continuants may share this matter with the other entities, if any, for which there do exist principles of conservation. With such principles and such entities we are not concerned. We are not even concerned here with any continuants ('open textured' as they have been called) that do not admit of definite answers to persistence questions. These lie outside the ambit both of the argument and of **D**(ii). That which is explicitly excluded from the province of the principle **D**(ii) can be characterized independently of **D**(ii). It can be characterized in terms of determinacy and indeterminacy with respect to identity and persistence—and so without jeopardizing the content of **D**(ii). We shall not be saying that **D**(ii) holds except when it doesn't.

We pass close here to the problems of the continuance of stuff. There are profound and difficult questions to be asked about this. It is allowed in *Longer Note* 1.12 that these questions cannot help but interact with some of the most difficult questions in the philosophy of chemistry and physics. It would be a wonderful thing, if life, will, and the mixed economy lasted so long, to embark upon them. But those questions are not these questions. And these ones are easier. [Footnote continues on page 66

Having detected this assumption let us declare that too. And rather than pursue undecidable fantasies about what it would be like if the assumption did not hold, or search for every conceivable pretext not to take it seriously, it would be better to observe and marvel at the near unanimity that has been reached, and is almost effortlessly extended to a whole range of new cases, about what constitutes the ceasing to exist of an everyday or Aristotelian continuant of this or that kind. What furnishes such determinacy to such questions? The answer to this question has now been begun, but it will not be fully complete until the end of Chapter Three.

6. *Lot's wife: and the notion of existence*

This argument for **D**(ii) may now be made less abstract by applying it to the case of Lot's wife. The amazing thing about the story as it is credulously envisaged by the sceptic of **D**(ii) is that an entity starts off with the whole principle of persistence for one kind of thing, and then exchanges that whole principle of persistence for the whole principle of persistence for another kind. Describing the events this way we get a contradiction. There are three other ways of describing them:

(1) the identity of Lot's wife and the pillar of salt may be denied;
(2) a sortal predicate like 'woman pillar' may be invented to cover the identity and supplant the self-contradictory descriptions we began with;
(3) the very coherence of the whole story may be challenged.

(3), which entails or pre-empts (1), is an option that the next chapter will make more and more attractive. It will suggest the importance of the fact that the story as told violates actual laws of nature. The immediate concern, though, is with the unattractiveness of option (2) and the consequential attractiveness of (1). If one can invent sortal concepts at will, if he does not have to discover or validate against nature those that he invents, then the real content of the assertion that something lasted till t and then ceased to exist will be trivialized. If one were really unconstrained in the invention of some substantial sortal-predicate by which to represent that the thing persisted, he

---

For a careful exploration of an attempt, by what he calls the Relational Theory, to circumvent the claim in the text to which the present note is affixed, see Tyler Burge 'Mass Terms, Count Nouns and Change' (*Synthèse* 31, 1975, see especially p. 74)—a gratifying vindication also of the constitutive 'is' and of the constitutive approach to things and their matter that was advocated in Chapter One.

would be equally unconstrained in the invention of a substantial sortal predicate by which it failed to persist. He could have it either way, so to speak. We do not at the moment think of matters like this, however. And we cannot, if we want to maintain the right sort of distinction between the true and the false. Enamoured as we are of this distinction, we want not to invent but to *discover* the answer to the question: what is this entity in the story of Lot? It is sometimes right to say that discovering the answer to such questions involves inventing (at the world's prompting) the right concept to apply to the world in order to discover that answer. That does not undermine the point that is being urged. (See also Chapter Five in this connexion.) The answer itself must still be something we can discover 'in spite of ourselves'. That is what it is to take existence and identity seriously—and likewise truth.

The story of Lot's wife raises a question to which sortal concepts are no less relevant than they are to identity. What is it to cease to exist? An orthodox account says: to cease to have any properties. But this is not necessary. Of Aristotle, the author of *Nicomachean Ethics,* I believe that he was bald. So this Greek, though long since dead and inexistent, has the property of being now believed by someone to have been bald. Similarly Heraclitus is still misunderstood and Frege has become famous since his death. Are these not properties? And even if ceasing to have any strict properties in some revised definition of a strict property were necessary and sufficient for ceasing to exist, that would still not be the stuff of a satisfying answer to the original question. The question surely arose from the desire to know what it *was* to cease to have properties (or to cease to have any of some relevant range of properties). Perhaps one cannot have everything he wants here when he wonders what it is for an individual to be *no longer available* to have such and such properties. But surely there is a better answer to be had than the orthodox twentieth-century account of tensed existence, if we will only respect the distinction between predications in the category of substance and predications in the category of quality or relation. Recognizing this distinction we shall be tempted to follow an older tradition and say that an individual a's having ceased to exist at t is a matter of nothing identical with a belonging to the extension at t of the ultimate individuative kind (or to the extension at t of any sufficiently high individuative kind) that is a's kind.[13]

13. Note that 'a exists at t' is not on the theory we have advanced here an incomplete assertion. It says $(\exists f)$ (f is a substantial concept for a and a is in the extension at t of f).
[Footnote continues on page 68

7. *Further* **D** *principles*

The next chapter will inquire how any predicate could possibly measure up to all the responsibilities that go with the title of standing for a substance concept. But it will be useful to assess first the magnitude of the office that it now appears the substance concept must discharge, and to reckon up in some further principles, without any regard to economy or independence of statements, the duties that have already been laid upon it. Here, as in section 1, the prospect we are pursuing is that we may exploit our *a priori* or formal knowledge of the equivalence and congruence properties of the identity relation to describe a notion of f-coincidence (for variable f) that will elucidate simultaneously such notions as *sort, substance, material substance, identity of substance* and *persistence*. Having abandoned any project of external characterization we are to build up a description of these notions as it were from the inside—from the inside of a working conceptual system. And we succeed where something familiar to us is recognized as such from its theoretical description.

> **D**(iii): *a* is identical with *b* if and only if there is some concept f such that (1) f is a substance concept under which an object that is an f can be singled out, traced, and distinguished from other f entities and other entities; (2) *a* coincides under f with *b*; (3) ⌐coincides under f⌐ stands for a congruence relation: i.e. all pairs ⟨*x,y*⟩ that are members of the relation satisfy the Leibnizian schema $\phi x \equiv \phi y$.
>
> **D**(iv): f is a substance concept only if f determines (with or without the help of further empirical information about the class of fs) what can and cannot befall an *x* in the extension of f, and what changes *x* tolerates without there ceasing to exist such a

---

This is a complete, though quantified, assertion, and it well reflects the apparent completeness of actual denials and assertions of existence. Someone bent on rejecting **D**(ii) might advance a theory to be sharply distinguished from mine. He might claim that '*a* exists' is indeed an incomplete assertion, and then propose a doctrine of *relative existence*. By this theory of existence the distinction we have drawn between phased and substantial sortal concepts is, as we have drawn it, simply misconceived: for then, *whatever* concept f is, a thing may always cease to exist as an f and continue to exist as a g. About this proposal I should remark that it is the only consistent course for someone bent on rejecting **D**(ii); and that it would constitute a daring reconstruction both of the principles of the continuant ontology and of the whole way we at present think and speak. **D**(ii) was intended to reflect the ontology implicit in our *present* way of thinking and of puzzling ourselves about first-order identity questions. According to that, many things do definitely stop existing.

thing as x; and only if f determines (with or without the help of further empirical information about the class of fs) the relative importance or unimportance to the survival of x of various classes of changes befalling its compliants (e.g. how close they may bring x to actual extinction).

Any predicate which both fails these requirements on f and restricts no sortal predicate that passes them will be incompetent to cover judgements with the sense of *identity*-judgements concerning continuant material substances. Clause (3) of **D**(iii) answers to the requirement that community of properties should be not the basis but the consequence of the satisfaction of an acceptable criterion of identity. It may seem either emptily unattainable—in the case where it is not allowed that any sortal predicate guarantees the satisfaction of the Leibnizian schema—or magic of some sort. But we shall see in due course that it is not magic. **D**(iii) simply recapitulates the principle on which in our actual practice, as that is sustained by the idea of a lifespan, predicates are applied to a and b (or withheld from a or b, as the case may be) in respect of any instant or period belonging to the life history of this (these) persisting continuant(s).

The sceptic may say that our practice has no business to be sustained by such ideas as these, however filled out in particular cases, and that any practices founded in them must be precarious in the extreme. But our sole concern is to describe within a structure of theory the ideas that the sceptic attacks, and to enumerate such sources of support as they do have, not to render them impregnable from doubt or difficulty, or minimize the considerable commitment that someone incurs when he says what something is. It is perfectly true that no sortal concept that qualifies by **D**(iii) as a substance predicate and as determining a principle of tracing is likely to come up to the standards a positivist would propose for *observationality* or direct *experiential confirmability*. (Very few of the predicates we normally employ do come up to that standard of observationality—not even 'white', or 'flexible', or 'soluble'.) This does not prevent a good sortal predicate that illustrates **D**, **D**(i) and **D**(ii), and satisfies **D**(iii), from furnishing a principle of individuation for members of its extension. Nor does it prevent the said principle from determining and organizing intelligibly the relevant empirical tests for whether a or b is an f thing, and whether a is the same f as b.[15]

---

15. From the same source, I believe we shall also have the wherewith to investigate further the *hidden attributivity* of all the predicates that philosophers have conspired to pretend are in no degree attributive (in the sense employed by Geach in 'Good and Evil', *Analysis* 17, 1956, pp. 33–42). An off-white wall or piece of paper is whiter than a white man or white bread. Standards of being coloured this or that colour depend in a manner still needing to be described on the kind of entity in question.

With **D**(iv) it should become finally clear why, in the sense of 'coincides' that I

Connoisseurs of the literature of identity and individuation will have noticed that little room has been left in the formulations attempted so far to accommodate the distinction, of which so much has sometimes been made, between criteria of distinctness, or synchronic principles of boundary drawing, and diachronic principles of reidentification or identity. This is not an oversight.[16] It is my contention that, as principles that purport to be of one or the other sort are filled out in the direction of adequacy, the distinction disappears. The distinction as a distinction between incomplete accounts may be not without interest. But we have been concerned with what substance-predicates actually stand for—with the counterpart of reference, that is.

Where the sense of substance words is concerned and where grasping their sense is concerned, this must wait for the beginning of Chapter Three, as must the justification of the next **D**-principle:

D(v): f is a substance concept only if f determines either a principle of *activity*, a principle of *functioning* or a principle of *operation* for members of its extension.

The Leibnizian echo of 'activity' is deliberate, as will emerge when in due course the *activity* of natural things is distinguished from the

---

employ to elucidate identity, a thing does not coincide with its matter. Coinciding is not simply being in the same place at the same time. Just as there is no such thing as mere continuity so there is no such thing as coinciding otherwise than under a concept. A house, for instance, does not coincide with its bricks and mortar. For in 'the house is bricks and mortar' the *is* is constitutive. We do not have identity. Cf. Chapter One, section 6.

16. Suppose we have the judgement that the horse that was to be found at place p at time t is the same as the horse that was to be found at p' at t'. This may be partially explicated as a judgement that these horses coincide, or are continuous, *in the fashion of a horse*, insisting always that it is the kind *horse* which carries the whole burden of explicating the particular character of the persistence or continuity that is required. The claim that is registered by this explication against those who have employed the distinction between synchronic and diachronic principles of articulation is that the opposite dependence between the concepts *continuous* and *horse* is simply inconceivable. For, as stated already, there *is* no such notion as pure continuity: and *a fortiori* there is no purely general notion of continuity and no primitive purely synchronic notion of horse such that (a) the second of these notions is insufficient to explicate diachronic judgements of identity, but sufficient for judgements of the forms 'this thing that is here now is a horse' and 'this [presently demonstrated] horse is not the same as that [presently demonstrated] horse', (b) the two notions taken together do suffice to reconstruct the notion of genuine continuant horses. See my 'The Individuation of Things and Places', section V, *Proceedings of the Aristotelian Society Supplementary Volume XXVII*, 1963 (reprinted in Loux, ed., *Universals and Particulars*, New York, Doubleday, 1968); see also M. J. Woods's reply, *ibid.*, and his 'Identity and Individuation' in R. J. Butler, ed., *Analytical Philosophy*, 2nd series, Oxford, Blackwell, 1965. Cf. also *Longer Note* 1.11.

fulfilment of function that is characteristic of organs and artifacts.[17] A key role will be played in that discussion by a principle that is a direct consequence of **D**(iii):

> **D**(vi): If f is a substance concept for *a* then *coincidence under f* is determinate enough to exclude this situation: *a* is traced under f and counts as coinciding with *b* under f, and *a* is traced under f and counts as coinciding with *c* under f, while nevertheless *b* does not coincide under f with *c*.

Consider what happens when an amoeba divides exactly in half and becomes two amoebas. We are committed by **D**(vi) and the other doctrines of this chapter to find that neither competitor fully qualifies as coinciding under the concept *amoeba* with the parent amoeba. It will become clearer in Chapter Three how the peculiar facts about amoebas, discovered *a posteriori,* will support this ruling. But two things are immediately obvious. The first is that, since not both amoebas can be identical with the original amoeba, and since neither has a better claim than the other, no sensible theory will want either amoeba to be identical with the parent.[18] The second is that, if in our theory coincidence under f is to be a sufficient condition of being the same f, then the judgements of coincidence and identity must not be withheld *ad hoc* simply because transitivity is threatened. There must be something independently wrong relative to amoeba coinciding, as the formal and empirical constraints (the facts about amoeba division) combine to determine what that is. In Chapter Three an account will be given of how these constraints can combine in this way.

8. *Counting and some related concerns*

The chapter may conclude with some miscellaneous deductions, and a doubt.

From the falsity of **R** we have

> **D**(vii): there are no essentially disjunctive substance-concepts (f *or* g) coincidence under which might allow *a* to be the same (f *or* g) as *b*, and the same (f *or* g) as some *c* that was distinct under every covering concept from *b*.

---

17. See below, Chapter Three, sections 1, 2, 3. See also Ian Hacking's important article 'Individual Substances' in Harry G. Frankfurt, ed., *Leibniz: A Collection of Critical Essays,* New York, Doubleday, 1972.

18. See page 72.

Some disjunctive sortals are innocuous in this respect, e.g. when the f is subordinate to a higher sortal. (For example *animal or mouse* is innocuous—*a* cannot be the same mouse as but a different animal from *b*—and this complex sortal reduces simply to *animal*.) They will be innocuous when the corresponding conjunctive sortal is a satisfiable concept (e.g. *animal and mouse,* which reduces in the opposite direction to *mouse*), but in that case disjunctive sortals seem to be as superfluous as they are innocuous. (It is sometimes objected that we must have disjunctive sortals for certain kinds of counting operation. But 'There are 7 women or shadows here' means 'The number of women *plus* the number of shadows = 7'. We do not need disjunctive sortals to find our way here.) Perhaps it will be well to emphasize that this is not an argument against essentially disjunctive (f *or* g) being *a concept.* It is an argument against its being a *sortal* concept.

D(viii): If f is a substance-concept for *a* then, however indefinitely and unforeseeably the chain of *a*'s f coincidents *a, a', a'', a'''* . . . extends, whatever is truly or falsely applicable to one member of the chain must be truly or falsely *applicable* to every member of the chain whatever. But then all fs must belong to one *category.*

This follows *a fortiori* from Leibniz's Law, and is trivial. But it is worth deducing for the sake of what it brings out against certain allegedly possible metamorphoses, for instance that of Proteus into fire at *Odyssey* IV, 453–63. These difficulties will be pursued in Chapter Three.

I now come to the doubt. It would be all of a piece with the speculative tradition to which the individuative theory presented here belongs to add

D(ix)?: f is a sortal concept only if there always exists the theoretical possibility of a definite and finite answer to the question 'How many fs are there in region *r* at time *t*?'

This is the claim of **C** of the first section of Chapter One. Many or most of the concepts that it is the aim of this and the next chapter to characterize do satisfy this principle. For all I know, everything

18. Contrast Prior, *P.A.S.* 1965–66 (*op. cit.* at footnote 7). The view I have put in the text conforms with the only thorough attempt to work out a logic of division and fusion, that of J. H. Woodger, *The Axiomatic Method in Biology*, p. 61. One amoeba becomes two amoebas, but 'becomes' receives an analysis making it correspond to ordinary 'becomes' as constitutive 'is' corresponds to the ordinary 'is' of predication and identity. The matter of the original amoeba—the 'it'—is the fusion, or the matter, of the two new ones taken together. There is matter such that first *a* was constituted of it, and then *b* and *c* were constituted of it.

Further light is shed on the amoeba problem by the 'only *a* and *b*' rule of Chapter Three, section 4.

traditionally accounted a concept of material substances satisfies it. But it is difficult to see that it is necessary. It is one thing to be able to say how many fs there are in a determinate context. But it is another thing to have what D(ix) seems to require: that is a perfectly general method of enumerating fs. Subject to any doubts that Hobbes's puzzle of Theseus' ship may start concerning artifact kinds (see Chapter Three, section 3), the concept *crown* gives a satisfactory way of answering identity-questions for crowns. But there is no universally applicable definite way of counting crowns.[20] The Pope's crown is made of crowns. There is no definite answer, when the Pope is wearing his crown, to the question 'how many crowns does he have on his head?'

Given that a man knows how to count and can be relied upon to count correctly in a certain situation, then to see if he gives the right answer to the question 'how many fs?' is to see whether he locates fs and isolates them correctly from their background and from one another. That is what carries C of Chapter One, section 1, and D(ix) so close to the truth. But a man could answer very well whether this or that f-compliant is the same as that or this one, and still find far too many different ways of articulating the f-compliants which are generally to be encountered in the world.

Frege wrote in *Foundations of Arithmetic*, § 54, 'only a concept which (a) delimits what falls under it in a definite way [der das unter ihn Fallende bestimmt abgrenzt], and (b) *which does not permit any arbitrary division of it into parts* [und kein beliebige Zertheilung gestattet] can be a unit relative to a finite number'. His first condition

---

20. Cp. *wave, volume of fluid, worm, garden, crystal, piece of string, word-token, machine.* This is a ragbag. These are all individuals decomposable into matter, but there is a good sense in which several of them are not substances. But, so far as the general doubt is concerned, it must be worth taking note of all the homeomerous items in other categories, such as colours and their shades, quantities, wanderings, wonderings, readings, insults.

With the exception of this one minor disagreement about countability as a necessary condition of a concept's being a sortal concept, there is here no disagreement (*pace* Griffin's accusations at *op. cit.*, p. 216, founded in the idea that Leibniz's Law for $x =_f y$ needs a further justification which he thinks I try to provide by an argument based in a new account of sortal predicates) with Strawson's account, or with the written and oral tradition concerning these predicates. The intention has not been to cut loose of that tradition, but to draw attention to an important and so far relatively neglected mark of the sortal predicate, viz. its role in covering identity sentences. It is worth adding that, just as a devotee of Leibniz's Law for $x =_f y$ frequently needs Leibniz's Law to detect deviant 'is' in 'is the same f as' sentences and put these aside for special treatment, so the test does not import any new argument independent of that given in Chapter One, section 3, and footnote 6. As always we are exploring the consequences and prospects of the Leibnizian view.

is very close to what we have intended by our conditions upon being a sortal predicate. There is no reason to think that the second condition, italicized here, is superfluous, or already entailed, or for Frege's purpose otiose. His purpose concerns counting, and the second condition, marked (b), is precisely what is needed for there to be a universally applicable distinction between right and wrong answers to the *special* question 'how many?' But this requirement definitely goes beyond the condition that Frege rightly puts first. His first condition corresponds well to our own interest in this chapter: namely, concepts that delimit whatever falls under them in a definite way—the concepts with which we articulate or segment the reality of our experience.

The barley drink disintegrates and loses its nature unless it is constantly stirred. (Heraclitus, Diels fragment 125.)

Nothing is permanent in a substance except the law itself which determines the continuous succession of its states and accords within the individual substance with the laws of nature that govern the whole world. (Leibniz, Gerhardt II, 263.)

That which is a whole and has a certain shape and form is *one* in a still higher degree; and especially if a thing is of this sort by nature, and not by force like things which are unified by glue or nails or by being tied together, i.e. if it has in itself the cause of its continuity. (Aristotle, *Metaphysics* 1052^{a22-5}, as translated by W. D. Ross.)

CHAPTER THREE

Sortal Concepts: and the Characteristic Activity or Function or Purpose of their Compliants

1. *The sortal predicates of natural kinds*

Among the best candidates to play the roles of sortal and substantial predicates, as these roles were described in Chapter Two, are natural kind words. We now reach the question whether even these will fill the bill. Given a kind k, associated with sortal concept c, how does c determine what is at issue, what the matter turns on, when it is asserted or denied that some pair (x, y) which is a subset of the extension of k belongs to the identity relation? **D**(iii) as glossed by **D**(v) calls for something to be latent or implicit within the sense of a natural kind identification that will determine, for x, for y and for every other typical member of the kind, a principle of activity. It seems that here the natural kind concept c must make some conceptual link between the relevant questions of identity and the empirically ascertainable causal and dispositional properties of members of the kind as we find them in the actual world. But how can the concept make this link? And, even supposing that it does do so, how will that provide a principle that is necessary and sufficient to articulate, to individuate, and to trace through their life-histories the members of k?

What is certain is that if we look to the sortal concept to do this there is no help to be got with the problem from accounts of natural kinds in the tradition of nominal essence (as traditionally conceived), or from accounts that seek to specify the sense of 'sun' or 'horse' or 'tree' by a description of such things in terms of manifest properties and relations, or appearances. It is now a very familiar point that these are unsatisfactory even in their own terms. When we read proposals of this sort literally, and as they seem to ask to be understood, they always fail either of necessity or of sufficiency for membership in the intended kind. And this is not their only failure. By the very form in which nominal essence accounts are given, it is impossible that they should reconstruct our actual understanding of natural kind substantives. They leave unexplained, not only the way in which our conceptions of the compliants of a sortal predicate can evolve while still being conceptions *of* the very same natural kind, but also the non-arbitrariness of that evolution. In the second place there is too little room in such accounts for the contextual conditions or the cultural, technological and other background conditions of our catching hold of one another's meaning when we make reference to kinds[1]—indeed of kinds being discerned at all in nature.

Hilary Putnam's counter-proposal is now well known.[2] It is that *x*

---

1. 'To be sure—there has to be a great deal of stage-setting before one can read a [dictionary] definition and guess how a word is used. But in debunking . . . the fact that something so simple . . . *can* convey the use of a word [certain philosophers] forget to be impressed by it . . . there is a great deal of stage-setting, but it is rarely stage-setting specifically designed to enable one to learn the use of *this* word.' (Hilary Putnam, 'How is Semantics Possible?', *Metaphilosophy* 3, 1970, p. 198.)

In subsequent writings Putnam has stressed how any good theory of these matters must incorporate not only stage-setting but also the division of labour and the dependence of non-experts on experts in the identification of natural and other kinds. At the time of writing his latest formulation is this ('Reference and Understanding', typescript, p. 24):

The ['probability theory of meaning'] cannot as it stands incorporate *either* the linguistic division of labour (the fact that confirmation procedures for *being gold,* or *being aluminium,* or *being an elm tree,* or *being N.N.* are not the property of every speaker . . . speakers defer to experts for the fixing of reference in a huge number of cases), *or* the contribution of the environment (the fact that the extension of a term sometimes fixes its meaning and not *vice versa*). In my view, the criteria used by experts to tell whether or not something is gold are not 'part of the meaning' of *gold* (e.g. the word doesn't change its meaning in the language if the experts shift to a different set of tests for same metal), yet they are part of a mechanism for fixing the extension of gold.

Compare Leibniz *Nouveaux Essais:*

le nom de l'or par exemple signifie non pas seulement ce que celuy, qui le prononce, connoist; par exemple: un jaune très pesant, mais encor ce qu'il ne connoist pas, et qu'un autre en peut connoistre, c'est à dire un corps doué d'une constitution interne, dont decoule la couleur et la pesanteur, et dont naissent d'autres proprietés, qu'il avoue estre mieux connues des experts (3.11.25).

C'est comme si l'on disait qu'un certain corps fusible, jaune et très pesant, qu'on appelle or, a une nature, qui luy donne encore la qualité d'estre fort doux au marteau et a pouvoir estre rendu extremement mince (3.10.17).

Aristotle too seems to have held that we can seize upon a phenomenon, e.g. a certain noise heard in the clouds, as what a word means, 'thunder' for instance (*Posterior Analytics,* 93^{a22}), and then work back to a nature or essence, such as *quenching of fire in the clouds* (the rudiments of what Aristotelians call a real definition and Leibniz a causal one), which the word indicates or points to. See Robert Bolton, *Philosophical Review* 1976, op. cit. in footnote 7, *Preamble.*

2. See also Saul A. Kripke, Lecture III, 'Naming and Necessity', in Davidson and Harman, eds, *Semantics of Natural Languages,* Dordrecht, Reidel, 1972. Compare

is an f (horse, cypress tree, orange, caddis-fly . . .) if and only if, given good exemplars of the kind (this, that and the other particular f), the most explanatory and comprehensive true theoretical description of the kind that the exemplars exemplify would group x alongside these

---

Leibniz, N.E. 3.6.14. Related conclusions have been reached by Vernon Pratt in 'Biological Classification', *British Journal for the Philosophy of Science* 1972, pp. 305–27. See also W. V. Quine, 'Natural Kinds' in Rescher, ed., *Essays in Honour of C. G. Hempel*, Dordrecht, Reidel, 1969; and Hide Ishiguro, 'Leibniz and the Idea of Sensible Qualities' in S. Brown and G. Vesey, eds, *Reason and Reality*, London, Macmillan, 1972.

It will forestall much confusion to propose a definite terminology here. The terminology will coincide with Frege's usage wherever Frege had a serviceable term, and may sometimes diverge from Putnam's. A sortal predicate has a *sense*, a *reference* or *designation*, and an *extension*; and there pertain to it both a *concept* (which may have *marks*) and a *conception*.

[1] The *reference* or *designation* of a sortal predicate such as 'horse', or 'what "horse" stands for', is the concept *horse* or *what it is to be a horse*.

[2] The *extension* of a sortal predicate such as 'horse' is the class of entities falling under the concept which it designates, i.e. the class of horses.

[3] The *sense*, or *contribution to truth-conditions*, of a sortal predicate may be elucidated by specifying what concept the predicate stands for.

[4] A *conception* of horse is a theory (or, if 'theory' is too grand, then an account or prototheory) of what a horse is, or what it is to be a horse. The conception is in no way the same as the concept. The conception is *of* the concept. Almost any appreciable change in people's beliefs about horses might constitute a shift in their conception of horses. But only rarely could a change in conception result in anything so extreme as a shift in the reference of 'horse'. (Though it may result in a correction of previous conceptions of that extension. But that is different, and will sometimes be determinately distinguishable from the rarer occurrence, which is a change in the extensions *correctly* associated at t and t' with a predicate that lives on in the language from t to t'. In practice we do leave room for such correction. Cf. G. Sommerhof, *Analytical Biology*, Oxford, 1950, p. 32: 'While vagueness must be condemned, *elasticity* may yet be highly desirable. The use of a concept is elastic if its users are prepared in the light of experience to consider alternative definitions for it.') As regards the connexion between conception and *sense*, however, it is not hard to envisage that a shift in beliefs about horses can be substantial enough to make the interpretation 'horse' inappropriate, e.g. if people's new conceptions of horses are mismatched with all the conceptions that go along with 'horse' as we now have it and use it in interpreting the language of others. On these matters see, *mutatis mutandis*, J. H. McDowell, *Mind* 1977, 'On the Sense and Reference of a Proper Name', and my 'Frege's Problem of the Morning Star and the Evening Star' (*op. cit.* (4), Preface).

[5] Finally a *mark* ϕ of a concept f is any ϕ such that $(\forall x)(fx \supset \phi x)$.

I have tried to present Putnam's theory in a manner that (a) is compatible with a supplementary doctrine of his about the stereotypes which support human understanding of substantives (stereotypes being standardized sets of beliefs or idealized beliefs associated with terms, and belonging with *conception*); (b) leaves sense itself relatively insensitive to minor shifts in conception, and to minor changes in the criteria used by experts; but (c) involves no unnecessary or dubious claims to the effect that the sense (contrast reference) of a natural kind word is invariant through change in theories, beliefs, or conceptions.

exemplars. It is fully compatible with this suggestion that the theoretical description that is in question in a given case should make reference to both the microphysical and the macrophysical. (Some of the most useful theoretical notions in this area are covertly both microphysical and macrophysical, *gene-pool* for instance.) I should also stress that it is not an implication of Putnam's doctrine that the people who use a natural kind word will know what the true theory of the kind is—only that, if they take the word seriously *as* the name of a natural kind, then their linguistic practices depend finally upon the however inexplicit supposition, not always borne out,[3] that such a theory is there to be found. But, according to the doctrine, the determination of a natural kind stands or falls with the existence of lawlike principles, known or unknown, that will collect together its actual extension around an arbitrary good representative of the extension. For the name to stand for a natural kind, everything depends on whether there is some nomological grounding for what it is to be of the kind. If there is, and if the predicate is worthy to survive as a natural kind term, then the holding of the relevant principles is nothing less than constitutive of its exemplification by its instances. To be something of that kind is to exemplify the distinctive mode of activity that they determine.

In this conception we are driven back to an unmysterious but pre-empiricist notion of substance which it would have been both possible and advantageous for Aristotle to distance from his concern with final causes:

> Things which exist by nature . . . such as animals and the organs of these or plants and the elementary stuffs . . . have in them a principle of change or rest (in respect of place or growth and decline or alteration generally) . . . the nature of a thing being the source or cause of non-accidental change or rest in anything to which it (the nature) belongs . . . (*Physics Book II*, ch. 1),

and which Leibniz did divorce from all final causality except that of God's decree:

> Aristotle has well called [nature] the *principle of motion and of rest,* though that philosopher seems to me to take the term more broadly than its accepted meaning and to understand by it not only local motion and

3. Witness what befell 'caloric', 'phlogiston', and Leuwenhoek's 'hominids'. On such terms see Kripke, *op. cit.* (footnote 2), and Lecture One, *ibid.,* paragraph one, and his addendum at pages 763–4. See also G. Frege, *Nachgelassene Schriften* (ed. H. Hermes, F. Kambartel, F. Kaulbach), Hamburg, Felix Meiner Verlag, 1969, p. 133; and *mutatis mutandis* my *Preface, op. cit.* (4), p. 232, and J. H. McDowell, *Mind* 1977.

rest in a place, but change and *stasis* or permanence in general (p. 499). . . . [The] divine law once established . . . has truly conferred upon [things] some created impression which endures within them, or . . . an *internal law* from which their actions and passions follow (p. 500). . . . if the law of God does in fact leave some vestige of him expressed in things . . . then it must be granted that there is a certain efficacy residing in things, a form or force such as we usually designate by the name of nature, from which the series of phenomena follows. (*On Nature Itself, or on the Inherent Force and Actions of Created Things*, Gerhardt IV, 504ff., as translated at p. 499 follg. by Leroy E. Loemker, *Leibniz Philosophical Papers and Letters*, 2nd edn, Dordrecht, Reidel, 1969.)

Putnam's account of natural kind words, as combined with the importance ascribed here to the *what is it* question, provides a fresh understanding of one part of the point of these doctrines; and rough and unfinished though his suggestion may be compared with the variety and complexity of all the classifications that are implicit or explicit in our linguistic practices, it has the signal virtue of revealing or recalling to us a possibility that has been scarcely envisaged by those who have preferred to theorize in abstraction from particular kinds of substantive, or preferred to erect transcendental arguments upon the foundation of such supposed truisms as 'because all our concepts are tools for the intellectual handling of our sensory intake, we cannot make sense of any statements about the world except ones admitting of a broadly phenomenalistic analysis'.[4]

4. Jonathan Bennett in 'The Age and Size of the World', *Synthèse* 23, 1972. Of the numerous philosophers who have been party to this conception I know only one who dared to draw the proper conclusion, viz. Nietzsche.

We speak of a 'serpent'; the designation fits nothing but the sinuosity (the *serpere*), and could therefore appertain also equally to the worm. What arbitrary demarcations! What one-sided preferences given sometimes to this, sometimes to that, quality of a thing. . . . What therefore is truth? A mobile army of metaphors, metonymies, anthropomorphisms; in short a sum of human relations which become rhetorically intensified, metamorphosed, adorned, and after long usage seem to a nation fixed, canonic and binding; truths are illusions of which one has forgotten that they *are* illusions. (*On Truth and Falsity in the Ultramoral Sense*.)

Ingenuity and elaboration of the phenomenal conception can postpone this conclusion. The conclusion Nietzsche draws about truth can be *blurred* by the deliverance of common sense that worms do not in fact belong to the extension of 'serpent'. But might they just as well have? If the semantical conception that sustains Nietzsche's inference to his conclusion is in violation of common sense—and in the presence of an alternative conception of the working of substantives it becomes all the easier to suspect that the phenomenal conception enjoys no special obviousness—the deliverance of common sense is irrelevant and the ingenuity is misplaced. It is a mere postponement of the startling conclusion that Nietzsche draws.

Semantical fact is almost always more interesting than transcendental philosophical

Putnam's account of these matters has been anticipated several times in the history of philosophy; but what earlier attempts have lacked, with the exception of Leibniz's perhaps, is the explicit combination of two distinctive features; (1) the component of *deixis,* which requires of any candidate f that it be relevantly like something that is directly or indirectly identifiable and is actually an f, and (2) the explicit acknowledgment of the indispensable part played in the determination of standards of relevant likeness by the lawlike statements that hold in the real world. With or without this feature, however, all have the distinctive consequence, which is attested by experience, that it is possible for what appear astonishingly like fs to be not fs, and that (because hidden structure dominates apparent, as Heraclitus puts it at fr. 54 Diels) the most improbable seeming specimens may turn out to be fs after all. It can also be a matter of prolonged and difficult inquiry gradually to improve currently accepted standards or conceptions of what it is to be an f.

On Putnam's account, the semantics of a kind word will accommodate all this. There is room for one and the same concept of *what it is to be an f,* anchored to examples that are grouped together in virtue of resemblances that are nomologically grounded, to be unfolded gradually in a succession of different and improving conceptions. As the primitive mentality gives way to the protoscientific, Putnam's theory can predict that men may decide that it is extraordinarily mysterious what even the most ordinary objects are, or feel that they are awakening from a state in which they never grasped properly what they encountered nor comprehended it even when they learned to recognize it.[5] The doctrine also illustrates in a schematic way how a word can enter the language on the slenderest and most provisional basis of theory—just enough to yield what is required for the recognition of an extension (which can itself be subsequently purified)—and draw credit on a draft that Nature may *or may not* finally honour.

Once one has seen the possibility of a natural kind word having such a debut, one will be tempted in the case of natural things to replace all doctrines that distinguish in the customary way between

---

fiction; and for the imagination a hundred times more potent. We do not really have to choose between (1) the phenomenal *cum* reductive way of Berkeley and Mach, which assimilates the criterion for being an f to some set of tests for f-hood, (2) the opposite way, which assimilates what would be required by way of a real test for f to the criterion for f-hood.

5. Cf. Heraclitus fragments 17, 26 Diels; and Leibniz '[les hommes] sont empiriques et ne se gouvernent pas que par les sens et les exemples, sans examiner si la même raison a encor lieu' (*Nouveaux Essais,* Gerhardt V, p. 252).

real and nominal essence by an account of the different *stages* in the unfolding of what it is to be an f. Maybe it would be better to describe instead the process by which clear but indistinct knowledge—knowledge sufficient for recognition but without itemized enumeration of distinguishing marks—is replaced by clear, more distinct (better itemized) or more adequate knowledge, and by which the nature of the extension of the predicate becomes more unmysterious to us.[6] It will pose no difficulty to suggest that one could pick out, say, a tadpole, identify its kind by saying 'its members are anything relevantly like this', leaving the actual standards of relevance to be scientifically determined at macrolevel and microlevel, and then be led to discover, with surprise, a principle of individuation for members of the kind that commits one to count into the kind a frog—not of course as a present tadpole, but as a member of the very same kind as the Batrachian specimen recently demonstrated. The discovery here may or may not amount to a modification of the sense. But all that it *need* be is a realization of the possibility, which was always there, of fuller or more detailed specification both of what it is to be an f and of *which* things are f.[7]

Frege said that the sense of an expression determined its reference, and not the reference the sense. If Putnam's theory is correct, this is not normally true of natural kind words. Just as the sense of a proper name (contrast definite description) is best explained by saying what its reference is, so in the process of the teaching and elucidation of the sense of a natural kind predicate everything depends upon the actual extension of the predicate (viz. all past, present and future compliants of the predicate), or on what Frege would have called its reference— the *what it is to be an f*. It does not follow that reference is *prior* to sense. (The principal effect of this would-be salutary exaggeration is only to raise difficult and perfectly irrelevant questions about the possibility of prelinguistic *deixis* and the preverbal categorization of

6. Leibniz describes this process in several places and connexions. See especially his account of clear but indistinct knowledge at *Meditationes de Cognitione Veritate et Ideis,* Gerhardt IV, especially p. 422.

7. Again someone might pick out an amoeba under a microscope, say '*that* cell [or *that* creature], and anything [relevantly] like it, I call an amoeba', and commit himself only to there existing some (as yet unknown to him) standard of scientific similarity. What he commits himself to is to live with that standard and the associated principle of activity when it *is* discovered, and to arbitrate persistence questions, when he graduates to these, in empirical and logical accord with these. We have seen how this minimal commitment leads into a new commitment in this case—the commitment to count every splitting of an amoeba as the demise of that amoeba. The commitment, though its working is logically constrained, is empirically grounded. It is grounded in the actual activity of these unicellular creatures. Cf. also here my *Preface, op. cit.* (2).

experience.) It follows only that sense and reference are here mutually dependent correlative notions.

Suppose that all this is even roughly right. Then it contains most of the answer to the problems that we have posed about the demands of D(iii), D(iv), D(v) and all the other D principles. If there have to exist true lawlike principles in nature for the actual extension of a natural kind predicate to be collected together around the focus of an actual specimen, and if this is a requirement even for the sense of the predicate, then it is a condition of the very existence of fs, so defined, that certain lawlike sentences should hold true. Again, if these lawlike sentences are to have the character they are required to have for the sense of the predicate standing for the concept f, then they must determine directly or indirectly, in ways that we can uncover by empirical discovery, the characteristic development, the typical history, and the limits of any possible development or history of any compliant of f. It follows that if f is a natural kind then, when we consider the problem of the identity through change of things falling under f, the semantics of the predicate that stands for it must exempt us from taking into account any situations other than those conforming to the relevant laws of the actual world. A situation that transgressed them would undermine the very applicability of the predicate.

The conclusion is not a novel one:

> I also maintain that substances cannot be conceived in their essence as bare or without activity, that activity is of the essence of substance as such . . . above all it is necessary to consider that the modifications that can befall a subject naturally or without miracle derive from limitation and variation in a real kind, or from a constant and absolute original nature . . . and wherever one finds some quality in a subject, one must believe that if one understood the nature of the subject and of the quality then one would understand how the quality could result from them. So in the order of nature it is in no way arbitrary whether substances have these qualities or those, and God will only give them those qualities which naturally befit them, that is the qualities which could be derived from the nature of the substances themselves as intelligible modifications of them . . . everything that is must be such as to be intelligible distinctly, if only one were admitted to the secret of things. . . .[8]

---

8. Leibniz, *Nouveaux Essais,* preface, Gerhardt, p. 59. Compare, in connexion with the contentions of the preceding paragraphs, Leibniz in Couturat, *Opuscules et Fragments Inedits de Leibniz,* Paris, 1903, pp. 16–24:

> I think that in this series of things there are certain propositions that are most universally true, and which not even a miracle could violate. This is not to say that they have any necessity for God; but rather that when he chose the particular

The interest of this conception of the activity of a substance, and of Leibniz's idea that the nomological foundation of activity is always something supervenient upon fundamental laws of nature (see Gerhardt II, 263, quoted at the head of this chapter), utterly transcends all the particularities of Leibniz's finished view of substance (which in the end dethroned Aristotelian continuants, seen as imperfect from this point of view, in favour of monads). Its implication for the theory of individuation outlined in Chapter Two may be summed up in an idiom that is alien to this book but, for the purposes of this particular thought, very concise. Where fs make up a natural kind, the only possible worlds we need consider, being the only possible worlds having within them any entity that is an f, are worlds sufficiently similar in nomological respects to the actual world to exhibit specimens relevantly similar to actual specimens. This means that, for the special case of natural kinds, we find that ordinary necessity nearly coincides with physical necessity, and ordinary possibility with physical possibility.[9] It was difficult, until we thought about the sense of natural kind words in Leibniz's or Putnam's fashion, to imagine how the requirements of the last chapter could possibly be satisfied. But the principal difficulty that now remains is epistemological, and is shifted to another point, which is at once right and familiar: how to assure oneself, once one realizes what a considerable commitment such an identification may involve, that any particular entity really is an f, or a g, or whatever.

It may be instructive to try to illustrate here how the theory of individuation and the most general findings of theoretical biology are in a certain way made for one another. (A way whose significance exceeds the pleasure a biologist may have in any anticipations he can read into such Leibnizian formulations as Gerhardt II, 264: 'For there to be a certain persisting law which involves the future states of that which we conceive as one and the same continuant, this is what I say constitutes a substance's identity'.) Starting off with the idea of a sortal predicate whose sense is such as to involve its extension, and which is the candidate *par excellence* for real definition, we are led to speculate what holds together the extension. So soon as we find that,

---

series of things he did choose, he decided by that very act to observe these principles as [giving] the specific properties of *just this particular series of things*. (Cf. Gerhardt II, 263 quoted at the head of this Chapter Three.)

I have followed here the interpretation of Leibniz's view that is defended in chapter IV, especially § 3-4, of Hide Ishiguro's *Leibniz's Philosophy of Logic and Language*.

9. Cf. Ishiguro, *loc. cit.* For the impact of this point upon the problem of splitting, see *Longer Note* 3.09.

we also find lawlike norms of starting to exist, existing, and ceasing to exist by reference to which questions of the identity and persistence of individual specimens falling under a definition can be arbitrated. Such norms will be supervenient on basic laws of nature, we have supposed, and represent certain so to say *exploitations* of these laws. But then we have been led by simple conceptual considerations to precisely the kind of account of living substances that biologists can amplify for us *a posteriori*, seeing these as systems open to their surroundings but not in equilibrium with them and so constituted as to be able, by dint of a delicate self-regulating balance of serially linked enzymatic degradative and synthesizing chemical reactions, to renew themselves on the molecular level at the expense of those surroundings—the renewal taking place under a law-determined variety of conditions and always in a species-determined pattern of growth and development towards, and/or persistence in, one particular form. (In certain cases there may be definite alternative forms keyed to different environments, e.g. locust/grasshopper, axolotl/salamander, but again this is something that is founded in a lawlike basis.)

2. *The other sortal predicates*

What has been said so far has been directed mainly at words standing for the various species of natural substances. The account could be extended and adapted without overwhelming difficulty to predicates of *genera*, where these were still determinate enough to be autonomously individuative. (See especially requirements **D**(iv) and **D**(v).) And *mutatis mutandis* certain of the claims so far made would apply both to words for the natural organs, *heart, liver, foot, brain*, and even to geographical or geological terms like *river, lake, spring, sea, glacier*, or *volcano*. In the latter case it will not be wildly inappropriate to speak of principles of activity. In the former we can honour **D**(viii) in terms both of principles of *activity* and of *modes of functioning* or *operation*. It would be interesting to enter into detailed questions about just how well these predicates measure up to the **D** requirements of the previous chapter; and to enter all the appropriate and considerable reservations.[10] But apart from the intrinsic interest of

10. There need be no one physiological theory to cover all animal hearts of all kinds. There is no one specific structure which a heart must have, nor any one fully specific mode of biological functioning that a heart must as such exemplify. To be a heart simply—contrast a human heart, a sheep's heart—an organ need only be an organ of

these kinds of entity it would be distractive, and it would be seen as mere postponement by those who hold that it is above all on artifact kinds that the individuative theory proposed in Chapter Two must stumble.

Consider ordinary artifact-words like *clock, chisel, drinking vessel, drill, stove, pen, spade, table.* Putnam's account cannot apply to these. Admittedly the easiest way to explain what a tool or artifact of some sort is may be by reference to an example. But *deixis* is scarcely indispensable—indeed it could be positively confusing under some circumstances: and there are virtually no lawlike sentences to be had about particular utensil, implement or tool kinds *as such.* There scarcely could be. Clocks, for instance, may be made of a variety of different kinds of material and may function by radically different kinds of mechanism (cf. Locke, *Essay* 3.6.39). Although artifacts are things to be encountered in nature, and subject to its laws, they are not collected and classified together *as this or that artifact* by virtue of resemblances of any scientific or nomological import. Artifacts are collected up not by reference to a theoretically hypothesized inner constitution but under functional descriptions that have to be indifferent to specific constitution and particular mode of interaction with environment. A clock is any time-keeping device, a pen is any rigid ink-applying writing implement, and so on. The description gives what it is usually impossible to specify in the other cases, an explicit *nominal essence*: whereas a finite and determinate set of marks suitable for definitional purposes is precisely not what the members of natural kinds endowed with a scientifically palpable real essence have in common.[11]

For the theory of individuation generally, and for the theory here advanced especially, there is then a crucially important difference

---

some definite physiological kind or other playing a particular role in the circulation of the blood.

Such terms seem then to be hybrid between functionally defined terms shortly to be characterized and natural kind terms. Compare certain complexities of the concept *person*; see below, Chapter Six, section 8.

11. Cf. *Preface, op. cit* (3) page 336, and (8). Concepts of artifact kinds, being verbally analysable in a way that is excluded for concepts of natural kinds, offer more prospect of generating truths that are analytic (in the strict sense of 'analytic', viz. truths reducible by explicit definitions to truths of logic). Even here though, and in the place where such truths would be less interesting, the matter is not unproblematic—if only because of the high degree of actual vagueness and indeterminacy in the definitions of artifact kinds and all the scope there is here for innovation. In any case, neither here nor in other chapters does anything whatever hang on analyticity. It would do no damage whatever to the doctrines of nature, substance and necessity put forward in this book if the only analytic truths were the logical truths.

between natural things and artifacts, both in respect of conditions of identity through time and in respect of the satisfaction of the requirements upon sortal predicates sketched in Chapter Two. Where there is any dispute concerning an object identified as a member of a natural kind one can readily conceive of getting more scientific facts. Consider the nineteenth-century discovery that the elvers *Leptocephali* were in fact the young of the species Conger Eel, or the humbler but in some sense proto-scientific discovery that tadpoles become frogs. These discoveries changed conceptions (not concepts); and on the exemplar theory we can see how they not only related to the semantics of 'eel' or 'frog' but also represented improvements in the understanding of concepts (what they revealed having been always allowed for by the fixing of the designation of the kind-word).[12] We can see why identity questions about members of natural kinds may be expected to find the notion of identity at its best, and, empirical discovery playing the part it does play here, it is plain why they are the most unsuitable of all candidates for conventionalist treatment. By reference to the nomological foundation of the natural kind concept we can make a clear distinction between normal activity and interference; at least for the case of normal autonomous activity we can set ourselves to find out what is *involved* in persistence, and enjoy complete confidence that this will decide everything that needs to be decided. It is in no way up to us what to count as persistence through change or through replacement of matter. Contrast the identity problem of artifacts. To some limited extent there may be shadowy counterparts of what a natural kind concept furnishes straightforwardly, but in the case of damage to a watch, say, or extensive replacement of its parts, there is nothing theoretical or extra to discover, once the ordinary narrative of events is complete. For there is no such thing as the natural development of a watch or a natural law concerning watches as such.

It will be useful, before we grapple with the problems of artifact identity, to return to the first chapter of Book Two of Aristotle's *Physics*:

> . . . animals and their organs and the elementary stuffs . . . differ from what is not naturally constituted in that each of these things has within it a principle of change and of staying unchanged, whether in respect of place or in respect of quantitative change, as in growth and decay, or in respect of qualitative change. But a bedstead or a cloak or whatever, *qua*

---

12. Here and throughout the terminology proposed in footnote 2 of this chapter is being maintained.

receiving the designation 'bed' or 'cloak' . . ., i.e. in so far as it is the
product of craft, has within itself no inherent tendency to any particular
sort of change. But in so far as an artifact happens to be composed . . . of
whatever mixture of natural elements, it does incidentally, as so considered, have within itself the principle of change which inheres in its
matter. So nature is a *source or principle of change and staying unchanged*
in that to which it belongs *primarily*, i.e. in virtue of the thing itself and
not in virtue of an incidental attribute of the thing. I say 'not in virtue of
an incidental attribute' because, for instance, a man who is a doctor
might cure himself. Nevertheless it is not in so far as he is a patient that
he possessed the art of medicine. It was incidental that he satisfied both
descriptions. And something similar holds of everything that is an
artificial product (192^{b8-28}).

There is an insight here that is so important that it deserves a
formulation free of the locutions 'qua', 'in so far as', 'considered as' at
which Aristotle clutches so desperately to give voice to his thought.
(These are the locutions by which some Aristotelians still persist in
obfuscating this and many other good thoughts; cf. the discussion in
Chapter One, section 7 under (λ).) Let us say instead that a particular
continuant x belongs to a natural kind, or is a natural thing, if and
only if x has a principle of activity corresponding to the nomological
basis of that or those extension-involving sortal identifications which
answer truly the question 'what is x?'. For purposes of this chapter,
and for purposes of the theory of individuation, it is not the question
of whether a thing was fabricated but the difference between satisfying and not satisfying this condition that makes the fundamental
distinction. Loosely, and because there is no other handy term, I shall
continue to call all objects that fail this crucial condition 'artifacts'.
*But this is without prejudice to the question, which is scientific not
philosophical, of the possibility of the artificial synthesis of natural
things.* I must stress this particularly, not only to protect the present
chapter from misunderstanding, but also to protect Chapter Six.
    It should go almost without saying that the distinction natural
thing *versus* artifact is presented here in a fashion conformable at
every point and in every particular with the plausible scientific belief
that, however a thing is conceptualized, it is subject to the fundamental laws of physics and chemistry. For that belief, there is no more
difficulty in our distinction between natural things and other things
than there is in making a further distinction, *within* the class of
natural things, between those things which, being alive, are not in
chemical and energy equilibrium with their surroundings, but suck
from their environment the energy they need for their typical activity

and molecular self-renewal and replacement, and those natural things that maintain a typical mode of activity without being alive and cannot help but be in equilibrium with their surroundings. It is true that live things exemplify most perfectly and completely a category of substance that is extension-involving, has characteristic activity, and is unproblematic for individuation. But not all extension-involving concepts are concepts of live things and I should stress that non-equilibrium with surroundings is an additional and special distinguishing mark. In fact terrible confusion will result generally from any assimilation of the *live/not live* distinction to the other two distinctions. *Extension involving* or *not extension involving, synthetically produced* or *not synthetically produced*, and *live* or *not live* (as elucidated in terms of non-equilibrium and of self-renewal at the molecular level)—these are *three* distinctions, for all that live animals fall on the same side of each of them.

3. *Problems of artifact identity*

Our pressing concern now becomes the problem of the individuation of artifacts and of other things that cannot furnish the theorist of identity with a principle of activity. Summing up the argument so far in the claims that natural things are individuated by reference to a principle of activity naturally embodied, and that ordinary artifacts are individuated, with less logical determinacy and considerably greater arbitrariness, by reference to a parcel of matter so organized as to subserve a certain function,[13] we shall be tempted to exaggerate the degree to which questions of artifact identity are matters of arbitrary decision. Even here I think that unqualified conventionalism is not overwhelmingly plausible. But artifact identity does present some difficult problems.

D(iii) requires that what an artifact-word like 'clock' contributes to the semantical determination of the relation 'x coincides with y under the concept *clock*' should be such as to make this relation both an equivalence relation and a congruence relation. But how can this be secured? And how are we to get the effect for artifacts that was got for natural things by the notion of activity? (The conceptual effect, I mean.) It would be unrealistic and absurd to suppose that coincidence under the concept *clock* required a clock's continuous functioning, or that the functioning spoken of in D(v) was more than

13. Contrast works of art, which do not normally, *qua* works of art, have any *function*. See below, Chapter Four, section 10.

remotely analogous to the activity of natural things. A clock may stop because it needs winding up. Such a pause does not prejudice its persistence. A clock can also stop because it needs to be repaired; and again it persists, however long the lapse before the repair. (The nominal essence of *clock* does not make 'broken clock' problematic for existence or peculiar in the manner of 'dead person'.) The nominal essence of *clock* must involve a stipulation of some sort concerning the capacity to tell the time. But surely the uninterrupted continuance for all t of the capacity at t to tell the time at t will not be stipulated. This is too strong. What counts to any appreciable degree against the persistence of a clock is only an *irretrievable* loss of the time-keeping function, or a loss of function which is, if not irretrievable, then finally and irrevocably unretrieved.[14] The coincidence-condition for clocks that results from all this, and the limitation this condition imposes upon the reorganization or dissipation of the matter and parts of a clock, is extremely weak.

Another reason why a clock-persistence condition has to be weak is that the repair of a clock apparently permits both *disassembly* and *replacement of parts*. We do not look back to the time when a clock was being repaired and say that the clock's existence was interrupted while it was in a dismantled condition. For a thing starts existing only once; and in the case of a clock its proper beginning was at about the time when its maker finished it. In the case of dismantling there is not even a time limit upon reassembly.

When these several points of discontinuous functioning, disassembly, and part replacement have been accommodated, the condition of coincidence and persistence for clocks that remains is not merely weak. It is so weak that there seems to be nothing to prevent one clock, identified by a description applying at the time when it was functioning normally, from *clock*-coinciding (i.e. coinciding in a manner supposedly sufficient for identity) with two distinct clocks, each identified under a description applying to it after some radical repair or muddled reassembly in an only moderately disorderly clock maker's workshop. But the coincidence of one thing with two things breaches requirement **D**(iii), **D**(vi), and almost every other interesting declaration made in Chapter Two. (It is worth noticing that it would even flout the weaker requirements that relative identity theorists would place upon the relation *is the same clock as*.) Nor is there one piece of clock—the spring, the regulator, the escapement, the face,

14. Perhaps some definite limitation is also required upon the particular *manner* of functioning by reference to which the condition is stated, but I do not see a good way to achieve this restriction.

the case . . . which the concept *clock* could suggest that we should revere as the 'focus' or 'nucleus' of a clock, and which can help us past this difficulty. Here, and in the extremes of ingenuity and opportunism to which such problems pushed the Roman laws of *accessio* and *specificatio* (cf., for instance, Justininian, *Institutes* Bk II, 1.34 *et passim*), we see that, however questionable it may be, Leibniz's transition in the decade of his writing the *Discourse of Metaphysics* from Aristotelian substances to Leibnizian monads, and his demotion of things with parts to the status of mere aggregates (for a characteristic statement see Gerhardt II, 261), did not arise from a simple misconception of the logical level of the predicate 'one'.

A good place to embark on the difficulties of artifact identity is with a case that Thomas Hobbes put forward expressly against those who regarded 'unity of form' as a *principium individuationis*: on this view,

> two bodies existing both at once would be one and the same numerical body. For if, for example, that ship of Theseus, concerning the difference whereof made by continued reparation in taking out the old planks and putting in new, the sophisters of Athens were wont to dispute, were, after all the planks were changed, the same numerical ship it was at the beginning; and if some man had kept the old planks as they were taken out, and by putting them afterwards together in the same order, had again made a ship of them, this, without doubt, had also been the same numerical ship with that which was at the beginning; and so there would have been two ships numerically the same, which is absurd.[15]

The unity of form theory that Hobbes means to attack here is not dissimilar from ours; and in our version of the theory coincidence under the concept *ship* has to be the makings of a sufficient condition of being the same ship (unless the concept *ship* were to be not a sortal concept). It might seem that in our theory the difficulty Hobbes mentions is escaped, because it favours the repaired ship. For the constant availability of this ship, and its uninterrupted service as the sacred ship by which the annual voyage was made from Piraeus to

---

15. *De Corpore* II, 11 (Molesworth, p. 136). Hobbes's source for the puzzle is Plutarch's life of Theseus:

> The vessel in which Theseus sailed and returned safe with these young men went with thirty oars. It was preserved by the Athenians up to the times of Demetrius Phalerus [floruit 280 B.C.]; being so refitted and newly fashioned with strong plank, that it afforded an example to the philosophers in their disputations concerning the identity of things that are changed by addition, some contending that it was the same, and others that it was not. (§§ 22–23; Cf. Plato, *Phaedo* 58ᴬ; Xenophon, *Memorabilia* 4.8.2.)

Delos may seem to mark this ship out as the one that is continuous in the manner of a ship with Theseus' ship. Subject to one reservation consequential upon the 'Only *a* and *b*' rule, which is due to be introduced as **D**(x) in the next section, it may seem that the explanations that the theory has already tendered for 'coincide' place us very well to reject as not good enough the claim of the reconstructed ship; and that, as applied to the concept ship, they do this independently of the threat to **D**(iv).

But this is scarcely the end of the matter or the whole answer to Hobbes' challenge. Suppose it were decided, in an age that no longer believed in Apollo but still believed in Theseus, to erect a monument to Theseus and to put his ship upon the monument. Surely some people would say that the ship put together from discarded planks was the right one to raise up there. And dispute might break out about this matter between priests who favoured the working ship and antiquarians who preferred the reconstruction.[16] The difficulty is then a certain incomparability between their positions. It may seem that one party would be looking for an archaeological relic and the other for a functionally persistent continuant; and that the dispute was to be traced to a disagreement about what it is for something to be a sacred ship. The antiquarian who favours the reconstructed ship has a different interest, it may be said, from the priest who favours the

16. A mereologist making reference to the mereological definition of identity

$(a = b) =_{df} [(a$ is a part of $b) \& (b$ is a part of $a)]$

might well side with the antiquarian and against the priests. As will appear, I do not want to say that the priests are on the right side of the argument and the antiquarian on the wrong side. But it is a precondition of the acceptability of the mereological definition of identity invoked on the antiquarian's behalf that, for any non-empty class of individuals α, there should be one and only one sum of all elements of α. That is to say that the sum axiom of mereology must be unrestrictedly true, whatever entities we admit into the class α, including continuants that persist through loss or gain of parts. (The sum axiom is the second postulate in the tenseless presentation of mereology given by Tarski op. cit. in footnote 22 of Chapter One. See text of Chapter One for the definition of 'sum'.) I hope that it no longer looks obvious that this axiom is true, unless 'part' is given some technical sense that simply fixes the truth value of Tarski's postulate II. (But in that case the mereological definition of identity that depends upon the axiom loses all direct usefulness for the antiquarian cause.)

Relative identity theorists are apt to claim for their view of such puzzles as Theseus' ship a particular naturalness. Griffin in *Relative Identity* p. 178 provides what he calls the "simple and appealing" solution that the original ship of Theseus is not the same ship as the reconstruction, though it is the same plank collection. There is then nothing peculiar at all about the case. The reader will have to decide for himself whether it is a virtue or a vice in the relative theory that it so readily parts the disputants from the issue which they suppose they disagree about—and from the ontology of absolute identity.

continuously repaired continuant.[17] Both are stuck with the identification *ship* but, having different interests, they seem not to mean quite
the same thing by 'ship', and neither can base his view upon the 'law
of development' of a ship, or suggest a programme of scientific
research to force one particular resolution upon the question. There
may then be a temptation to dismiss the question as merely psychological.[18] But we must not confuse the fact that it is in some sense a
psychological matter whether *we* adopt the priests' or the archaeol-
ogists' view with its being a merely psychological matter which one is
Theseus' ship—or an arbitrary matter. And problem cases involving
exchange of parts point to a need to soften somewhat the doctrines of
Chapter Two, at least where artifacts are concerned.

4. *Two approaches to the problem of artifact identity*

There are two different ways with this kind of difficulty. The first
involves a departure from the spirit of Chapter Two and involves our
seeing a certain further complexity in the notion of f-coincidence. It
proposes that we start with the relation in which x and y stand just in
case y is a coincidence-*candidate* (of type f) for identity with x. We
then say that x *veritably coincides under·f with* y if and only if y *is an
f-coincidence candidate for identity with x and nothing distinct from y is
an f-coincidence candidate for identity with x.*[19] If one wanted to
proceed like this then one could elaborate the theory further with an

17. Once we have perceived that the dispute about the ship is like this, we may even
start looking in the direction of the possibility that priest and archaeologist find
different entities with different principles of individuation in one and the same place.
That will not quite do. In this case at least, the archaeologist's concept is derivative
from the concept used in active daily life, and it is not so easy as it may seem to restore
determinacy and order. For a sophisticated discussion of this case see Brian Smart,
'How to Reidentify the Ship of Theseus', *Analysis* 32.5, April 1972, pp. 145–8 and 'The
Ship of Theseus, the Parthenon, and Disassembled Objects', *Analysis* 34.1, Oct. 1973,
pp. 24–7.

18. Compare Frege, *Foundations of Arithmetic* § 26:

'The objectivity of the North Sea is not affected by the fact that it is a matter of our
arbitrary choice which part of all the water on the earth's surface we mark off and
elect to call the 'North Sea'. This is no reason for deciding to investigate the North
Sea by psychological methods. . . . If we say 'The North Sea is 10,000 square miles
in extent' . . . we assert something quite objective, which is independent of our
ideas and everything of the sort. If we should happen to wish, on another
occasion, to draw the boundaries of the North Sea differently . . . that *would* not
make false the same content that was previously true.' (Cf. Dummett, *Frege op.
cit.*, p. 576.)

19. See *Longer Note* 3.19.

account of the degrees of strength in a candidature, and arrange to distinguish best from second best, third best . . . claimants. Such proposals abound in the literature and, for artifacts at least (contrast persons), they may well seem attractive. But their attraction is illusory. It derives entirely from the apparent lack of an alternative.

The most fundamental objection to the 'best candidate' approach is that it licenses the following as a possibility: we could walk up to the antiquarian's relic, seen as a candidate to be Theseus' ship, and say that, but for the existence of its rival, i.e. the distinct coincidence-candidate that is the constantly maintained working ship plying once yearly to Delos, it would have veritably coincided as a ship with Theseus' original ship. But the idea that in *that* case it would have been Theseus' very ship seems to be absurd.[20] There is a temptation to add as a *step* in this argument: nothing might have been a different entity from the entity it actually is. But the temptation is to be resisted. We are discovering in this argument, which for what it is worth is complete as it stands, the real intuitive grounds for doubting that anything might have been a numerically different entity from the one it actually is. The doubt is not a premiss or step, but something brought to light by the argument; and it is grounded in the violence the contrary supposition does to the understanding of '=' that is implicit in everything we think and say about identity (at least when we are not struggling with paradoxical cases). It *underlies* the impossibility of conceiving of an entity's not being identical with that with which it *is* in fact identical.

It is important to make clear that the argument just offered is directed solely against the 'best candidate' type of theory. It is not intended to muster support for the decision (provisional in any case) in favour of the working ship and against the reconstituted one. *Mutatis mutandis* the same argument would be available if the antiquarian's were preferred to the working ship.

Before coming to this other method of dealing with the difficulties posed by artifact identity, it will be useful to state the moral of the

---

20. Compare Arnauld, letter of 13 May 1686 to Leibniz:

> I can as little conceive of different varieties of myself and a circle whose diameters are not all of equal length. The reason is that these different varieties of myself would all be distinct from one another, otherwise there would not be many of them. Thus one of these varieties of myself would necessarily not be me: which is manifestly a contradiction. (Gerhardt II, 30, translated by H. T. Mason.)

Cf. also B. Williams, 'Personal Identity and Continuity', *Analysis* 21, 1960, a discussion antedating in the philosophical literature of identity the rediscovery of Miss Barcan's *J.S.L.* 1947 proof of the necessity of identity.

breakdown of the first method. What we need, if *identity* is what we want to elucidate, is a criterion which will stipulate that for a relation R to be constitutive of the identity of *a* and *b*, *a*'s having R to *b* must be such that objects distinct from *a* or *b* are irrelevant to whether *a* has R to *b*. Let us call this the *Only a and b* condition and add it as **D**(x) to our list in Chapter Two. This condition is violated by the 'best candidate' proposal in all variants.

I shall start out upon the other approach I have promised with the remark that in all the literature of the subject that I have been able to see there is not a single proposal which (a) justifies the whole corpus and every reasonable seeming extension of the corpus of identity judgements about artifacts we commonly accept as true, (b) allows total freedom of disassembly *and* part-replacement, (c) meets **D**(iii), and (d) satisfies the *Only a and b* condition.[21] Even if one were to relax a jot or two the demands we have been placing on identity criteria, cautiously but perceptibly, in recognition of the tolerance that so many linguistic practices require and in real life so rarely abuse, there would still be no chance of ordinary artifact terms both meeting the modified requirement and making indefinite allowance of disassembly, repair *and* discontinuance of function.

Does this mean that we are faced with the choice between the laws of identity and abandoning, in the spirit of the maxim *no entity without identity,* the whole ontology of artifacts? Is it simply an illusion that this ontology and its associated ideology are well-founded? At best the data will only support a more modest heresy.

21. This may not be quite accurate. One possible exception is a condition proposed by Brian Smart (*Analysis* 1973–74) and by Graham McFee (*Flesh: An Essay on Personal Identity,* M.A. thesis, Keele, 1975) which protects the continuity of form condition in the Theseus' ship case by ruling that planks removed serially from the ship are not necessarily parts of the ship any longer. ('A replaced part is no longer an actual part at all, just as an ex-convict is no longer a convict . . . the 'continuity of parts' condition applies but *actual* parts must be used', McFee, *op. cit.* Cf. part III, § 8 of D. P. Henry, *Medieval Logic and Metaphysics,* London, Hutchinson, 1972.) The trouble with this approach is that it presupposes some other account than the purely mereo-logical account of what it is for a ship to survive disassembly. But it is clear that the continuity of form condition is not strong enough (or correct enough when strong enough) to arbitrate all the questions of survival and identity which arise in all the problem cases that have challenged the ingenuity of contributors to *Analysis* and the *Journal of Philosophy.* The continuity of form condition as Smart and McFee construe it is never incorrect, but it can only be applied without paradox or contradiction to the full range of cases where these writers have supposed that the ship *survives* disassembly etc., if there is available *another* account (or some supplement of this account) saying what it is for it to survive so. This other account of what constitutes identity in the problem cases must not protect itself from refutation by pleading the laws of identity. The shoe is on the other foot. The laws of identity as applied to the relation *is the same ship as* have to flow from the nature of this account.

Most of the judgements that it is necessary to suggest that we should block or revise concern cases which are either extreme or paradoxical (in the way in which the case of the ship of Theseus is both). It is not even obvious that outside philosophy anybody has really made any of the judgements which the proposal that is due to be presented will proscribe as incorrect.

What supports the ontology of artifacts, and what has made it possible in the first instance to treat artifacts as continuants, is the availability of an indubitably sufficient condition of artifact identity that may be constructed on the lines of a criterion that has been suggested for quantities in the category of stuff by Helen Morris Cartwright. The condition does not exclude change, but it excludes all addition or subtraction of matter whatever; and, as adapted to artifacts, it also requires the however vestigial continuance of the capacity to subserve whatever roles or ends the artifact was designed as that very artifact to subserve. (Cf. **D**(v).)

This condition can be relaxed a little without our facing either the difficulty of necessary conditions or the danger that condition **D**(iv) will be breached. Some matter may be exchanged, perhaps, provided all replacement of material parts is referred back to the first state of the finished artifact, and provided only, if the reader will forgive the comical precision of this first attempt, the artifact retains more than half of that original matter. (Or retains, where such is definable, the material of some individuatively paramount *nucleus*.) Finally, perhaps some physical adaptation of an artifact can be allowed in response to shifts in the social or technical purpose for which it was designed. But I shall not explore in detail the question how far this and other relaxations may go before we get to the irreclaimably paradoxical situations like the case of Theseus' ship. (Nor shall I inquire here what other precautions, if any, it will become necessary to take against the paradox of the heap, *Sorites*.) My point is that, by reference to a *strict* condition like the condition we began with, we can see our linguistic practices as underhung by a sort of safety net that will justify our confidence in a certain capacity of ours for controlled opportunism. (If we fall from the heights where we take conceptual risks in our management of artifact identity, then there is provision for redescribing puzzle cases in terms of the disposition and redisposition of their constituent matter. Another possibility, which Edward Hussey has proposed to me that one might consider, is that talk about artifacts should be seen as replaceable by talk about *episodes* in the careers of the sets of objects or aggregates that make up their constituent matter.) For, if we resist the temptation to suppose that we can find in favour of identity even in the most puzzling of the puzzle situations yet devised, then the sufficient condition that we do have justifies us in treating artifact-kind words as sortal predicates properly and generally competent to explicate coincidence, to determine persistence conditions, and to cover judgements of absolute identity for artifacts.

No admissible relaxation of the strict condition will account for each and every judgement of artifact identity by which we are rationally tempted. But in the case of at least some of the more audacious judgements of artifact identity, where the concept exceeds its strength and takes us too far from the original function or material constitution of the artifact,[22] it is not obvious that judgements always demand to be read literally as statements of identity. Certainly it is not difficult to find a reinterpretation of such judgements. When a man gives his watch to the watchmaker to clean and repair, what he wants back may, on a very sober and literal minded construal, be *either* that very watch (by the unproblematic criterion) *or* a watch with a certain obvious relation to his (a watch of the same kind, in better working order, enjoying considerable community of parts, etc.). If he wants more than that, if he thinks of his watch as an antiquarian or historical relic from a better age, or as a work of art, then he should take more precautions than we normally do take. Which is to say that, for many practical purposes, we normally do not care very much about the difference between artifact survival and artifact replacement. (A negligence that in no way undermines the real distinction between these.) In so far as this provokes the suggestion that convention reigns here, there is at least a point to be found in Aristotle's doctrine that natural things are the real beings *par excellence* to which everything else is secondary—even perhaps in the extraordinary sounding doctrine that the title of *real unity* must be reserved to 'animate bodies endowed with primitive entelechies'.[23]

This is how matters seem to stand with the normal artifacts that in everyday life, and outside the museum, we freely permit to be repaired, altered and even (without our realizing it very well) re-placed. But could there not be artifact concepts that were less per-

22. See *Longer Note* 3.22.
23. Cf. Leibniz, *Nouveaux Essais* 3.6.24: 'Il est vray qu'il y a apparemment des especes qui ne sont pas veritablement *unum per se* (c'est a dire des corps doués d'une veritable unité, ou d'un estre indivisible qui en fasse le principe actif total) non plus qu'un moulin ou une montre le pourroient estre'; 3.6.42 'En un mot, l'unité parfaite doit estre reservée aux corps animés, ou doués d'Entelechies primitives'; cf. 2.24.1, on which see R. Coburn's article cited at Chapter One, footnote 13.

missive in their definition (as required by **D**(iv) and **D**(v)), were more like natural kind terms in the specificity of what they required of their compliants, and did not raise the problems that are raised by artifacts subject to disassembly, part-replacement and cessation of function? The answer to this question is that there surely could be, though I have not been able to find any normal artifact terms that do require of their compliants anything like unremitting obedience to some specified law or principle or activity implicit in the artifact kind predicate itself. One very special kind of artifact whose survival-requirement is at any rate extremely detailed and specific is the *work of art*. But we shall postpone the special features of this and all cognate concepts until the last section of Chapter Four, which is the chapter where we explore the essentialist consequences of all the conceptual stipulations we have so far been motivated to make for natural things and for artifacts. We shall maintain that the conceptual need which a natural law will supply for the identity of a natural thing and which goes more or less unsatisfied for an ordinary artifact kind, the artist's conception of his activity and its eventual product can supply for the work of art. But, among artifacts, works of art and their like are in a category of their own, and most especially perhaps for purposes of the theory of individuation. Rather than explore this or other analogies with a principle of activity (e.g. that furnished by such social artifacts as an *administration,* or a *governing body* recruited and replenished by a formal procedure), it is much more urgent to provide now an outline of what is supposed to have been achieved in the first three chapters.

5. *Summary of conclusions to date: and a methodological remark*

(i) The formal properties of identity, both ' $=$ ' and ' $\overset{=}{f}$ ', are transitivity, reflexivity, symmetry, and the congruence defined by Leibniz's Law. Whether or not the meaning of the notion of identity is completely exhaustible by these formal principles (and there is good reason to doubt that it is), these principles at least are integral to the purport of both 'the same' and 'the same f'.

(ii) If (i) above is true, then **R** is false.

(iii) There are two distinct standpoints from which **D** as stated at the beginning of Chapter Two can be maintained. It may be held that *a* could be the same f as *b* without being the same g. That is **R**. Or it may be held that to say what *a* is is to subsume *a* under a predicate which either gives *a*'s principle of continuity or individuation—its principle of activity or mode of functioning—or restricts some other predicate that gives this principle.

(iv) A substance-predicate f in the sense of (iii) above has to fulfil the condition that a's coincidence with b under the concept f will entail the community of all of a's and b's predicates. Thus f-coincidence will be not only an equivalence relation, but also a congruence relation. Nothing less will suffice for a theory of individuation of the continuants of our accepted ontology.

(v) The requirement is satisfied by sortal predicates whose definition is extension-involving and deictic-nomological in the manner described by Leibniz, Putnam, Kripke and others.[24] These are natural kind terms. The requirement is not so straightforwardly satisfied by ordinary artifact concepts, which are not extension-involving or nomologically founded; and here a small amount of revision of what might appear to be our current linguistic practices or intuitions is required. It may be that tacitly these practices already respect some corresponding restriction.

(vi) All this has been explained by reference to the coinciding of entities under a concept. The locution 'coincides', rare though it is by comparison with the other words and forms we are using it to elucidate, and technical though my use of it may be, is not an invented one. And whenever we have written 'x coincides with y under the concept f' our sentence could be rewritten (without loss of anything but the strictest synonymy and occasional convenience) in the form 'x coincides with y as an f—in the manner, that is, of an f'. All that this can do is to make a reader who thinks he needs something more remind himself of what is already there, hidden in his own understanding of 'the same f'. Perhaps 'coincides' could drop out of my object-language if a better observed and more complete account than I have managed to give were achieved of what it is to say what a thing is. But, until that is achieved, it is only by talk of coinciding that I see any way for substance, identity and individuation to be prised far enough apart to give a view of the many strands by which they are connected. I would draw attention here to the relative perspicuity of the right-hand side of the schema by which 'coincides' is explicated in section 1 of Chapter Two.

6. *Transition to Chapters Four and Five*

It will be instructive to try to apply all this to persons, to works of art

24. For further discussion of the deictic nomological doctrine, see *Longer Note* 4.24.

and to other special cases of natural and artificial things. But first the view of individuation that has begun to emerge must be brought into some relation with the larger questions of Realism, Idealism and Conceptualism to which a theory of individuation is finally answerable.

Call the philosopher who denies **R** and denies **D** the Bare Absolutist. Call an upholder of my position a **D**-Absolutist. Chapter Four draws out certain of the individuative and essentialist consequences of **D**-Absolutism. Chapter Five seeks to communicate my conviction that the **R**-theorist typically exaggerates the autonomy of thought in the singling out of objects of reference; that Bare Absolutists, if they genuinely believe in continuants at all, are disposed by their denial of **D** to take too lightly the conceptual preconditions of singling out; and that it is the role of the **D**-Absolutist to see the articulation of reality in a way that corrects both faults at once. The mind *conceptualizes* objects, yet objects *impinge* upon the mind.[25]

25. One who defends such a thesis can scarcely fend off too soon certain misreadings of what he means to be committed to. Perhaps 'the mind conceptualizes objects' will appear to carry the suggestion that *the very same objects* could have been conceptualized in different ways, had the mind been differently constituted. But, if so, then the suggestion that appears to be carried is hereby cancelled. That is not what the sentence in the text means or implies.

Nature loves to hide. (Heraclitus, Diels fragment 123.)

We despise obvious things, but unobvious things often follow from obvious things. (Leibniz to de Volder, Gerhardt II, 183.)

CHAPTER FOUR

Essentialism and Conceptualism

1. *Independence from the explicitly modal of the foregoing theory of individuation*

We have made little or no use up to this point of the notion of necessity, and have resisted the idea that a theory of individuation must be a set of judgements about all possible worlds, or try to occupy itself with the problems that are special to the making of statements of explicit necessity *de dicto* or *de re*. In the case of natural kinds and their members we went to some lengths to show that it is enough (criteriologically sufficient) to obtain a set of true generalizations open, counterfactual-sustaining, and ranging over all past, present and future entities of *this* world. (That at least in the way I will put the point to adherents of the orthodox view of laws and empirical generalizations.) It is true that in connexion with artifacts, and at the point when the argument for the *Only a and b* Rule was introduced, something modal appeared to be involved. But the appearance was deceptive. In so far as a modality obtruded itself there, it was as a consequence not as a premiss of the argument for that rule, the sole basis of which was the natural, intuitively manifest constraints on what we can recognize as an elucidation of identity.

Marking the end of modal abstinence, I now seek to deduce certain 'essentialist' consequences of the theory of individuation expounded in the preceding chapters. Someone who finds these incredible will have the choice between criticizing the theory for entailing them and criticizing the derivation that is about to be attempted. But what results from the derivation is a very extensional variety of essentialism, and a very modest one. (Gaps in the derivation should be criticized as such, rather than filled by principles or premisses supplied from the works of these who aim for something stronger.) To the adherents of *possibilia,* possible worlds, and stronger essentialisms that instantly entail such conclusions as the conceptual indispensability to anything of its actual origin, the outcome may seem to be a doctrine of laughable timidity.

2. *Principles and maxims governing the derivation of a modest essentialism*

I begin with an enumeration of the principles and assumptions that will govern the derivation of essentialism to be attempted in later sections. I believe that it is only empiricism as empiricism misconceives itself, not nominalism or extensionalism, that could find anything here to cavil at.

(A) The first maxim is to dispense, in everything relating to the derivation, with *possibilia*. Compare Arnauld

> I have no conception of these purely possible [individual] substances, that is to say the ones that God will never create. . . . One can conceive of possibilities in the natures which he has created . . . but I am much mistaken if there is anyone who dares to say that he can conceive of a purely possible substance, for I am convinced in my own mind that although one talks so much of these purely possible substances, nonetheless one never conceives of any of them except according to the notion of those which God has created.[1]

(B) The second principle is the requirement that the argument should nowhere rely upon possible worlds.[2]

(Γ) The third principle or assumption I shall make is given succinctly by A. J. Ayer:

> We can significantly ask what properties it is necessary for something to possess in order to be of such and such kind . . . the answer may be to some extent arbitrary, but at least some answer can be looked for. On the other hand, there is no such definition of an individual.[3]

It is the consequence of this that, to make clear which thing a thing is, it is not enough (*pace* the friends of logically particularized essence) to say however lengthily that it is *such,* or *so and so.* We have to say that it is *this* or *that such.* This is perfectly obvious when we think of trying to determine one entity by mentioning short or simple predicates (other than *identical with x* or such like). But it is difficult to see

1. Arnauld to Leibniz, 13 May 1686, Gerhardt II, 31–2, as translated by H. T. Mason. Cf. W. V. Quine, 'On What There Is' in *From a Logical Point of View,* Cambridge, Mass., Harvard, 1953.
2. See *Longer Note* 4.02 for the reason for this.
3. *The Central Questions of Philosophy,* p. 197.

any reason to believe that by making ordinary predicates ever longer and more complicated we shall be able to overcome the obvious non-sufficiency or non-necessity for identity with just x that infects all the relatively simple predicates true of x.

(Δ) The fourth assumption or principle can again be given in alien words:

> I can think that I shall or shall not take a particular journey, while remaining very much assured that neither one nor the other will prevent my being myself, So I remain very much assured that neither one nor the other is included in the individual concept of myself.[4]
>
> [But] we have to maintain some anchorage in reality if our references are to be successful. . . . There appear to be no *general* rules for deciding what this anchorage may be. . . . One could imagine that the Pyramids were built at a different time, or perhaps even in a different country. If one anchors Dickens to other items in his biography one can conceive of his not having been a writer: if one identifies him by his writings one can perhaps conceive of his having lived in a different century. But could we consistently place him in the distant future, or in prehistoric times? . . . It is a rather arbitrary question in this sort of case.[5]

Appearances perhaps to the contrary, what Ayer is claiming here does not depend upon the theory of reference as such. Nor, even if Ayer expresses the point in a way that perhaps invites this charge, does it depend at all upon a confusion between a supposition about what might in fact be the case, the world being what it actually is, and what might, contrary to fact, have been the case, if the world had been different. Of course one can counterfactually conceive at t of an individual x not having those properties by which, for the very purpose of conceiving of its being otherwise, one does at t identify x in the actual world. But if serious conceiving is to have to do with conceptual possibility and if it is excluded that anything can be just *anything*, then we shall need to arrive at an understanding of conceiving such that, for any entity, there are some properties or complexes of properties which nothing counts as the conceiving of the entity as having. What the Chapter Three discussion of the *Only a and b* Rule suggested, for instance, was that one of the excluded conceivings is the conceiving of a thing as not the very individual that it is. The point will be argued fully in this chapter, as will the exclusion of the conceiving of an individual's having a different principle of individuation from its actual principle. But the immediate point is only that

4. Arnauld to Leibniz, Gerhardt II, 33, translated by H. T. Mason.
5. A. J. Ayer, *op. cit.*

one can claim such things without incurring the confusion mentioned above.

The point of agreement between Ayer and me may be put as follows then: Where a thinker A conceives of an individual x as ϕ (and by moving from 'refer' to 'conceive of' we only make Ayer's claim more secure), ϕ cannot assume just any value. There are restrictions on ϕ and they depend on which entity in particular the entity x is. What we then have in (Δ) is not a reduction or elimination of necessity and possibility (that is not our concern), but the following elucidation of possibility and necessity *de re*:

  (i) x can be ϕ if and only if it is possible to conceive of x that it is ϕ;
 (ii) x must be ϕ if and only if it is not possible to conceive of x that x is not ϕ;
(iii)   The position of the boundary between what one can conceive of x and what one cannot conceive of x depends on x, i.e. depends on which or what thing x *actually* is, and may sometimes depend on a matter of degree, or be somewhat arbitrary: in which case, it must be unsurprising that at least some of the properties that it is definitely impossible (i.e. well beyond the last point of possibility) to conceive of x's not having are rather *unspecific*.

(E) The next guiding principle for the construction to be attempted is that the relation *A conceives of x's being* ϕ or *A conceives* (λz) $(z$ is $\phi)$ *of x* may be cleared of all extensionalist and nominalist suspicions by viewing its connexion with *A conceives that* on the model of Quine's theory of the relation holding between *believing of* and *believing that*. The relation we are concerned with is then between the thinker A, the entity x (however described), and an attribute $\hat{z}(\phi z)$ or $(\lambda z)(\phi z)$. The relation is triadic. Quine has shown how, at a certain price, the attribute which is its third term can be nominalistically reconstrued.[6] Similarly, 'x is such that it is possible to conceive (λz) $(z$ is $\phi)$ of x' represents a complex dyadic relation between x and this attribute.

(Z) Ordinary intuitive grammar suggests that 'necessarily' and 'possibly' can either govern a complete sentence (as in the sentences that submit naturally to treatment within the first grade of modal involvement) or govern a simple or complex predicate. If it is asked

6. See 'Quantifiers and Propositional Attitudes', *Journal of Philosophy* 53, 1955, reprinted in *Ways of Paradox*, New York, Random House, 1966, at pp. 183–94. For an important amplification of the theory, see Brian Loar 'Reference and Propositional Attitudes', *Philosophical Review* 1972, p. 57.

what is meant by the latter usage, which lies altogether outside Quine's enumeration of the three grades of modal involvement,[7] then I reply first that this is something the reader is already familiar with under the verbal forms 'x can be ϕ' and 'it is possible for x to be ϕ'; second, that (Δ) above was already a partial elucidation of some such usage; third, that anyone who speaks English is already deeply committed to a whole range of locutions that resemble this one in lying outside Quine's enumeration.[8] For, if we supplant *de re* 'possibly ϕ' and 'necessarily ϕ' by 'can (be) ϕ' and 'must (be) ϕ' ('cannot help but (be) ϕ') we shall notice that, so far as logical form goes, they seem to have formal affinities with the *de re* predicates of ability, obligation, capacity or disposition, which people who have heard nothing of possible worlds apply effortlessly to the actual things of the actual world when they say that A can do otherwise than he is doing, that D could not help but strike C, or that X, Y and Z are soluble or fragile or fusible.[9] None of these claims has a natural *de dicto* translation.

---

7. See W. V. Quine, 'Three Grades of Modal Involvement', *Proceedings of the XIth International Congress of Philosophy, Brussels 1953*, Amsterdam, North Holland Publishing Co., reprinted in *Ways of Paradox* (see footnote 6), p. 157. See also 'Reference and Modality' in *From a Logical Point of View*, Cambridge, Mass., Harvard, 1953, 1st edn (rewritten for the 1961 edition).

8. And the truth predicate is defined for a language containing this 'necessarily' in my 'The *De Re* "Must": A Note on the Logical Form of Essentialist Claims', and for a richer language containing it by C. A. B. Peacocke in 'Appendix to David Wiggins' "The *De Re* 'Must'" ', both in Gareth Evans and John McDowell, eds, *Truth and Meaning: Essays in Semantics*, Oxford, 1976.

For the idea of treating 'necessarily' as a modifier of predicates or the copula, see 'The Identity of Proposition' in P. T. Geach, *Logic Matters*, Blackwell, 1972, p. 174; R. Cartwright, 'Some Remarks on Essentialism', *Journal of Philosophy* 65, 1968; my *Identity and Spatio-Temporal Continuity*, 1967, p. 42; R. Stalnaker and R. Thomason, 'Abstraction in First Order Modal Logic', *Theoria* 3, 1968; G. E. Hughes and M. J. Cresswell, *An Introduction to Modal Logic*, London, Methuen, 1968, note 131; John Woods 'Essentialism, Self-Identity and Quantifying In' in Milton K. Munitz, ed., *Identity and Individuation*, New York University, 1971; my *opp. citt.* Preface (3), (5), (9). Compare also Ian Hacking 'All Kinds of Possibility' (*Philosophical Review* 1975) for an analysis which is amenable to the same truth-theoretic treatment and delivers the same results as the present chapter seeks to establish. See also Christopher Kirwan, 'How Strong are the Objections to Essence?', *Proceedings of the Aristotelian Society* 71, 1970–71; Tyler Burge, 'Belief *De Re*', *Journal of Philosophy* 1977. For the historic sources of this view of the matter, see for instance Aristotle, *Prior Analytics* 30^{a15-23}; *De Interpretatione* 21$^{b26ff.}$; *De Sophisticis Elenchis* 166^{a23-3a}.

9. For a more extended attempt to describe the transition of other *de re* locutions into that limiting case which is the essentialist 'must', see pp. 349–50 of my 'Identity, Continuity and Essentialism', *Synthèse* 23, 1974.

(H) I represent with the sign NEC the undifferentiated *de re* 'must' or 'necessarily' that I presume to underlie as a genus the various species of *de re* concept. For the corresponding *de re* 'can' and 'possibly' I use the sign POSS. NEC and POSS are conceived here as working with predicates abstracted in a manner now to be described.[10] To form the expressions to which NEC and POSS are to apply we take any open sentence, say 'x is a man' or 'if x is a man then x has genetic make-up G' or 'x is identical with y' and bind the free variable or free variables in the open sentence with an abstraction operator λ. Thus: (λx)[Man x] or (λx)[Man $x \supset Gx$] or $(\lambda x)(\lambda y)[x=y]$. These abstracts may as well be read 'the property that any x has just if x is a man', 'the property that any x has just if, if x is a man, then x has genetic make-up G', 'the relation in which any x and y stand just if x is y' respectively. (Nothing will hang on whether explanations are given in this second level fashion or not.) We may now express the judgement that an entity or a sequence of entities $\langle \ldots \rangle$ falls in the extension of some property or relation so designated as follows:

Caesar has (λx) [Man x]
Everything has the property (λx) [$M(x) \supset G(x)$]
$\langle$the evening star, the morning star$\rangle$ have $(\lambda x)(\lambda y)[x=y]$,

or more handily and conventionally by simple juxtaposition thus:

(λx) [Man x], $\langle$Caesar$\rangle$
$(z)((\lambda x)$ [$M(x) \supset G(x)$], $\langle z \rangle)$
$(\lambda x)(\lambda y)[x=y]$, $\langle$the evening star, the morning star$\rangle$.

So far these are mere λ-equivalents of simpler sentences, but putting NEC or POSS to work on these abstracts, and leaving the subject term incontrovertibly outside the scope of the modality, we have

[NEC (λx) [Mx]], $\langle$Caesar$\rangle$
(z) ([NEC (λx) [$M(x) \supset G(x)$]], $\langle z \rangle)$
[NEC $(\lambda x)(\lambda y)[x=y]$], $\langle$the evening star, the morning star$\rangle$.

The last says that the evening star and the morning star *necesssarily*

---

10. The decision to signal these occurrences specially by this particular notation is quite without prejudice either for or against the appropriateness of $\square$ and $\diamond$ to this role. It is not implied but it is in no way excluded by the syntax or semantics of NEC and POSS that the pairs NEC and $\square$, and POSS and $\diamond$ will prove to be related very much as the theory of truth relates say predicate-negation and sentence-negation.

have that relation which any x and y have if and only if they are identical, or that it is *necessary for* the evening star and morning star to be identical. Thus the modal enrichment of the first order logical framework is explained in the first instance, not in terms of possible worlds, but rather in terms of the English vernacular. It is also managed in such a way that the *de re* 'necessarily' at least starts life with credentials no worse than those of Quine's own relational senses of saying and believing. Just as Ralph believes of the man in the brown hat (or of the man seen at the beach—it makes no difference, for they are identical), that he has the attribute λx (x is a spy), or the man in the brown hat (*alias* the man at the beach) is such that he is believed by Ralph to have the attribute spyhood; so, in this *prima facie* innocuous sense of 'necessarily', Caesar is such that he necessarily has the attribute *man*—or Caesar is such that it is necessary for him to be a man. Following the parallel, we can say that '[NEC (λx) [Mx]], $\langle$Caesar$\rangle$' is to '$\square$ (Man (Caesar))' as the relational '(λx) [Man x] is universally believed of Caesar' ($\approx$ 'It is universally believed of Caesar that he is a man') is to the *notional* 'It is universally believed that (Man (Caesar))'. Compare (E) above.

3. *The necessity of identity, and some asymmetrical necessities*

Taking Leibniz's Law in the form

For all F such that F is a genuine property of x or y,
$(x=y) \supset (Fx \equiv Fy)$

and making the assumption (against which no effective argument now remains) that NEC properties are genuine derived properties, we have the following proof of the complete coincidence of the necessary satisfaction and the actual satisfaction of the predicate of identity— that is the NEC counterpart of the quantified modal theorem:

$(x)(y)((x=y) \supset \square(x=y))$.

Consider any individuals H and P (Hesperus and Phosphorus say) such that

H = P.

Now the following is a truth about H:

$$[\text{NEC } \lambda x \, \lambda y \, (x=y)], \, \langle H, H \rangle;$$

and, the scope of this NEC being confined to the abstract, there then exists the abstractable property

$$(\lambda z) \, [\text{NEC } [\lambda x \, \lambda y \, (x=y)]], \, \langle z, H \rangle].$$

But H itself has this property, and what applies to H applies to P. So

$$(\lambda z) \, [\text{NEC } [\lambda x \lambda y \, (x=y)], \, \langle H, z \rangle], \, \langle P \rangle.$$

Then by the rule of λ-abstraction, we have

$$[\text{NEC } [\lambda x \, \lambda y \, (x=y)]], \, \langle H, P \rangle.$$

But now, since nothing depended on the particular choice of H and P which were such that H = P, we have the necessity of identity:

$$(x) \, (y) \, ((x=y) \supset [\text{NEC } [\lambda x \, \lambda y \, (x=y)]], \, \langle x, y \rangle)).$$

This proof adapts almost line for line a famous proof of the necessity of identity which was given by Ruth Barcan Marcus in 1947. It was received with incredulity by those committed to the mutual assimilation (much criticized in more recent times by Kripke and others) of the categories of *necessity* and *a priority,* and rejected on the grounds that the identity of evening and morning star was an *a posteriori* discovery. But even if *statement ascertainable a priori to be true* and *necessarily true statement* coincided perfectly in their extensions, Miss Barcan's theorem could still stand in our version. For the conclusion is not put forward here as a necessarily true statement. It is put forward as a true statement of *de re* necessity.[11] And what the proof comes down to is simply this: Hesperus is necessarily Hesperus, so if Phosphorus is Hesperus, Phosphorus is necessarily Hesperus. The only conceivable point left to argue is whether there is a *de re* use of 'must' in English. But the onus is on the contingency theorist and the anti-essentialist at last. He has to dispel as illusion what seems to be fact—that in English there exist many such *de re* uses.

It is a matter of some importance that this proof is unobstructed

11. See *Longer Note* 4.11.

even if we suspect that within its own scope NEC itself creates an opaque context. All substitutions in the proof are on *manifestly* extensional positions lying outside that scope.[12] But the proof also does much to disarm all suspicions of that character. For, it *sets free* the modal intuition that, even *within* a context governed by NEC, we should expect NEC identicals to be inter-substitutable. And we now know that all actual identicals are NEC identicals. So we have earned the right to make the substitution, and have justified what is simply taken for granted by those who prove Miss Barcan's theorem by reference to a fully fledged possible world semantics providing *ab initio* and *ab extra* for the identification of particular individuals across all the possible worlds where they occur under no matter what description. In lieu of assertion (or of claiming that the only test there can be of theories of modality is a holistic comparison of finished theories) we can go some way to *explain* how variables of quantification standing outside NEC contexts can reach into them. For proof and modal intuition *taken together* suggest that NEC contexts are really referentially transparent. As a result there is also no obstacle to the expression of asymmetrical formulae such as

$$(x) \, (\alpha) \, (x{\in}\alpha \supset \text{NEC}[(\lambda z) \, [x{\in}z]], \, \langle \alpha \rangle),$$

which claims that if a set contains an individual it necessarily contains it. We may also state and prove such variants of the Barcan theorem as

$$(x) \, (y) \, (x = y \supset [\text{NEC} \, [(\lambda z) \, (z = x)]], \, \langle y \rangle).[13]$$

12. This holds of both the deduction and the truth theory required for that minimal fragment of first order logic which adjoins NEC to abstracts of the form $[\lambda x \, \lambda y \, (x = y)]$ in the object language. In the metalanguage the only additional requirement is to adjoin NEC to abstracts of the form
$[\lambda x \, \lambda y \, (x \text{ satisfies } y)]$.

13. The discovery that we can after all get the effect of quantifying into NEC contexts may suggest the charge that this collapses the distinction between the symmetrical sentence

[Necessarily $[\lambda z \, \lambda y \, (z{\in}y)]]$, $\langle t, \alpha \rangle$,

the unquestionable sentence (where $t{\in}\alpha$ in fact),

[Necessarily $[\lambda y \, (t{\in}y)]$, $\langle \alpha \rangle$

and the false asymmetrical sentence

[Necessarily $[\lambda z \, (z{\in}\alpha)]]$, $\langle t \rangle$

But this charge would rest on an assimilation of the in principle separable ideas of the scope of 'Necessarily' and of the opacity or transparency of positions lying within the

4. Conceivability, theory and essence

As good a place as any in which to try to advance and to illustrate the mutual congeniality of essence and extension is indeed the area in which extensionality reigns absolutely, namely set theory. Let us explicate the *de re* 'necessarily' by reference to the explanations that those friends of extensionality who are also set theorists give of the identification and individuation of classes.

> What sets attributes apart from classes is merely that whereas classes are identical when they have the same members, attributes may be distinct even though present in all and only the same things.[14]

> We use the word 'set' in such a way that a set is completely determined when its members are given.[15]

(Suppose that we try to apply these criteria, and that we are invited to think of a thing α, identified as the entity (whether class or attribute we do not yet know) to which there belong the items *x* and *y* and only these.[16] Then it seems that, if we are to envisage α for what it is, what we have to ask is whether α, the very thing α, could have dispensed with the particular items *x* and *y*. If it could—if α could lack *x* or could lack *y*—then α is not a class. That is the

---

scope of 'Necessarily'. That such a distinction is possible may be illustrated by reference to a temporal modifier 'always', which certainly does not create opacity. Consider

(*x*) (lives in London *x* ⊃ [always [(λ*z*) (*z* lives in London)]], ⟨*x*⟩),

which is true just in case nobody who ever lives in London during his natural lifetime ever leaves the city to dwell in another place; and

(*x*) (lives in London *x* ⊃ [always [(λ*y*) (*x* lives in *y*)]], ⟨London⟩),

a sentence which is to be interpreted in such a way that it is obviously false. Take anything which is ever an inhabitant of London; then London, for so long as London exists, can number him or her among its living inhabitants.

14. W. V. Quine, *From a Logical Point of View*, Cambridge, Mass., 1953, p. 107. Cf. *Word and Object*, Cambridge, Mass., 1960, p. 209: 'Classes are like attributes except for their identity conditions.'

15. Patrick Suppes, *Introduction to Logic*, Princeton NJ, Van Nostrand, 1957.

16. Suppose we decided that α was not an attribute. We could then test whether α was a class or a mereological whole. We could ask whether *x* and *y* had parts. If they did then, since we were told that *x* and *y* were *all that belonged* to α, we should have disproved that α was a mereological entity. Cf. p. 151 of Goodman's new 'A World of Individuals' (*Problems and Projects*, p. 151, Bobbs-Merrill, 1972): 'While a class of individuals is uniquely a class of just those members, a whole made up of individuals may also be made up of quite other parts.'

thought that is suggested both by Quine's distinction of classes and attributes, and by the usual justification of the axiom of extensionality in terms of membership *determining* set-identity.

The idea that motivates this whole way of talking is that, whereas there is no criterial connexion between actual extension and being this or that property, or between an actual particular position in space-time and being this or that man (this contrast is important), there *is* a criterial connexion between membership and set-identity. But neither the test nor the thought which prompts it can even be stated within the first grade of modal involvement, or in terms that the Quine of 'Reference and Modality' (1953) would regard as respectable.[17] What is needed is the thought that, if α is a class containing x and y, then α could not have lacked x.[18] This is a *de re* modal assertion, and the penultimate formula of section (3) above is a proposal about how to understand it. That formula is true as well as significant. Set theorists who say that it is a peculiarity of sets to be determined by their members, or who distinguish sets from attributes in Quine's way, are surely saying at least this. And it need occasion no surprise that, in order to delimit an area within which extensionality will reign, or to justify intuitively the axioms of extensionality for sets and exclude attributes from the intended interpretation of Greek letter variables, one has to trespass for a moment outside the delimited area and talk in a language of richer expressive resources.)

---

17. In pursuit of a different purpose, Cartwright has put what I think is a cognate point, as follows:

$(x)\,(y)\,(z)\,((z{\in}x{\leftrightarrow}z{\in}y){\rightarrow}x{=}y)$ . . . will be a theorem of any pure theory of classes but presumably of no pure theory of attributes . . . but it is a difference between theories, and I know of no coherent way in which it can be supposed to carry over to the objects dealt with in the theories. It does, of course, reflect a difference between the *concepts* class and attribute.

Richard Cartwright: 'Class and Attribute', *Nous* I, 1967. See also R. Sharvey, 'Why a Class Can't Change Its Members', *Nous* II, 1968.

18. A proof that, for all finite classes α, if α has x as a member then α necessarily has x as a member can be framed by employing the pairing axiom and the axiom of extensionality, plus the same meagre resources of modality as were employed in the proof of the necessity of identity. (Similary it is implied by the modalization of the sum axiom in mereology—on which see Ch. Three, note 16—that any part of a mereological sum is necessarily a part of it.) Such a proof does not improve on the following informal argument: Suppose someone doubted the necessity of the membership relation. How could he combine the doubt with a reasoned affirmation of extensionality, or advance on behalf of extensionality such claims as 'a set is nothing more than a unity constituted by its members' (Richmond Thomason, *Symbolic Logic*, London, Collier Macmillan, 1970, p. 284)? If there is no other way of identifying such a unity than via its constituents, then its identity is derivative from these in a way in which the identity of a perceptibly demonstrable horse or tree is not derivative from that of any particular cells or sequence of spatio-temporal positions or sequence of paired space-time positions and material components. There is no sense then in the idea of a set $\{x, y\}$, with actual members x,y, turning up in another possible world lacking x or y.

Given (Δ) of section 2, there is a natural way to express the modest and reasonable essentialism that we find lurking in the set theorist's explanations of the claim that the extensionality principle helps determine what is intuitively meant by 'class' or 'set': The pair set {Eiffel Tower, Crystal Palace} is essentially a set, and essentially a set with just these members, because nothing whatever could count as envisaging that very set in a way that implied that it was not a set, or that it lacked these members. For (i) *set* is the most fundamental identification of this entity, and a more unrestrictive answer to the Aristotelian question what this thing is is not available; and (ii) once it is conceded that this set is necessarily a set, the principles of set theory bring it about (*qua* definitive of what sets are and of how they are individuated) that the actual membership of the pair is its only possible membership.

Let it be clear at this point that I am not claiming that it is impossible to envisage such sets as {Eiffel Tower, Crystal Palace} under any other *description* than 'pair set whose sole members are Eiffel Tower and Crystal Palace'. One might conceive of it under the description 'the pair set whose members are in Z's opinion the most remarkable works of nineteenth-century engineering in the capital cities London and Paris', or in indefinitely many different ways. But to show that this set might *lack* the Eiffel Tower as a member one must envisage it under a description that actually *excludes* the description 'pair set consisting of Eiffel Tower and Crystal Palace'. And then the question will be concerning *what* would one be envisaging that it might have lacked Eiffel Tower?

It may seem for a moment that one can envisage anything of anything, even 'lacking Eiffel Tower' of {Eiffel Tower, Crystal Palace}, provided that the identification he starts off with is as vague as, say, 'entity mentioned or had in mind at *t* by F. Hausdorff'. But starting off with so vague a description of the thing mentioned by Hausdorff should not make it easier but harder for the would-be envisager to be sure that he has, in the serious sense, conceived of that entity under the description 'lacking the Eiffel Tower'. The sort of possibility we are interested in should not be such as to be *augmented by ignorance*.[19] The same goes for the necessity and possibility Ayer was discussing in his own enunciation of principle (Δ). The conceiving must be with regard to a definite and actual compliant of the identification; and what it is possible to envisage with regard to that depends on what the particular entity is, whether Dickens, the Pyra-

19. Cf. Arnauld's Objection 'De Natura Mentis Humanae', against Descartes, at p. 201, vol. 7 of *Œuvres de Descartes*, edited by Adam and Tannery.

mids, or whatever. But then, if it is true that any description that the thing is envisaged as satisfying must, *qua* seriously envisaged of it, respect the identity-link holding between the entity of the envisaging and the actual entity with respect to which the envisaging takes place, then it seems that the description must not be *incompatible* with absolutely every description actually individuating the entity in question as 'this f' or 'that g' or whatever.

There is no intention here to claim that determining which thing x is, or singling x out, requires the explicit announcement of a predicate that specifies what the thing is, only that an explanation of which thing x is must be such that one can trace the explanation back to some sortal specification, or some set of sortal specifications, all of them (on pain of identity becoming relative) determining some single principle of identity.

Whatever the strength of this as a general doctrine, the argument about classes has displayed at its best this conception of the individuation of particulars. For the argument turned upon bringing {Eiffel Tower, Crystal Palace} under one of the fundamental concepts of some theory outside which the entity was not envisageable or individuable or identifiable at all, and then applying that theory.

These claims are intended to gather some of their strength from earlier chapters. And by the time the reader is some way through Chapter Five, I hope that his conception of what singling out is and involves will cause him to share my conviction that the denial of these claims will involve either (i) the senseless fiction of characterless substratum; or (ii), the relativity of identity; or (iii), both (i) and (ii); or (iv), the rejection of an ontology of separate particulars. If, proceeding in the way that I have, I claim to see more necessity than Ayer does, this is almost entirely due to the emphasis placed here on the role of the *what is x?* question in picking out or identifying x; and to the fact that I view the specification implicitly determined by a *saying which* as having a canonical form with two elements—both a sortal component *(What is x? It is an f thing)* and a deictic or particularizing component *(Which f thing is x? It is this f: or It is the f which is φ)*. To put the point again in Aristotle's or Strawson's way: every particular is a *this such*.

5. *Conceivability continued*

A handy way of summing up (Δ) (E) and (Z) as they combine with our conception of individuation is this: x could be ϕ, or it is possible for x to be ϕ,[20] if and only if it is possible to conceive of x's being ϕ; and a thinker genuinely conceives of x as ϕ only if there is *some* sortal concept f such that: (i) f adequately answers the Aristotelian question what x is, and commits anyone who singles a thing out as an instantiation of f to a persistence condition; (ii) f and ϕ are cosatisfiable by x, and if x were ϕ then x could still be singled out or individuated as this or that instantiation of f.[21] The interest of this elucidation lies not in a claim to be an analysis or reduction of *de re* possibility—it is neither—but in the stringency of the necessary condition that it proposes for *de re* possibility. It illustrates how there might be such a thing as a *de re* necessity to which a concrete particular was subject. (On the supposition that predications in the category of substance and predications in other categories such as quality are mutually irreducible, the condition does not yet require that any one *qualitative* attribute be held constant.)

It is possible to conceive of Caesar's having a different career. It is possible to conceive of this very man's not being consul in 69 B.C., or his not conquering Gaul, or his not crossing the Rubicon, or even of his not in fact being male, not living through adolescence or not perhaps having his actual parents.[22] What then is it impossible to

20. See Hacking, *op. cit.*, for this variant. For the distinction of *could* and *can*, which could be made explicit here by the identification of a place for a *relative to what supposition* parameter ('could' representing here the bare supposition that x exists), see e.g. S. A. Handford, *The Latin Subjunctive*, pp. 130f. (cited by J. L. Austin at *Collected Papers*, p. 164) and Alan R. White, *Modal Thinking*, Oxford, Blackwell, 1975, ch. two.

21. What would refute this contention? A weaker requirement that arose equally naturally from a theory of particular identification, respected the absoluteness of identity, and represented the substantial requirement that (Δ) puts upon the *de re* relation of conceiver, object and attribute.

22. Kripke asked at page 314 of 'Naming and Necessity' (in Harman and Davidson, *Semantics of Natural Languages*, Dordrecht, Reidel, 1972) 'by what right' one would call a person sprung from different sperm and egg from the actual ones 'this very man'. If this implies that every counterfactual speculation about Julius Caesar involves the thinker who undertakes it in establishing his *title* to identify the individual concerned as Julius Caesar, then this is dangerously close to the 'telescope' view of cross-world identification of individuals. (See *Longer Note* 4.02.) The problem of entitlement is the very problem we have seen reason to applaud Kripke's method of avoiding. We do not have to find something *in virtue of which* the object of speculation is Julius Caesar. With the materials we are using we can go one step to meet Kripke, however, though not far enough yet to grant the conclusion that what a thing springs from it necessarily springs from (in so far as that conclusion goes beyond the necessity of *identity*). Perhaps the speculator has to be able to *rebut* the charge that he has lost his subject of discourse if he changes its parents or origin. But now I ask: can he not rebut the charge by claiming to speculate about how *the man whom Brutus murdered in 44 B.C.* would have fared if (say) Marius had been his father? To rebut the charge of losing the individual perhaps there must always be available to the speculator, *consistently with his speculation*, some

envisage of Caesar? The *this such* conception of individuation and the class paradigm of the previous section combine to suggest that what it is hard or impossible to conceive of Caesar's not being is man (human). For if anything plays here the part that we found the concept *class* to play in the earlier argument, then the concept *man* plays it. Or so it would appear. I allow that there is one doubt. Someone might concede to me that there must be *some* sortal concept f such that, whatever else Caesar is envisaged as being, no genuine envisaging of Caesar excludes his being this instance of f. But the questioner might wonder whether there was a less specific sortal concept than *man* that was capable of fixing the persistence conditions of this entity and answering the question 'what is Caesar?'. Could not the generic property *animal* serve in the role of f? (See section 11; and see Chapter Six for the other proposal, *person*.)

This is by no means the only obscurity or perplexity to be encounted in adapting the {Eiffel Tower, Crystal Palace} argument to the things to be encountered in nature. But before we prune back the doctrine it must be allowed to put on more leaf.[23]

6. *Individuative essentialism and its consequences*

Suppose that every natural thing x satisfies throughout its actual existence some sortal concept that those who single x out have to treat as invariant (cf. **D**(ii)), even when engaged in conditional and counterfactual envisagings of states and histories alternative to x's actual states and history; and suppose that this concept is a natural kind concept which not only says what x is but also leads *a posteriori* to a passable criterion of identity and persistence for members of its extension.[24] Then not only will such sortal concepts be owed much or most of the honour accorded by Aristotle and Leibniz to the *infima species* (cf. Aristotle, *Metaphysics* Z; Leibniz, *Nouveaux Essais* III, 6.36, III, 3.6)—provided that they really do represent the least specific account of their bearers that will suffice to articulate these very

---

such specification of which man he means by Julius Caesar. But even this principle, which may be slightly too strong, does not favour any particular specification of who Julius Caesar is.

23. There are anti-essentialists of a moderate persuasion who might let pass the set-theoretic argument of Chapter Four, section 4, on the grounds that sets are abstract things and not identifiable independently of a mathematical theory, but resist strenuously the extension I have attempted to material substances. It seems dubious, however, that conceptual dependence on a mathematical theory is the real principle of the distinction between abstract and concrete. Witness the entities of modern physics.

bearers from the rest of reality; it will also be possible to derive some surprising *a posteriori* consequences.

Suppose that 'man' (and every other natural kind term, whether species or genus) has its sense fixed by reference to some hypothesized generic constitution, which users of the term are committed to think of as exemplified under the physical laws of the actual world by the actual instances that they encounter and group together as men. (Suppose the simple fact of their use of the term commits them.) And suppose G is some (not too specific) genetic feature that is scientifically partially *definitive* of that constitution. Now consider anything that is a man. He is then necessarily if-a-man-then-G. It may be objected that the conditional governed by this 'necessarily' is no conceptual necessity, because it is contingent upon the laws of nature that actually obtain, and other laws might have obtained. But Chapter Three has confronted that objection. If the concept of *man* behaves in a manner consonant with the suggested mode of definition of 'man', then the very existence of men is contingent on the same thing. For it is on the same actual laws that the delimitation and significance of the man-definitive constitution depends.[25] Since G and *man* depend for their existence on the very same circumstance, and it is by indirect reference to G that (in the last analysis) anything counts as a man, it follows that a man is necessarily if a man then G. So, with this established, we can go on to the next step. We already have the beginnings of an argument to show that whatever is a man is necessarily a man. If that is right (see below, section 11), then we can necessitate the consequent of the conditional and say that anything that is a man is necessarily G.[26]

24. See *Longer Note* 4.24. I find that the argument of this section is anticipated by A. MacIntyre's article 'Essence and Existence' in Paul Edwards, ed., *Encyclopaedia of Philosophy*, vol. 3, London, Collier Macmillan, 1967.

25. See again Chapter IV of *Leibniz's Philosophy of Logic and Language* by Hidé Ishiguro.

26. For the NEC counterpart of $\Box(p \supset q) \supset (\Box p \supset \Box q)$ presupposed to the argument of the last two sentences of this paragraph, see p. 348 *Synthese* 1974, Preface op. cit. (3).

It is my hope that in this account of the *de re* 'must' and 'can' there resides some justification for modes of expression that are very natural to some scientists, and possibly indispensable to the attempt to describe how scientific theory explains *what* certain things are. For a passage susceptible of this interpretation and best explained, not by an implausible transposition into *de dicto* terminology, but by *de re* necessity backed with a notion of conceiving not open to the charge that the less you know the more you can conceive, consider Erwin Schrödinger's explanation, at p. 49 of *What is Life? The Physical Aspect of the Living Cell* (Cambridge, 1944), of the Heitler–London quantum theory of the chemical bond:

... a number of atomic nuclei, including their bodyguards of electrons, when they find themselves close to each other, forming 'a system', are unable by their very

It is sometimes complained that essences 'explain nothing'. But if the foregoing argument is correct then, apart from the least interesting and least controversial necessary properties (e.g. *identity with Caesar,* which is too special, and *self-identity,* which is too general), they do have a function. In the first place, there are predicates that stand for essential properties of a thing and register the condition whose satisfaction is a prerequisite of the very thing's being articulated *at all* from the rest of reality. These predicates are not in the business of explaining anything much, because they are presupposed to there being anything to explain. But, in the second place, there are more interesting predicates, like G above. These represent *a posteriori* or scientific accounts given by some (at the appropriate level) fundamental theory of the natural kind or articulative sort outside which x cannot be envisaged at all. It is to the satisfaction of this complex requirement that such properties as G owe both their focal place in the theory of individuation and their necessity.

We may add to the maxims of section 4 a principle long since acknowledged in every interesting or thoughtful essentialism.

(Θ) The practical scientist does the business; but the philosopher keeps the books. (Nelson Goodman, *Problems and Projects,* p. 168.)

I agree with those who deny that forms are to be used in seeking to explain specific and special causes (Leibniz, *Specimen Dynamicum.*)[27]

---

continues from p. 118]

nature to adopt any arbitrary configuration we might think of. Their very nature leaves them only a very numerous but discrete series of 'states' to choose from. . . . The transition from one of these configurations to another is a quantum jump. If the second has the greater energy ('is a higher level'), the system must be supplied from outside with at least the difference of the two energies to make the transition possible . . . the molecule will of necessity have a certain stability; the configuration cannot change unless at least the energy difference, necessary to 'lift' it to the next higher level, is supplied from outside.

27. Gerhardt, *Leibnizens Mathematische Schriften,* vol. VI, p. 235. Cf. *Discourse of Metaphysics,* ch. X (Gerhardt, *Philosophischen Schriften,* vol. IV). 'I agree that consideration of these forms is of no service in the detail of natural philosophy, and must not be used for explaining phenomena in particular. And it was in this that our scholastics failed, and the Physicians of past times following their example, believing that they could account for the properties of bodies by mentioning forms and qualities without going to the pains of examining the manner of operation; as if one were willing to content oneself with saying that a clock has the horodictic quality resulting from its form, without considering in what all this consists. . . . But this failure and misuse of forms must not make us reject something knowledge of which is so necessary in Metaphysics.' (Translation by Lucas and Grint.) Cf. also chapter XI *ibid.*

7. *That the logical impropriety and the uselessness of 'haecceitas' fully match the syntactic impropriety of the word*

Individuals have essences without which they would not 'be what they are'—would not exist; but (apart from logically particularized essential properties like *necessarily identical with Caesar*) their essences are shared or shareable. The requirement that essences should be unique to particulars (like almost any other attempt either to say anything or to deny anything by means of the absurd idea of *haecceitas*) is seriously contaminated with confusion. We get from the 'this' of 'this f' (where f is or determines some sortal specification) all the particularity which is required for anchorage to the actual entity that we conceive of in various counterfactual ways. Whether or not Strawson has ever demonstrated fully the conceptual necessity to thought as we know it of individuals, I believe him to have demonstrated conclusively that, wherever thought *does* recognize individuals, the functions of 'this' and 'such' are (regardless of any limited interchangeability of role) simply mutually irreducible. It is true that Russell's Theory of Descriptions may be seen as a proposal for redrawing the apparent frontier between predicating and designating. But whether we accept the theory or not, designating (which is a linguistic function that is *entity-involving* in a way in which predicating need not be) and predicating are *two* functions. A *haecceitas* would be the connotation of a predicate which, by attempting to absorb both, could perform neither function.

The non-particularized properties that pass the test of being invariant under all counterfactual speculations representing successful *de re* conceivings of Gaius Julius Caesar are those with negations *not* coconceivable with his sortal identification *man* (or, more weakly, not coconceivable with *animal,* see below section 11). All such properties are multiply satisfiable.

8. *The essentialist 'must' and 'can'*

The claim that Caesar is necessarily a man, that he cannot not (or cannot help but) be a man, is founded then, according to our elucidation of these matters, in Caesar's being such that it is impossible to envisage with respect to him his having any attribute or sortal property exclusive of his being a man. What kind of a 'must' is this?

Of course the locutions 'can' and 'must' are normally put to other work. The range of available meanings of these modalities is highly various. *De re* modal claims are usually based upon people's abilities or inabilities, capacities or incapacities as of some time and relative to the circumstances of that time, or upon their obligations or debts or compulsions of that time.[28] If a man must repay £5 then the source of the necessity is perhaps a borrowing transaction and consequential state of indebtedness from which he has not been released. Or if a man cannot help but slide down a slope then what necessitates his falling may be a trip, the gradient of the slope, and the man's lack of the strength he would need to regain control. This is more unalterable than a state of being obliged to pay money (except perhaps in Sicily). But what I suggest is that we should see the *de re* necessity of essence as the limiting case of the other *de re* necessities with which their form appears to group them. The essential necessity of a trait arises at that point of unalterability where the *very existence of the bearer is unqualifiedly conditional* upon the trait in question. Here, at this point, a property is fixed to its bearer by virtue of being inherent in the individuation of it—inherent in the very possibility of the drawing of a spatio-temporal boundary around it. The closer the source of the attribute to the singling out of the thing itself—the more it is bound up with the whole mode of articulating reality to discover such an object in reality—the more exigent, obviously, is the necessity that, *if there is to exist any such thing as the bearer,* it should have the feature in question. The *de re* 'must' of causal inflexibility here passes over at a certain threshold into an inflexibility that is conceptual (though only loosely speaking logical). There is no reason why this should make the essentialistic *de re* attribute any less of a real attribute of the thing itself.[29]

9. *Avoiding overspecificity*

I come now to the charge of overspecificity in the identification of

28. There are constant temptations to confuse differences in the grounds for modal attributions with differences in their meaning. It is not necessary to settle here the question whether we have here an array of distinct senses disposed around a focal idea, or a univocal idea which can conjoin with different parameters to yield a variety of different kinds of semantic output.

29. *Pace* Wittgenstein who, for the same sort of reasons as I give in this chapter, isolated such attributions but dubbed them *non*-descriptive.

There is a sense in which an object may not be described. This is that a description may ascribe to it no property whose absence would reduce the existence of the object itself to nothing. Description may not express what would be essential for the existence of the object. (*Philosophische Bemerkungen* § 93–4.)

man as the highest individuative sortal for Caesar. Why should not the link between an envisaging and the actual Caesar be secured by the object of the speculation being identifiable under the description *this mammal* or even *this animal*?

Suppose first that this objection were correct, and that one or other of these very unspecific sortal specifications were a good enough sticking point. Even then there would be *de re* necessities to be discovered. Animal excludes *stone, insect, paddle steamer, number* (and *mereological fusion of animal parts* too, in my judgement). The objector might say that the resulting essentialism lacked much of the interest of the position first stated. But our doctrine of natural kinds would still have a real point at the level *mammal* or *animal*; and, even at such a distance from the specific, there is still something to be made of scientific discoveries, however much more generic and abstract the choice for property G of section 6 would then have to be.

The damage the objection can inflict is limited then. But the proper reply to the objection is that our constraints on envisaging, taken in conjunction with our existing theory of individuation, do seem to suffice to rule out *this animal* as too weak a link between the envisaging and the actual Caesar if it is to sustain an envisaging of Caesar as not a man. The whole justification of our criterion for essential properties is the claim that there can be no envisaging this or that particular thing as having a different principle or individuation (different existence and persistence conditions) from its actual principle. Seen in this light, 'this animal' is by no means obviously a good enough identification of Caesar to sustain the envisaging of him as not a man. For it may be that 'that animal' is not itself *autonomously individuative*. Admittedly the words 'this animal' suffice to express a rough and ready identification in ordinary contexts of what things are. This is because 'animal' can take on an individuative force from the context, or from some other sortal predicate that is ready to hand.[30] But the designation 'this animal' is supported in all sorts of

30. Or because it does not matter very much to know more than roughly what the thing in question is. 'What's under that blanket?' 'It's an animal—I should sit on the other blanket if I were you.' In the context it is probably perfectly obvious that it is not a leopard say, or a gila-monster under the blanket. This is ordinary indoor life. (One can sit next to the blanket, for instance.) It doesn't matter whether it's a cat or a dog or even a nanny goat under the blanket. It doesn't matter *exactly* what is under the blanket. It is important to remember that here and throughout the individuative principle for a particular *x*, and the conditions of *x*'s existence and persistence, is not something special to the particular *x* with its particular life history, but something general which, according to the theory of individuation that I should defend, is required to determine the *point at issue* in matters of *x*'s existence and survival, and the

different ways, and it determines no single principle of individuation. How then could it work in the context of the claim 'N.N. conceived of this particular animal's not being a man', if 'man' were not available to supplement 'animal' in the anchorage of the object conceived to the conceiver and the property conceived by him *of* that object? In order that there be an envisaging of *Caesar* as not-a-man, there must be available, to link the actuality of Caesar and the envisaging, a new sortal identification of Caesar both autonomously individuative and co-conceivable with '*not* a man'.

Suppose that the new identification is an ultimate sortal predicate (in the terminology of Chapter Two). Then, in the case of natural things like Caesar, this ultimate predicate, however far it be above the level of *infima species,* must still be conditioned by some sufficiently specific causal generalization to provide conditions of identity and persistence for members of its extension. (These are the generalizations to which, whether he knows or wishes it, anyone who subsumes a thing under the concept is committed.) This requirement is breached in the attempted envisaging of Caesar as not a man unless there is a sortal term lower than 'animal' and higher than 'man' ('human') that is individuative and suffices to fix Caesar with Caesar's very principle of individuation. If someone can find such an ultimate sortal concept for Caesar, however, and it is higher than *man* then he is at liberty to substitute it for *man* throughout the argument of previous sections, and weaken all my claims accordingly. They will not have been diluted to nothing.

At this point it seems that an element of the indeterminacy that Ayer

---

point at issue in matters of the existence or survival of all the other things in the highest genuinely individuative kind to which *x* belongs.

At *New Essays* 3.3.6 Leibniz represents Locke as saying, 'les mots deviennent generaux lorsqu'ils sont signes d'idées generales, et les idées deviennent generales lorsque par abstraction on en sépare le temps le lieu, ou telle autre circonstance, qui peut les déterminer à telle ou telle existence particulière'. In his objection to this doctrine Leibniz exploits the distinction that I am pressing here. The principles we have to use in keeping individuals under continuous observation can be made to yield genus terms. There is abstraction from species to genus. (Cf. Ishiguro, *op. cit.*) But there is no abstraction from individuals to species. The principle we use in observing and tracing a particular does not come with a species concept which we get by *abstraction* from individuals. That would be impossible, for in so far as we have a species concept for an individual, the possession of this concept and the ability to pick out the thing under it cannot be *separated.* For genera terms, however, which *presuppose* individuation, there is no such difficulty. 'Je ne disconviens point de cet usage des abstractions, mais c'est plutôt en montant des espèces aux genres que des individus aux espèces. Car (quelque paradoxe que cela paraisse) il est impossible à nous d'avoir la connaissance des individus et de trouver le moyen de déterminer exactement l'individualité d'aucune chose, à moins que de la garder elle même.'

predicted (and we anticipated at (Δ) of section 2 above) has crept in. But it is no part of the essentialist's purpose to deny that in exploring the grounds of *de re* modal attributions we encounter vagueness, indeterminacy, and questions of degree. This is not a new admission on his part.[31] Nor does a problem of vagueness, confined now to the property that *must* attaches to, or the need to decide whether a certain threshold has been reached or not, entail that the choice to make a modal assertion, or not make it, is unprincipled or arbitrary, or a matter of no moment. The admission of vagueness does not undermine any point or interest we have succeeded in attaching to these questions, or degrade the complexity of what is involved in seeking to establish, well below the level of how things superficially appear to be, whether one can or cannot envisage some property ϕ of Caesar. Nor, finally, does it count against the claim that such envisaging is always with reference to the highest individuative kind which is sufficiently specific autonomously to determine identity and persistence condition of the sort that it was the function of principles **D**(ii), **D**(iii), **D**(v) to elucidate in Chapter Two.

10. *The essences of artifacts; and the essences of works of art*

Both by manner of argument and by example, we have concentrated so far upon entities belonging to natural kinds. After the distinctions made in Chapter Three, it will come as no surprise if artifacts need separate treatment.

If someone responds to the hardness of problems of artifact persistence rehearsed in Chapter Three, not with proposals about how to dispense with it in the more extreme cases of subtraction, addition and repair, but with a more demanding type of necessary and sufficient condition arrived at by some modification of the nominal essence for artifacts suggested by the Helen Cartwright criterion for quantities, then what results might seem to be an enrichment, at least in requirements concerning matter, of the essential conditions of survival of this or that particular tool or utensil or whatever. Here, however, we have to be on our guard against a confusion. We have tried throughout to distinguish the question of survival through change— how the object must be in stage $n+1$ *given that it was thus and so at stage* n—from the question what can be envisaged of an entity only conditionally upon the existence of the entity. Surely one can envisage in the *second* way,

---

31. Leibniz made it willingly in *Nouveaux Essais*.

Les passages d'espece en espece peuvent etre insensibles, et pour les discerner ce serait quelquefois a peu pres comme on ne sçauroit decider combien il faut laisser de poils à un homme pour qu'il ne soit point chauve. Cette indetermination seroit vraye quand meme nous connoistrions parfaitement l'interieur des creatures dont il s'agit. Mais je ne vois point qu'elle puisse empecher les choses d'avoir des essences réelles independamment de l'entendement, et nous de les connoistre: il est vray que les noms et les bornes des especes seroient quelque fois comme les noms des mesures et des poids, où il faut choisir pour avoir des bornes fixes (III.6.27. Compare also III.3.14, III.5.9, and III.6.38).

this table's not being painted white, not being quite so tall, not being chamfered at the corners. Can one envisage in this way its being not a table, or its not even being a piece of furniture fabricated for a cognate purpose, or its enjoying the negation of the disjunction of all predicates of being fashioned for cognate purposes? Surely one cannot envisage the last, and probably one cannot even envisage the first of these things. Can one then envisage its being made of different wood? (Of a different piece of wood, or even of a different type of wood?)[32] Here there is little or nothing we can postpone to the day of some empirical discovery. The problem is conceptual, and the facts upon which the problem is based are in. My tentative answer to the question of material constitution is that so much variation from the actual one can envisage without jeopardizing the identity of this very table. (Even though one cannot envisage, regarding this table, its having *almost wholly different matter this week from the matter it had last week*—which is a quite different envisaging.) Again, though, it will be no skin off the nose of moderate essentialism if it turns out to be a matter of degree how much variation from the actual features of the table one can unconditionally envisage.

Neither here, then, nor with natural things do we arrive at a genuine attribute ϕ such that some individual is necessarily ϕ and such that ϕ even approximates to being logically peculiar to that very individual. There was never any prospect of this, even before it became clear that even the species concept would have to cede the place of central theoretical importance to the highest autonomously individuative sortal concept. Nevertheless it is natural to ask: could there not be some special sort of artifact-kind for which, as a very special case, something closer to a Scotist theory of individual natures held?

To obtain even an approximation to the theory of individual natures we should have to think of a class K of things each particular member of which was such that countless particular details were conceived as so central to the aim or mission or nature of this particular member of K that its very existence depended on their presence. Being essentially conceived so particularly, any change in the central set of properties which were specific to its being *that* particular would then—for this is the consequence of the requirement—have to count as some definite step towards the destruction of the thing or the replacement of it by another particular (albeit another member of K). At the same time, if we are to have any approximation to particular natures, anything belonging to K must be an individual, a material *particular* (in some relevant sense of 'material'). It must not be a type or a recipe instantiable by different material particulars.

I have argued elsewhere that easel pictures, carved sculptures and frescoes come as close as anything can come to meeting this requirement.[33] In the culture of the West, and in certain other cultures, we think of the artist as making something which is calculated by him to have an effect which cannot be characterized in instrumental or non-aesthetic terms, and cannot be

32. See *Longer Note* 4.32. 33. *Preface, op. cit.* (8).

identified independently of some totality of relevant features that are the individuating features of this or that individual work. It follows that, once the work is finished and once the set of features is determinate, to visit any interference upon the set, whether for better or worse, is to threaten the work with obliteration, or with destruction by replacement, however gradual. (Note that there is vagueness here, because partial destruction, insufficient to bring the work to the point where it is right to speak of replacement *tout court,* is an idea that makes sense in this sort of case. That is the sad condition of many fine works.) At the same time we do not conceive of a picture as a template for the mere reproduction or multiplication of some particular image. And finally, at least in our particular culture, we attach even more importance to the artist's effect being brought about by materially the same means that the artist envisaged and contrived than to the effect itself remaining agelessly indiscernible from one age to the next. What a principle of activity does very completely for a natural thing, and what the function of an ordinary artifact does very imperfectly for the artifact (see above Chapter Three, section 4), the artist's conception of his own making of the work and of its outcome (and the effect that the artist envisages the work's presence having on an ideal spectator) must do for a painting. There are no lawlike sentences to be framed about paintings or particular paintings; and it is equally true that, being no ordinary artifacts, paintings and carved sculptures do not have a function. But any particular work has an aim, a highly *particular* aim, that is internal to its being that very work. This can generate very particular *de re* necessities. The work has necessarily—is such as to be *de re* inconceivable or unenvisageable as definitely lacking—any sufficiently rich complex of features that has essential occurrence in the artist's own implicit or explicit account (placed as it is in whatever context of cultural understanding and artistic theory) of this very piece of his work.

Quand nous ferons naître la pensée, elle naîtra ainsi dans un univers déjà rangé.

When we come to exhibit the birth of thought we shall find that it is born into a universe that is already ordered. (Simone Weil, *Leçons de Philosophie,* ed. A. Reynaud, Librairie Plon, Paris 1959, p. 24, translated by Hugh Price, *Lectures on Philosophy,* Cambridge University Press, 1978.)

The relation between my consciousness and a *world* is not a mere matter of contingency imposed on me by a God who happened to decide the matter this way rather than that, or imposed on me by a world accidentally preexisting and a mere causal regularity belonging to it. It is the *a priori* of the judging subject which has precedence over the being of God and the world and each and everything in the world. Even God is for me what he is in consequence of my own productivity of consciousness. Fear of blasphemy must not distract us here from the problem. [But] here too, as we found in the case of other minds, the productivity of consciousness does not itself signify that I *invent* or *fabricate* this transcendency, let alone this highest of transcendencies. (Edmund Husserl, *Formale und Transzendentale Logik*, Max Niemeyer Verlag, Halle (Saale) 1929, pp. 221–222.)

CHAPTER FIVE

Conceptualism and Realism

1. Anti-realist conceptualism and anti-conceptualist realism

Chapter Four was for the most part an exploration of the conceptual limits of our thinking about the particular natural things that belong to this or that particular ultimate individuative kind. It was also an attempt to point to the conceptual riches that will lie hidden within any individuative kind which is a natural or real kind. In the exploration of what plays the constraining role in thought about individuals of kinds having names that are incapable of verbal definition, we were discovering what plays the part that verbally explicit definitions play in the determination of nominal essence. In both sorts of case the constraints on thought are founded in meaning; but where a word is like 'frog' or unlike 'house', and has its sense fixed in a manner that is reality-involving, meaning is conferred in a distinctive way.[1] And this in its turn generates conclusions that appear to go well beyond the semantical. It seems to be a metaphysical, not a merely semantical, thesis that being a man, or having a certain genetic feature G (see Chapter Four, section 6), is an absolute individuative prerequisite for anything's being Caesar. For this reason, the derivations of Chapter Four will attract the hostility of at least two schools of thought. Designating my own position (simply for brevity and convenience) *conceptualist realism,* one of its likely critics may be called the *anti-realist conceptualist,* and another the *anti-conceptualist realist.*

The anti-realist conceptualist may or may not be an **R** theorist, and may or may not have found intelligible the defence of principle **D** attempted in Chapter Two. What he is certain to find questionable in the extreme is the purported absoluteness (non-relativity to context, level, or whatever), of the necessity that I have alleged (*exempli gratia*) to attach to the particular entity Caesar's being a man.[2] The

1. For some of the complications consequential on this view, see *Longer Note* 4.24.
2. See Bas C. van Fraassen, 'Essence and Existence', *American Philosophical Quarterly Monograph* 1977–78. Most unfortunately Michael Dummett's important article

anti-conceptualist realist on the other hand, whose position is addressed below at section 5 following, will see no special difficulty in any absolute notions of truth, necessity, substance or whatever that may have lurked in earlier chapters; but he will doubt (as Michael Ayers does, for instance)[3] the consonance with any serious realism of the conceptualism that has informed the argument for **D** and the whole method of derivation of *de re* necessity. A third form of opposition will come from latter day Humeans, and those who set store by some transcendental deduction, done by the method of *a priori* semantics, of the theoretical impossibility of any *de re* necessity which is not reducible to the analyticity of some sentence: but I have said my piece against this school, and shall now direct attention upon the other two.

'It is all very well', the two new opponents are likely to object, 'talking as you did in the previous chapter of the constraints on envisaging a thing. Suppose that the place marked by the z-variable in "it is possible to envisage z's being ϕ" *is*, as you claim, an extensional position and somehow confers extensionality upon "z" in "z can be ϕ". And suppose that when Quine claimed that to be necessarily greater than seven was not a trait of a number, but depended only on the manner of referring to the number (*From a Logical Point of View*, p. 148), he overlooked the kind of necessity that you have found outside the range of Quine's three grades of modal involvement. Suppose again that when a thinker genuinely conceives of z as ϕ there must, for purposes of the kind of possibility you were concerned with, be some sortal concept f such that z can be identified as this or that f-compliant and such that f and ϕ are coconceivable of z. This last requirement may perhaps justify you in adopting, for purposes of your brand of possibility, what Quine called an "invidious attitude towards certain ways of specifying a thing and favouring other ways as revelatory of its essence" (*ibid.*, p. 155). But these concessions, in the form in which you are trying to extract them, are perfectly

---

'Common Sense and Physics' (in Graham MacDonald's collection of essays for Sir Alfred Ayer, *op. cit.*note 3, Ch. Six) came to hand too late to enable me to reconsider my conception of realism and anti-realism in this area, or the classification of Van Fraassen's accounts of *de re* modality and substance. Scarcely less important to this and other themes of the present and previous chapters is another work, on whose soundness Chapters Four and Five partly depend: Gareth Evans, 'Identity and Predication', *Journal of Philosophy* 1975. Unluckily this relation of dependence is non-symmetrical.

3. See Michael R. Ayers, 'Individuals Without Sortals', *Canadian Journal of Philosophy* vol. IV, 1974–75. Nicholas Griffin has written a reply to this: 'Ayers on Relative Identity', *Canadian Journal of Philosophy* vol. VI, 1976.

unimportant. For the most you will be able to derive from them will turn out to be a conceptualism shaped by human powers of envisaging. These powers are the product, both time-bound and culture-bound, of a conceptual scheme which is determined by interests that are very special. However deep seated they seem to us, they are scarcely implanted in us by nature to mirror nature itself. What you are trying to do is to fabricate some strange engine with which to invest with real essences the concrete entities of the world, by investing with indispensability the particular conceptual scheme that, from our limited and cosmically insignificant point of view, *we* bring to bear upon the world. But these entities are independent of whether human beings exist or not, and perfectly indifferent to how human beings conceive of them. What is more, the conceptual scheme for which you are working to get this privilege is scarcely very different even now from the scheme that systematically delayed the progress of natural science beyond the jejune approximations of Aristotle.'

The moral the anti-realist appears to draw from all this is that the aspiration to contemplate, however distantly, the ultimate real essences of concrete things is best forgotten about—in nature itself there are no modalities. The anti-conceptualist on the other hand does not conclude that essentialism as such is mistaken, only that the realist aspiration, as fully seriously conceived, is inimical to any position like conceptualism. He will persist in the idea that the realist ideal is to be valued above any supposed conceptualist insight, and hold fast to his conviction that he will find some better approach than that which leads through proposition (Δ) of Chapter Four to the real essences of concrete things.

In answer to these critics, I shall be content for the most part to clarify the claims of my particular conceptualism to be one form of realism. For the objection I have just rehearsed comprehends a number of misapprehensions whose removal will be far more instructive and far more liberating of thought than an exhaustive response to all the accusations and countersuggestions that each critic could muster on his side. I believe that once conceptualist realism is recognized for what it is, its metaphysical plainness will be manifest.

2. *Four clarifications*

(a) The objection given in the previous section is not innocent of vestigial misunderstanding of one point that Chapter Four will have made familiar. The conditions that have been characterized as peculiarly central to the articulation of this or that particular thing from the rest of reality concerned not the world's need to contain (say) Caesar, but only the kind of thing Caesar had to be *if* there was to be any such thing as Caesar. The necessity in question is at once crucial with respect to the question of the individual's being extant to articulate, and peculiarly innocuous. In Kant's terminology it is a *conditioned necessity,* and its oddity resides only in the character of its condition. The condition comprehends all states of affairs in which the very entity in question exists.[4]

(b) To put a sentence forward as a true statement of *de re* necessity (or as a *de dicto* necessity for that matter, if the *de dicto* were in question) is not to put the sentence forward as in some special way proof from revision, correction, or the boredom of our descendants. Those who object in such terms to essentialism as an expression of the stick-in-mud mentality, or of ill-advised reaction, have insufficiently distinguished these several statuses.

(c) It is necessary to reiterate the sincerity of essentialist adherence to principle Θ of section 6 of Chapter Four. Essences of natural things, as we have them here, are not fancified vacuities parading in the shadow of familiar things as the ultimate explanation of every-

---

4. (For the sceptical.) If someone insists on converting the explanation here suggested for

(i) *a* is necessarily f

or

(ii) [NEC (λz) [fz]], $\langle a \rangle$

into some *de dicto* equivalent

(iii) $\Box$ $(\exists x)$ $((x=a) \supset fa)$,

then (iii) should be distinguished (cf. principles (Z) and (H) of Chapter Four, section 2) from the existentially harmless

(iv) [NEC (λz) [$(\exists x)$ $(x=z) \supset fz$]], $\langle a \rangle$.

Note also that the premiss

(v) $\Box$ fa,

which is distinguished by me from (i) and (ii), will not be available here, even if the (some think) disputable principle

(vi) $\Box$ $(fa \supset (\exists x)$ $(x=a))$

(existential generalization for good names) is considered valid. So there is no threat in any case of reaching the conclusion

(vii) $\Box$ $(\exists x)$ $(x=a)$.

Note finally that (vii) is itself to be distinguished from

[NEC (λz) [$(\exists x)$ $(x=z)$]], $\langle a \rangle$.

thing that happens in the world.[5] They are natures whose possession by their owners is the precondition of their owners being divided from the rest of the reality as anything at all. These natures are delimited by reference to causal or explanatory principles and purposes that are low level perhaps, but demanding enough for something to count as their being disappointed or frustrated. (Witness the longish list of sortal concepts that have definitely failed.) Whatever these principles may once have seemed to be, essentialists since Leibniz have recognized that the principles which Chapter Three called the laws of development of individual natural substances, and which were associated with individuative kinds of natural things (one at least for each kind), are not themselves the scientifically *basic* laws of the physical world. Nor in general are they reducible (in the strict and proper sense) to such laws. Such kind-bound laws of coming to be and passing away are nevertheless nomologically grounded. They are *supervenient upon*, and, as Leibniz would put it, *consentient with*, the more basic laws, which are immanent in all things.[6]

(d) The realist conceptualist may cheerfully admit that the sortal concepts of which we are possessed, and which he argues to be presupposed to our articulation of reality, are (in a certain fashion and sense—see section 7 below) the creatures of our interests: and also that there need be no one way in which we *must* articulate reality, nor any one level at which we must. But something which does not follow from any of this is that, *relative* to some particular set of determinate interests, there is arbitrariness in the discriminations we make, or in the existence conditions that we ascribe to the members of the natural and artifact kinds under which our interests determine that we shall conceptualize experience. For the supposed arbitrariness of whether or not this or that concept is brought or not brought

5. We do not look for scientifically ultimate explanations at this level of conceptualization. By the standards of 2,300 years ago it was not necessarily unscientific to look for them there, as Aristotle justifiably and non-vacuously did. (See the interpretation offered by Alan Gotthelf in 'Aristotle's Conception of Final Causality', *Review of Metaphysics* XXX, 1976.) What has been discovered since Aristotle is that the search for fundamental explanations and principles, and for mechanisms underlying the phenomena, requires not only a new vocabulary but also a new ontology. On this see below, section 7. None of this entails that science has shown that every explanation in any way worth having can eventually find expression at this deeper level.

6. Cf. Leibniz, Gerhardt II, 263, *op. cit.* at head of Chapter Two. Not only are these ideas separable from the teleological view of nature (see Chapter Two, section 1). They are separable also from the teleological conceptions of certain theorists of Natural Law about the levels of excellence that natural things may realize or attain to. For an amusing, summary account of these ideas see H. L. A. Hart, *The Concept of Law*, Oxford, 1961, p. 185.

to bear upon reality cannot be translated into a corresponding arbitrariness in the determination of the compliants themselves of the concept.[7] Any arbitrariness or vagueness that attaches to the determination of the extension of the sortal concept has a quite different source (see Chapter Four, section 6).

So put, no essentialist will find any of these confusions or misapprehensions very inviting—unless confusion (c) is irresistible. Their influence is more indirect now than direct. But it must also be allowed that the conception which the anti-essentialist opposes to the essentialist conception is sustained by the enchantment of an image that is vivid in the extreme.

3. *A conventionalist reconstruction of our modal convictions: a conceptualist anti-realist view of essence*

'At bottom, everything that can be said about the world, can be said in purely general statements, without modalities. There is no thisness beyond suchness, but every actual individual is individuated already by the properties it has in this world; hence can be denoted in principle by a definite description in which the quantifier ranges over actual existents alone. At this bottom level the only necessity we can countenance is purely logical or verbal necessity which, like God, is no respecter of persons. In this modality whatever Peter can do Paul can do also. A semantic representation of this will use a conventional identification of individuals in different worlds, but since every individual plays each possible role in some possible world, *every* choice of conventional identifications which does not violate the identity principle that no two existents in world α have all the same properties in α yields the same result.

'To make sense of our world in a *convenient* fashion, however, we raise certain regularities to the status of laws and (not independently) certain attributes to the status of natures. In the formal mode, this means that some statements assume the office of assumptions which may be tacitly used in all reasoning, and certain predicates are chosen to form a classificatory scheme. Once this is done, we produce relative or tacitly conditional modal qualifiers.... A proposition P is *peculiarly about* individual e if we can change the truth value of P by permuting e with another individual e' (while leaving all other individuals fixed), but cannot change that truth-value by any permutation which leaves e fixed.... In a full model, no proposition peculiarly about a particular

7. Cf. 'The *De Re* "Must": a Note on the Logical Form of Essentialist Claims', *op. cit.* (5) *Preface*, p. 288, and section 1 generally.

entity can be necessary, for [in a full model] the necessary proposition is closed under all permutations.'[8]

What Van Fraassen describes here is a sort of reconstruction in two stages of how it is possible for us to have our present ideas of substance and *de re* modality. The reconstruction also suggests to us what we should make of these ideas and of the fact that we have them. Not too much, he suggests. The reconstruction is not put forward by Van Fraassen as an ordinary historical hypothesis or even as a piece of psychogenetic theory. Taking it rather as it is intended, there is just one thing that would appear to be crucial to the reconstruction and to the attitude that it recommends towards substance and modality: the two stages of which it speaks must be intelligible to us and describable by us, the theorists, in just the relationship that the account postulates. How otherwise can we credit Van Fraassen's own words with even the semblance of intelligibility?

The difficulty in this respect attaches to the first stage. Here whatever Peter can do Paul can do also (Van Fraassen says)—indeed anything whatever can do. For anything, it seems, can do or be anything at this level, the only constraints being those imposed by logical necessity in the narrowest sense which, whatever dues it pays to 'indiscernibility at a world', is 'no respecter' of identity in the proper sense. The question then is: can we really understand this first stage of the reconstruction? Only, it seems to me, if we can make sense of an entity that is nothing in particular. (Cf. the justification and refinement of Δ of Chapter Four, section 2, undertaken in section 5.)

Van Fraassen's adherence to the Identity of Indiscernibles is important here. Contrast with his explicit reliance upon the principle everything that we have claimed in Chapter Two against the Identity of Indiscernibles and have elsewhere implied (in agreement with P. F. Strawson, *Individuals,* 'Monads' chapter and *passim*) about the indispensability and irreducibility of the demonstrative function. To turn *this* into *thisness* and, having found no way to understand *thisness* as a

8. Bas C. Van Fraassen, part IV of 'Essence and Existence', *American Philosophical Quarterly Monograph* 1977–78. Cf. part I:

The nominalist's first and basic move in this game is to say that all natural necessities are elliptic for conditional verbal necessities. This sheet on which I write must burn if heated, because it is paper—yes. But the only necessity that is really there is that all paper must burn when heated. This is so, but means only that we would not call something paper if it behaved differently . . . when sufficiently refined, the position that all non-verbal necessities are ellipses for conditional necessities *ex vi terminorum* can be held.

Cf. also the same author's 'The Only Necessity is Verbal Necessity', *Journal of Philosophy* Feb. 1977). Contrast Chapter Four, section 4.

sort of *suchness*, to seek then to patch matters up by espousing the Identity of Indiscernibles—this is a counsel of confusion, confusion that is needless. But there is scarcely anything unconfused that can be either said or denied by the use of the words *haecceitas* and *thisness*. What these words purport to help one to say *or* deny is as mixed up as the noises that they make are unlovely. (Cf. Chapter Four, section 7.)

Finally, I would claim that the whole charm of Van Fraassen's picture depends on one's allowing that one can first have an ontology of particulars conceived as bare, and then at a second stage introduce, as an instrument of understanding, explanation and discovery, what Quine and Geach have called an *ideology*. But is it not a mysterious suggestion that a whole range of attributions, including sortal attributions which say what various everyday things are, could be determined at this second stage (in radical dependence, Van Fraassen suggests, on some human viewpoint), and be superimposed upon a completed first stage ontology which is at once bare but existentially determinate? For one used to the idea that an ontology is by no means an empty or uncommittal thing, this is as strange as being asked to believe that one could distinguish between first a neutral or concern-uncontaminated ontology of jokes (what it is for x to be a joke, or for x and y to be the same joke, or for there to be such a joke as z), and second, a quite separate and interest-contaminated range of predicative attributions to jokes (including 'funny'). Is it compatible with a good theory of existence to suppose that the first stage (ontology) could have been provided for, leaving absolutely everything else to be determined at the second (ideology)?

Obviously, if ontology were completely insensitive to all changes in theory or conceptual ideology, and if one and the same fixed set of entities could be descried by conceptions of the world that were different to just any degree that you like, then that would refute the account offered in Chapter Two, section 6, of the relationship between existence and belonging to a sort. I should hope that the positive account there offered had the attraction of simplicity. There is a range of basic sortal attributions that we apply to various everyday things—'this is a horse', 'this is a tree', 'that is a man'. These belong to the level of ontology and, at least to this extent, ontology and ideology contaminate one another. What is strange is that the anti-essentialists whom I am attacking[9] accept all these attributions

9. Russell was an opponent of essentialism, but these paragraphs are not directed at his position. For he pursued the logic of his position (and the logic of my paragraphs here) to the point of rejecting the ontology which is presupposed to saying 'this is a man'. See 'The *De Re* "Must"', *op cit.*

in their unmodalized form, and then (one stage too late, in my opinion, for they have already consented to pick out the thing and to involve themselves, however minimally, in the relevant theory) adduce as a reason to deprecate the suggestion that any of these things *had* to be a horse, or a tree or a man, the anthropocentricity of the viewpoint that underlies and conditions the attributions. But here as everywhere the question is: of *what* one could ever be speaking if one allowed that it might equally well have been a prime number or a fire shovel, though it was in fact neither?

4. *A hypothesis concerning the sources of anti-essentialism*

I advance for the reader's consideration a hypothesis. It is that the anti-realist case against essential properties has rested on a sequence of three ideas.

(1) It is conceivable that, in the absence of creatures capable of thought as we know it, the particular kinds of individual substance that we ourselves recognize in this world would never have been discovered. (Indeed nothing forces anyone to discover in a place even what is there to be conceptualized in terms of his own concepts.) In that place, in the room of what we ourselves find there, and out of its matter, another race of creatures might have singled out and individuated quite other kinds of things with very different principles of articulation and individuation.

From this not implausible-seeming premiss the conceptualist anti-essentialist goes on to conclude:

(2) It is perfectly possible for what is there to be discovered in a given place, e.g. for a substance which is there, to be conceptualized in at least two quite different ways. The progress of science would precisely consist in conceptualizing it in better, and radically different, ways. So, he argues:

(3) The constraints arising from the conceptualization and individuation of the particulars that we recognize in the world, and can draw spatio-temporal boundaries around, must not be represented as necessities on what is actually there, independently of mind or thought. The most objectionable feature of all the objectionable features of essential attributions is that they purport to record such necessities.

It is at stage (2) that everything goes wrong here. What is this substance out there that can be conceptualized in radically different ways, which can be seized upon in thought by the anti-essentialist, but can have radically different principles of existence and persistence ascribed to it? This is surely an entity with inconsistent properties. If the charge of having a ridiculous conception of substance sticks anywhere, it sticks on anyone who argues via (2) from (1) to (3). But it is only by means of some such conception that an anti-realist philosopher can crowd out altogether the possibility, which is important but always neglected, that, even if (what is not in every case obvious) a conceptual scheme capable of exploring and understanding the physical world could dispense altogether with the articulation and isolation of x from its environment (because it could afford to ignore x altogether), still the essential attributions upon x record or reflect conditions at once fundamental and invariant upon x in particular's existing and being singled out in reality.

5. *An exaggeration of conceptualism, deprecated and mended by some truisms: and the reply to the anti-conceptualist realist begun*

If the preceding section succeeded to any significant extent, it gained some favour for some sort of conceptualist view of individuation. But conceptualism may seem to have strange consequences.

Leszek Kolakowski writes:

> The picture of reality sketched by everyday perception and by scientific thinking is a kind of human creation (not imitation) since both the linguistic and the scientific division of the world into particular objects arise from man's practical needs. In this sense the world's products must be considered artificial. In this world the sun and stars exist because man is able to make them *his* objects, differentiated in material and conceived as 'corporeal individuals'. In abstract, nothing prevents us from dissecting surrounding material into fragments constructed in a manner completely different from what we are used to. Thus, speaking more simply, we could build a world where there would be no such objects as 'horse', 'leaf', 'star', and others allegedly devised by nature. Instead, there might be, for example, such objects as 'half a horse and a piece of river', 'my ear and the moon', and other similar products of a surrealist imagination.[10]

I am bound to agree with any anti-conceptualist realist who asserts that what Kolakowski says here is impossible to believe. I should hold that any conceptualism which is bent on picking its way past the

10. Leszek Kolakowski, *Towards a Marxist Humanism,* New York, Grove Press, 1968, pp. 47–48. My attention was first drawn to this passage by Michael Ayers, who has doubted that my own conceptualism leaves me in a position to disagree with it.

confusions that have sustained for so long the conflict between
realism and idealism must indeed strive to do justice to the insight for
which Kolakowski is seeking expression. But it will see the whole
interest of these problems as residing in the problem of finding the
elusive, correct and unexciting formulation of that insight. A conceptualism that aspires to the title of a modest and sober realism must
keep at arm's length any such 'sense' as the sense in which horses,
leaves, sun and stars could be supposed to be artifacts. It must hold
on to the distinctions so laboriously worked out in Chapter Three. It
must leave itself room to express all the proper reservations (concerning the lack of appropriate causal and explanatory principles, etc.)
about the prospects of a genuinely sortal notion with the same
extension as *half a horse plus a piece of river*. And it must hold a nice
balance, adjusted to what is in fact a subtly reciprocal relation,
between the extent to which the concepts that we bring to bear to
distinguish, articulate and individuate things in nature are something
invented by us and the extent to which these concepts are something
we discover and permit nature itself to intimate to us and inform and
regulate for us. Conceptualism properly conceived must not entail
that before we got for ourselves these concepts, their extensions could
not exist autonomously, i.e. independently of whether or not the
concepts were destined to be fashioned and their compliants to be
discovered.[11] What conceptualism entails is only that, although
horses, leaves, sun and stars are not inventions or artifacts, still, in
order to single out these things, we have to deploy upon experience a
conceptual scheme which has itself been fashioned or formed in such
a way as to make it *possible* to single them out.

For a man to single out a leaf or a horse or a sun or a star, or
whatever it is, that which is singled out by him must have the right
principle of individuation for a leaf or a horse or a sun or a star. . . .
For to single out one of these things he must single *it* out. Such
truisms would scarcely be worth writing down if philosophy were not
driven from side to side here of the almost unnegotiable strait which
divides the realist myth of the *self-differentiating object* (the object
which announces itself as the very object it is to any mind, however
passive and of whatever orientation) from the *substratum* myth that is
the recurrent temptation of bad conceptualism.[12] It is easy to scoff at

11. Cf. Hobbes's definition: 'a body is that, which having no dependence upon our
thought, is coincident or coextended with some part of space'. *De Corpore* II, 11
(Molesworth, p. 136).
12. Rebounding from all this, there is a temptation to add nonsense to confusion and
say that a thing is nothing but a sum (in some inexplicable sense of 'sum') of properties

substratum. It is not easy to escape the insidious idea that there can be the singling out in a place of a merely determinable space-occupier awaiting incongruent or discordant substantial determinations (individuatively inconsistent answers to the question *what is it*).[13] But no substance has been singled out at all until something makes it determinate *which* entity has been singled out; and for this to be determinate, there must be something in the singling out that makes it determinate which principle is the principle of individuation for the entity and under what family of individuatively parallel sortal concepts it is to be subsumed (see Chapter Two, section 7).[14]

---

and/or appearances, or a set of universals each sitting in the next one's lap. (This is in fact the notion of thing favoured by some anti-essentialists. How it is to be combined with the idea that objects so conceived have no essences finally passes comprehension. Consider, for a start, the negation of the conjunction of these properties. And if the reply to that is that these collocations of properties have shifting membership, then inquire after the principle determining membership. The answer to this will smuggle back the notion of substance.)

13. There will exist too indefinitely many items with too many distinct principles of identity and persistence which you might find in that place—the thing, the parcel of stuff that makes up the thing, and the mereological sum of all the components of that parcel, to name but three. See also here A. M. Quinton, *The Nature of Things*, p. 67.

Against all such arguments, Michael Ayers has written (*op. cit.*, p. 132; and compare M. C. Bradley's critique at *Australasian Journal of Philosophy* 47 (1969) of the principles of tracing that have been defended in Chapter Two):

> it might be thought that in unravelling the sweater we remove or destroy one principle of unity, and [that] by cutting the [woollen] thread [of the ball of wool from which the sweater was knitted] we remove a second. Each operation is possible without the other, and so each principle of unity seems independent of the other [giving in one and the same place two different things of different kinds]. The latter and more realistic view, however, is that, if a sweater consists of a single thread, then this means only that the different parts of the wool hang together in more than one way, and so have a unity that is more difficult to destroy than would otherwise be the case. Roughly, the unity or structure of a sweater knitted from a hundred separate threads is destroyed by unravelling, and the unity of a single thread by cutting; while the unity of a sweater knitted from a single thread survives either operation but not both. Thus no serious doubt is cast on that apparently essential ingredient of a realist theory of the identity of physical objects, the principle that the same matter cannot be subjected to more than one principle of unity at the same time: i.e. cannot compose more than one individual simultaneously.

If this says that in some cases (composition from one thread) unravelling a sweater is not a way of destroying it, but that in other cases (composition from several threads of wool) matters are so different that unravelling is enough for destruction, then I am happy to let the reader assess the price of Ayers's 'realist principle'. I hope it will be clear why I believe that the principle is dispensable to realism, to objectivity, and to the nomologically grounded conception of substance. (Compare here certain difficulties that I claim to see in a similar principle of Eli Hirsch's. *Vide* footnote 4 of my *op. cit.* (3), *Preface*.)

14. A fallacy for the unwary: *It is indeterminate what thing A singled out; therefore A singled out something indeterminate.*

6. The perfect consonance of sober realism and sober conceptualism

An anti-conceptualist realist who takes exception to the essentialism arrived at by means of principle Δ of Chapter Four will view with suspicion any suggestion that there exist truisms which, in the presence of a strict notion of identity, will entail that what individuative scheme we bring to bear upon experience, or the fashion in which (as a race, or as a culture, or as a culture at a time) we have elected to articulate reality, can determine both what kinds of thing we shall single out (fs, gs or whatever) *and,* which for me is almost the same, what will be principles of individuation or conditions of persistence of what we single out.[15] Such claims may seem to the realist to be tantamount to saying that the active inquiring mind does not merely construe reality but constructs it—as if under certain conditions the mind could fashion not only concepts or conceptions but truth itself. But is this not a particularly unappealing form of idealism, he will ask? Have we not ventured to criticize others for venturing close to such infantility?

The literal purport of my claim which the realist has put under discussion is not that mind constructs reality. If it comes close to seeming to say that, this is only because the truth has here to rub shoulders with two opposing doctrines that are so similar in their underlying absurdity as to leave very little room between for the truth to stand. But there is just room for it to stand. For our claim was only that what sortal concepts we bring to bear upon experience determines what we can find there—just as the size and mesh of a net determine, not what fish are in the sea, but which ones we shall catch. The thesis is that the concepts under which experience is articulated and things are singled out determine the persistence conditions of what is singled only because such concepts determine *what* is singled out. But there is scarcely more than a trace of idealism in this doctrine—when the persistence condition itself is not joined to the concept by any creative act of the mind (neither postulating nor positing nor inventing) and is even on occasion given to the concept, in a reciprocity of the kind Chapter Three was meant to illustrate, by the compliants themselves of the concept.

Much hangs here on identifying correctly the point, if any, where there *is* choice or freedom in the articulation of reality. The near certainty of incomprehension of these tenets by a certain kind of realist is so great that even the reader who has long since seized what I would say here may forgive me for making one more attempt: Once a

15. For the grounds on which Michael Ayers takes exception to such claims, see *Longer Note* 5.15.

set of individuative concerns is determinate, and an interest and a set of sortal concepts is fixed upon, nothing that we who have the concept can do will determine whether or not something at a certain place actually *satisfies* a given concept or not. Any freedom we enjoyed was at an earlier point. Whatever may be the obscure truth to be found in the idea that what concepts a thinker applies to the world depends on his inventiveness in the fashioning of concepts and hypotheses, and whatever the truth of the idea that the accident or caprice of his interests and his conceptual daring and enterprise will carry him at his pleasure to places that nothing else would have carried him to; this *exhausts* his freedom. For, once arrived at a place, what he finds there is not at his pleasure. Whether there exist f compliants or not cannot depend on his invention or his concerns.

7. The realist requirement restated, refurbished and satisfied

It is not enough to remove confusions. The anti-conceptualist realist is not necessarily a man confused by anything at all except the difference between good and bad conceptualism. And he is most unlikely to think it relevant to what he has to say that one can count as objectively as you like, for instance, (and answer the question *what is it?* as accurately as you like) under sortal concepts of utterly provincial or frivolous provenance. His real preoccupation is not I think with objectivity (for it presupposes that, at least in the sense of there being a public canon for the correct application of a concept), but with something that arises after the point at which the objectivity has already been secured (i.e. after truth has been shown, as well as it can be shown, to be a feature which every statement that possesses it possesses independently of our means of recognizing it, and every statement that lacks it lacks independently of our means of recognizing it). For what concerns the anti-conceptualist realist is not so much to safeguard the mere objectivity of human thinking, as to preserve its prospects of passing beyond the most narrowly anthropocentric.[16] But here it seems to me that an essentialist of my persuasion can make common cause with him. For, as we have conceived this, an indivi-

16. For the distinctness of these concerns, and for the Peircean conception of the advance of science beyond and away from the anthropocentric, see section IX of my 'Truth, Invention, and the Meaning of Life', *Proceedings of the British Academy* 1977.

I have found that my conception of realism here is in some respect anticipated, albeit in terms more optimistic than I should think necessary or desirable, by Milton Fisk in 'The World Regained', *Journal of Philosophy* 1972, see especially pp. 667–8.

duative scheme for the articulation of reality and the singling out of natural things is wide open to reality. And if (as I claim) there is nothing to prevent it from being regulated and corrected constantly *by reality itself,* then there is a way for an overwhelming importance to reside in the distinction explored in Chapter Three between nominal or stipulative definitions, founded in the function of artifacts, and the real or causal definitions that we strive after, identifying them by 'tacit reference to the real essence of this or that species of body' (Locke, *Essay* III.10.19), and annexing them in the first instance by marks which *stand proxy* ('tiennent lieu', Leibniz, *Nouveaux Essais* 3.6.14), and always taking the risk in which our explanatory aspirations involve us that, where we are unlucky, there may prove to have been no one underlying constitution. Here surely the things themselves shape our conception of things.

You assert that the notion of substance is formed from concepts, and not from things. But are not concepts themselves formed from things? (Nonne ipsi conceptus formantur ex rebus?) You say that the notion of substance is a concept of the mind, or an entity of reason as they say. But the same can be said of any concept. (Leibniz to de Volder.)[17]

In so far as Leibniz is making a general claim here, it is falsified by the case that he always ignores (or, where he does not ignore it, underestimates), *viz.* artifact kinds and cultural objects where the onus of match is from compliant to concept not concept to com-

17. Gerhardt II, p. 182. Cf. *Nouveaux Essais* 3.6.13:

But whatever rules men make for the denominations and powers of names, and provided that the rule is properly followed, or is secure and intelligible, it will be founded in reality. Men will not be able to fabricate kinds which nature, which extends even to the possible, has not itself made or distinguished previously. As for the interior, although there is no external appearance which is not founded in inner constitution, it is true nevertheless that the same appearance may sometimes result from two different inner constitutions . . . if one were to concede that certain apparent natures which prompt us to give them the same name have no inner constitution in common, even then our definitions would not cease to be founded upon real kinds. For phenomena themselves are realities. We can say then of everything which we truly distinguish or compare with something else that nature also distinguishes it or makes it agree in the comparison, although nature has distinctions and comparisons which we do not know at all and which may be better than ours. . . . The more thoroughly one examines the generation of species, and the more one follows in classification the conditions which it requires, the closer one will approach to the natural order. . . . If we knew enough about things, perhaps we should find for every kind attributes which are common to all its members and always subsist in the same organism whatever alterations or transformations may befall it.

144   CONCEPTUALISM AND REALISM

pliant. But in the other case at least, surely human understanding does come ever closer to finding features of the world whose articulation is not sensitive to the practical or provincial explanatory interests with which thought first addressed itself to the world. It is true that the normal thing-kind concept (even though the understanding sees it not as the work of the understanding but as something in nature that the understanding has prepared itself to be able to discover or light upon) is rarely or never a scientifically basic concept—still less so fundamental a concept that we can assert that there is *no* understanding of nature sufficiently abstract or profound for its possessor to be in a position to look past the extension of this concept. It is true that for all we know, and however deep we go, an intelligence of a superior kind might always latch on to a more fundamental and explanatorily more basic class of things whose identifying attributes pulled their weight in a far better and more universal theory than any of the classes that we shall ever discriminate. To this extent, the causal cum explanatory interests that give us even the most sophisticated and scientific sortal concepts we possess might indeed be held by a certain kind of critic to be rather provincial. But the proper answer to the realist critic is not in any case that these concepts are not provincial to *any* degree, but that the critic has nothing to offer as a proof that all genuinely explanatory insights *have* to be framed at the deepest level of fundamental theory. This is just as unlikely to be true in the pure theory of science as it would be unmanageable in the daily practice of expounding the relatively fundamental theories we do possess. The condition of acceptance that we do impose on the sortal notions we continue in practice to employ is not an empty one. And equipped with these notions, our conceptual scheme surely represents a respectable, however unimpressive, stage in some however gradual process of the revelation of reality. Only some dissatisfaction with all human thought or speech as such, or as any sort of a representation of reality, could prompt someone to deny this.[18]

18. A very good idea of what it would be for this condition to go unsatisfied, and for a system of concepts to lack this kind of endorsement, may be derived from a consideration of a system of classification which Foucault mentions in a well known passage that Borges ascribes to a 'certain Chinese encyclopaedia.' In this it is written that

animals are divided into: (a) belonging to the Emperor, (b) embalmed, (c) tame, (d) sucking pigs, (e) sirens, (f) fabulous, (g) stray dogs, (h) included in the present classification, (i) frenzied, (j) innumerable, (k) drawn with a very fine camelhair brush, (l) *et cetera*, (m) having just broken the water pitcher, (n) that from a long way off look like flies. In the wonderment of this taxonomy, the thing we apprehend in one great leap, the thing that, by means of fable, is demonstrated as

8. *Concluding suggestions*

By way of partial summary of this and the previous chapter, I shall close with some suggestions concerning the relation of the scientific world view and the less theoretical view of reality, which lags behind it but has always to sustain the meaning that can be attributed to our thoughts.

(i) Many of the scientifically significant shifts in our conceptions of the world represent not shifts in our conceptions of a settled ontology, or shifts in the individuative conceptions proper to one and the same set of entities, but the abandonment for certain explanatory purposes of the old set of entities and the old ontology. The ingredients that compose such things may then be inventoried, if that is the question, in other counts of the stuff of the world. Their matter does not have to be reckoned as the matter of these particular entities. In so far as questions about the old set of entities are answered rather than simply abandoned, the answer is given under the new order by bridge principles (whose *ad hoc* character it will do no harm to acknowledge), or by recourse to considerations (again *ad hoc*) of a mereological kind.

(ii) Where a shift in conception is a genuine revision of the old conception of the old entities, and where the same entities are recognizable, i.e. where the shift is an improvement or development of the individuative conceptions which were *constitutive* of the old ontology, the old ontology can happily take over the improvement. (Cf. property G of section 6 of Chapter Four.) If the Leibnizian cum essentialist account of concept-formation is correct, then conceptual schemes are designed from the outset to allow for this improvement.

(iii) Scientific progress towards an explanatorily more fruitful conception of the world which abandons an old ontology does not always or necessarily *discredit* the ontology of the older, less theoretical conception of the world. That may still count as adequate in its own terms. And it may well be cotenable with the more theoretical conception. It is important to contrast the discrediting of entities of some kind, palpable or impalpable, with the discovery of new entities

---

the exotic charm of another system of thought, is the limitation of our own, the stark impossibility of thinking *that*.

M. Foucault, *The Order of Things,* New York, Pantheon, 1970. It is not really the difficulty of thinking these concepts (for as Foucault himself says they are perfectly well defined), but the difficulty of conceiving that such a taxonomy could make any headway with causality—with the *explanation of anything*.

at the atomic or subatomic level, a level to which the macroscopic is not reduced in fact (in the serious sense), but which for every macroscopic event promises some explanation of it. The second sort of discovery leaves high and dry but perfectly unharmed the familiar macroscopic entities in which we cannot abandon our interest. Indeed there are some practical interests we *cannot* become blind to, and some entities in which it is impossible for us to lose our interest (most notably perhaps the entities to be treated in Chapter Six).

(iv) A new conception of the world and its accompanying ontology will not come bare of individuative concepts or of *de re* necessities of its own. As always, what generates these will be the requirement that everything conceivable of the new entities be coconceivable in the new ontology with what is their most fundamental sortal identification. Principle Δ of Chapter Four concerned a necessity that is not in the narrow sense logical necessity. But its *strength* (contrast certainty) is equal to that of logical necessity. For once the theoretically fundamental sortal property f is fixed upon and its extension comes to light, it is not for thought to renege even hypothetically upon the determination of how a thing falling within that extension had to be in order to an f (belong to f). That would weaken thought's grip of its object. If f determines an ultimate sort (in the sense that f is a concept that determines a principle of individuation, is purged of phasal and temporal restrictions, and is as high as it can be consistently with being autonomously individuative), then there is nothing else that a particular entity falling inside the sort could oblige the conventionalist by acquiescing to become instead. To *be,* for such a thing just is to comply with this ultimate or near ultimate concept f. Falling under that, the individual is not conceivable at all as *not* an f compliant. And now I should add that, if that is what it means to say that the individual *a* is necessarily ϕ and the explanations of Section 2 are borne in mind, then the idea that there is somehow a further question about whether necessity does or does not reside in the world, in so far as the world is conceptualizable, is surely an illusion—an interesting illusion, but an illusion whose parallels in other areas ought, I believe, to make both the anti-essentialist and the actualist uneasy.

It is only in its proper body that mind is revealed. The [idea of the] migration of souls is a false abstraction, and physiology ought to have made it one of its axioms that life had necessarily in its evolution to attain to the human shape as the sole sensuous phenomenon that is adequate to mind. (Hegel, *Introduction to the Lectures on Fine Art*, Stuttgart, Jubiläumsausgabe, 1953, vol. XII, p. 118; translated by B. Bosanquet.)

Most people are natural metaphysicians, and it is an easy passage for them from the unassailable methodological doctrine, that physics and chemistry are applicable to biological objects, to the metaphysical doctrine, that living organisms are 'nothing but' physical systems. This . . . retards the search for explanatory hypotheses on the biological levels, just as a purely behaviouristic approach to psychology retards and discourages the search for other hypotheses in that science. . . .

There is one more point to be mentioned in connexion with the doctrine of the reducibility of biology to physics and chemistry: people who hold the doctrine do not in fact believe it. If you want to reduce biology to physics and chemistry, you must construct bi-conditionals which are in effect definitions of biological functors with the help of those belonging only to physics and chemistry; you must then add these to the postulates of physics and chemistry and work out their consequences. Then and only then will it be time to go into your laboratories to discover whether these consequences are upheld there. From the fact that people do *not* do this, I venture the guess that they confuse *reducibility* of biology to physics and chemistry, with *applicability* of physics and chemistry to biological objects. (J. H. Woodger, *Biology and Language*, Cambridge, 1952, pp. 336–8.)

CHAPTER SIX

Personal Identity

1. *John Locke on persons*

Locke defined a person as 'a thinking intelligent being, that has reason and reflection, and can consider itself as itself, the same thinking thing, in different times and places' (*Essay* II, xxvii, 2). To many who have been excited by the same thought as Locke, continuity of consciousness has seemed to be an integral part of what we mean by a person. The intuitive appeal of the idea that, to secure the continuing identity of a person, one experience must flow into the next experience in some 'stream of consciousness' is evidenced by the number of attempts in the so called constructionalist tradition to explain continuity of consciousness in terms of memory, and then build or reconstruct the notions of person and personal identity with these materials. The philosophical difficulty of the idea is plain from the failure of these attempts. Hindsight suggests that this was as inevitable as the failure of the attempt, if anyone ever made it, to make bricks from straw alone—and, considered simply as a failure, just as uninteresting. But the question is what moral we are to draw from the failure. To some memory theorists, it may impart the sense that most of the difficulties have arisen from their leaving the flesh and bones that are the stuff of persons out of the Lockean construction. Others may have drawn other morals, or even abandoned the Lockean conception of personhood. But surely the various obstacles that the memory theorists have encountered attest much more directly to the shortcomings of their excessively constructional approach to the subject of persons (constructional, I mean, in contrast with descriptive) than they attest to the mutual irrelevance of experiential memory and what constitutes the temporal persistence of a person.

There is a distinction, well founded in the texts of Locke and Descartes on the one hand and Hume, James, Russell and Ayer on the other that is sometimes put as the distinction between 'subject' and 'no subject' theories of the self. (It is not happily put so, because no-subject theories aim not so much to reject as to reconstruct the subject, and it comes back into discourse as a complex.) But in this chapter the continuity of persons is to be discussed on a level at which this division in the traditions of speculation about the nature and persistence of selves is irrelevant. Where either tradition accords to experiential memory some relevance to personal identity, the similarities eclipse all differences. When William James, for instance, writes that 'the continuing identity of each personal consciousness is treated as a name for the practical fact that new experiences look back on old ones, find them warm and appropriate them as mine', and that subsequent experiences must judge that 'these feelings are the nucleus of me', his 'no-subject' theory is founded in just the same sorts of question as Locke's version of the 'subject' theory.[1] It must be admitted that among these questions are several that are misconceived[2] or arise out of serious confusion between how we know something and what it is for that thing to be so. But it does not follow that either tradition is wholly wrong to interest itself in the idea that memory and reflection help to constitute the continuity of the persisting self.

The first aim of this chapter is to examine in their connexion with the problems of substance and sameness the charges of circularity and manifest absurdity that have been brought against the theory that the kind of continuity that Locke describes is part of the essence of persons and their identities. Of these particular charges I think the theory can be cleared absolutely. The second aim is to pursue a potentially conflicting insight that is suggested by the defence of Locke against the charge of circularity. Even though this conflicting insight finally subverts the memory theorists' conception of what personal *identity* is, it will be powerless to refute the Lockean conception of what it is to be a person with a sense of his own identity. Here we shall agree with Locke, while rejecting the more extreme positions that he has inspired.

There is something so interesting about the notion that a person is an object essentially aware of its progress and persistence through time, and peculiar among all other kinds of thing by virtue of the fact that its present being is always under the cognitive and affective influence of its experiential memory of what it was in the past; and this notion is so closely related, not only to profound contentions of

1. Like the role in which James casts 'stream of experience', 'the transition of one experience into another', 'coconsciousness', 'conjunctive relations'. See *Essays in Radical Empiricism*, Longmans, 1912.
2. See Sydney Shoemaker, *Self-Knowledge and Self-Identity*, Ithaca, N.Y., Cornell University Press, 1963.

Leibniz and Kant,[3] but also to deeply ingrained ordinary ideas of life as something to be reviewed and looked back upon; that I believe we should look with some suspicion at the contention that a continuity of consciousness condition of personal identity is irreducibly circular. What seems not merely suspect, however, but almost inconceivable is the suggestion that this sort of mental connectedness is simply no part of the concept of a person. The pretheoretical conception of mental connectedness is an intuitive idea that we bring to philosophy. The hard question is not the question of its relevance to philosophy but of just what, if anything, it implies about the nature of personal *identity*.

If one defines a person in Locke's manner, and if one also attaches so much importance to the self-recording faculty of experiential memory that active exercise of the faculty becomes a criterial property for being a person, then it will be very natural to expect that, by virtue of being counted as part of the condition of existence and persistence, this active exercise will register upon the identity conditions for persons. This will seem to follow from certain truths that are now very familiar (though due to be scrutinized afresh in section 12) about the intimate relation holding between an account of *what a thing is* and the elucidation of the identity-conditions for members of its kind. In the end, though, this natural expectation is disappointed. Memory registers only faintly on identity conditions. Indeed I shall urge in the last section of the chapter that the issue of mental connectedness, considered as a mark of what it is to be a person, has to be separated from the main issue of identity and survival, and that, even though experiential memory is one component in an inner nucleus of conceptual constituents of what it is for a person to continue to exist or perdure, there is no strictly necessary or sufficient condition of survival that we can formulate in its terms. I hope that it will be the result of this separation, not only to disrupt the even flow of controversy between friends and enemies of the Lockean concep-

---

3. Cf. Leibniz, *Discours de Metaphysique* XXXIV (Gerhardt IV, p. 460); J. Bennett, *Kant's Analytic,* Cambridge, 1963, p. 117, 'the notion of oneself is necessarily that of the possessor of a history: I can judge that this is how it is with me now, only if I can also judge that that is how it was with me then. Self-consciousness can coexist with amnesia—but there could not be a self-conscious person suffering from perpetually renewed amnesia such that he could at no time make judgments about how he was at any earlier time.'

For the affective role of memory, and for the crucial importance of the function of memory in placing us under the influence of the past in our development into the persons we at any point become, see now Richard Wollheim's 'Memory, Experiential Memory, and Personal Identity' in Graham MacDonald ed. *Perception and Identity* (London 1979).

tion, but also to refine our general understanding of the intimate but complex relations of the notions of sameness and substance.[4]

2. An objection by Joseph Butler: the charge of circularity

Bishop Butler wrote in criticism of Locke that: 'One should really think it self-evident, that consciousness of personal identity presupposes, and therefore cannot constitute, personal identity, any more than knowledge, in any other case, can constitute truth, which it presupposes' (*First Dissertation* to the *Analogy of Religion*). Here many interpreters have taken Butler to be pointing to a difficulty of principle that attaches to stating any Lockean condition whatever of personal identity. But there is even room for disagreement about what exact objection this is. Bishop Butler's famous sentence does not seem to recapitulate the point made in his preceding sentence, which reads: '. . .though consciousness of what is past does thus ascertain our personal identity to ourselves, yet to say it makes personal identity or is necessary to our being the same persons, is to say that a person has not existed a single moment nor done one action but what he can remember; indeed none but what he reflects upon. And one should really think it self-evident. . .'. We shall come to this earlier sentence shortly. But the ensuing sentence about what is self-evident and which I began by quoting appears to concern some different and self-sufficient point of logic or horse-sense that, according to Butler, Locke ought to have been able to see even before he embarked on his hopeless project—something that Butler holds to be as manifest as 'knowledge presupposes truth'. The point would appear to be that one cannot define A's identity with B in terms of A's *being conscious*

---

4. The disagreement that I have noted here between myself and some other friends of Locke's conception of what it is for a person to continue in being concerns in part the *phenomenology* of the concern to survive, a matter so important and so distractive that with just one observation I shall postpone it to another occasion. The observation is this: If we ask what is so good, either absolutely or to me, about my mental life's flowing on from now into the future, the answer either imports what makes me dear to myself—and with it my idea of myself as a continuant with certain moral or other qualities that make me fond of myself—or imports something as instinctive and irreducible as the commitment to make prudent provision for the future. These are commitments that we need reasons to opt out of rather than things that we have to look for deep reasons to opt into. But what is the content of the instinct? The content is surely that the animal that is me should not cease to be. Either way then—whether the answer goes through one's idea of oneself or through instinct—the phenomenology of the concern is bound up *inextricably* with the identity relation. Cf. my 'Note on the Concern to Survive', *Midwest Studies in Philosophy* 1979.

of having been identical with B or A's *remembering being* B.[5] But if that is the objection, then why should a friend of John Locke not make the definition of A's being the same person as B in terms of A's *really or apparently remembering X-ing at time t if and only if X-ing is something B in fact did at time t?* There may well be obvious and extreme difficulties about this, but they are not the difficulties of circularity or presupposition that Butler claims to have perceived. For a definition like this one does not even mention A's consciousness of *identity* with B.

At this stage in the argument other philosphers have been willing to amplify or extend Butler's argument. Antony Flew writes: 'It is absurd to say that "he can remember that he is the same person". The absurdity is usually slightly masked since expressions such as "I remember doing, feeling, seeing something" do not contain explicit reference to the fact that what is remembered is that the speaker is the same person as did, felt, or saw whatever it was.'[6] But this does Locke the same injustice as Butler did him, misses completely the point of linking experiential memory with personhood, and imports also a new claim: that 'A remembers X-ing' is a disguised or 'masked' version of what should be rendered explicitly as 'A remembers A's X-ing'. And it seems to me that, so far from 'A remembers X-ing' having 'A remembers A's X-ing' as its canonical and equivalent form (or 'A remembers B's X-ing' implying the identity of A and B,[7] *pace* Flew, p. 56), the two locutions are importantly different in both construction and sense. This is a complicated matter on which there is much to be said. But the difficulties of equating A's remembering X-ing with A's remembering A's X-ing or remembering his X-ing, are part of a larger phenomenon deserving of more attention than philosophers have given it. Is my imagining being Moses, or an elephant, equivalent to my imagining (the impossible state of affairs of) *my*

5. It may be suggested that the general difficulty is one attaching to the attempt to build into the definition of a thing-kind f a reference to the capacity of a typical member of f to have at *t* a certain relation to its own states before *t*. If the thought is supposed to be that there is a systematic difficulty about an 'its' like this one, then see section 5 below and footnote 15.

6. See A. G. N. Flew, 'Locke and the Problem of Personal Identity', *Philosophy* XXIV, 1951, p. 55.

7. For more comment on this see B. A. O. Williams, 'Personal Identity and Individuation', *Proceedings of the Aristotelian Society* 1956–57, and my *Philosophy* 1976 (*op. cit.* (6) *Preface*), p. 134. Concerning the logical form of *imagining*-sentences and cognate matters, see also B. A. O. Williams, 'Imagination and the Self', *Proceedings of the British Academy*, 1966, and the divergent interpretation of the grammatical phenomena offered by Richard Wollheim in 'Imagination and Identification' in *On Art and the Mind*, Allen Lane, 1973.

being Moses or an elephant? Compare also foreseeing, visualizing, conceiving. Here, as with imagining, an inability to leave oneself out of the picture may in some cases disable one from achieving anything at all.

To say that there can be no acting or suffering anything, and no being Moses or being an elephant, without *some* subject's doing or suffering or being these things is not the same as to say that the subject must be specified within the claim that someone imagined or remembered the acting, being or suffering; or even that the subject must, *if* specified, be the same as the subject of the psychological verbs *imagine* or *remember*, where these are used in the senses of imagining and remembering 'centrally' or 'from the inside'. What is more, even if one always could rewrite 'A remembers X-ing' as 'A remembers A's X-ing'—which one can't, but even if one could—it would still be right to ask: why *should* one rewrite it so?

3. *Another line of objection, and the requirement of continuity of consciousness restated to counter the charge of absurdity*

Butler also claims in the same passage of the *First Dissertation* that to say that 'memory makes personal identity, or is necessary to our being the same persons, is to say that a person has not existed a single moment, nor done one action, but what he can remember; indeed none but what he reflects upon'. This is a charge not of circularity in the memory condition of personal identity but of outright absurdity in the verdicts that it implies: and now the proper response is to concede that some of Locke's formulations lay him open to such objection, but inquire whether this is an irremediable fault.

One might think it a decent first attempt at adjusting Locke's development of his conception, and more than enough to secure something like the continuity that Locke desired between person P_{t_j} and person Q_{t_k}, to amend the theory to say that, for some *sufficiency* of things actually done, witnessed, experienced . . . at any time by P_{t_j}, Q_{t_k} should later have *sufficient* real or apparent recollection of then doing, witnessing, experiencing . . . them.[8] Let us call this relation (suitably tidied up, with more about 'sufficiency', and glossed some-

---

8. 'P' (or 'Q') stands in for a definite description of a continuing person, not of a 'slice'. The subscripts t_j, t_k . . . index the *time with respect to which* the definite description *applies* to the continuing person. The subscript will be omitted where this does not need to be indicated. The notation leaves it an open question whether 'P' and 'Q' stand in for the same or different descriptions.

how to allow for sleep and other forms of inattention) the relation C of *strong coconsciousness*; and let us symbolize its holding as (Q_{t_k}) $C(P_{t_j})$. Then anyone bent on grasping the nerve of Locke's conception of person would see, as some but not all of Locke's critics have seen,[9] that the identity-condition he had to refute was one that made the persistence of a person P depend only upon P's being related at each successive phase of his biography in this C-relation to P at each previous phrase. C itself is a non-transitive relation; but *C, the ancestral of the C-relation, which is the weaker and transitive relation of *x*'s being either C-related to *y* or C-related to some *z* which is C-related to *y* or . . .—I shall call it coconsciousness simply—provides us with all we need for the statement of a general neo-Lockean identity-condition:

I_p: P is the same person as Q if and only if (Q)*$C(P)$.

The shortcomings of this will become evident, and they are rehearsed in section 4; but they are not the defects of circularity, logical impropriety or outright absurdity; nor are they obvious symptoms of a defect inherent in all further elaborations of I_p in which *C might be employed. What they will really signify is the unexpected *richness* and *concreteness* of the requirements on a satisfactory realization of Locke's original idea of personal identity. It will appear that these requirements are radically inconsistent with the immaterialist conception of persons that Locke himself described. But it is not that aspect of his theory that this chapter is to discuss. The defects relate to (i) the formal inadequacy of (x)*$C(y)$ to define an equivalence relation like identity, and (ii) the need to fortify *C in order to secure what is actually intended by the continuity of consciousness requirements.

4. *The inadequacy of I_p, as of any pure or physicalistically uncontaminated 'remembering' condition of mental continuity. The involvement of remembering with the physical*

Defining *C as we have, but bracketing the expectations created by the proposal I_p, do we have positive reason to think that *C is

9. Even though it is a possible elucidation of 'extend' in Locke's words at *Essay*, II, xxvii, 2 (p. 449 Frazer). Locke did not have the logical apparatus for a ready distinction between C and *C. This is no reason for holding him to C, even though it is clear from the sequel (Frazer, p. 450) that Locke himself was miles away from formulating the distinction.

symmetrical and reflexive and transitive? Unless *C has all these properties, its obtaining between some x and some y is certainly insufficient for their identity, and may be insufficient even for what was originally intended by continuity of consciousness.[10]

Suppose $(\exists y)\,((x)\text{*C}(y))$. Then does it follow that $(x)\text{*C}(x)$, i.e. that x sufficiently remembers doing a sufficiency of what x has done? Even if we scale this down a little to require only that x has the *potentiality* to recall sufficiently at each stage a sufficiency of what x has done just before, there is already a problem. If a person is knocked down in a road accident and never recovers consciousness or memory at all, can he not remain biologically alive in hospital for years afterwards? Is he not an unconscious, or memoriless person? Some will find Locke's disqualification of this person strained or absurd, or will complain that it smacks of legislation, which it does. But it is not necessarily pointless legislation. It is not with reflexivity that the obvious or immediate difficulty lies (though we shall see in the end that there is a difficulty). Symmetry and transitivity are the immediate challenge.

Nothing in our definition of *C seems to have ruled out the following possibility: A stream of consciousness divides at some point and flows into a delta of two consciousnesses that are separate therafter. Here we have, say,

$$(Q_{t3})\ \text{*C}(P_{t1})$$

and also

$$(R_{t3})\ \text{*C}(P_{t1}).$$

Perhaps the best way to give oneself the impression that one can conceive of this is to begin by conceiving of a Lamarckian state of affairs in which children inherit some substantial experiential memories corresponding closely to the life of the mother up to the

10. The reader may have believed it to be an objection to I_p that *C is already an asymmetrical relation. Here we must guard against a misconception of what was meant by P_{t_j} and Q_{t_k}. What such descriptions stand for are not time-slices of people or 'person-moments'. They are people, persisting three-dimensional things which are born, live for some time, and then in one manner or another die. Similarly *C is only defined for *people* as terms. In a more detailed treatment C and *C would be explicitly tensed.

If P_{t_j} and Q_{t_k} are the same person then, regardless of the fact that these descriptions may pick out the person by reference to predicates which hold of the person at the different times t_k and t_j, their references are one and the same. Everything true of one is true of the other and, with certain merely grammatical adjustments, the designations are everywhere intersubstitutable *salva varitate*.

moment of giving birth.[11] Having fully conceived of that, one may go on to the harder exercise and imagine the twinning of an adult, then try to conceive this in fuller and fuller detail. We shall raise some doubts in section 7; but if the division of a stream of consciousness is fully conceivable, then *C cannot be both transitive *and* symmetrical. If the stream of consciousness of someone who (say) planted the fig tree beside a certain wall divided, and if there were later two people who claimed to remember planting the tree (and did indeed remember planting it—all the factual and circumstantial and causal require- ments of memory being somehow satisfied in the fantasy), then the criterion I_p would force us to identify the two claimants with one another. But one may shout and the other may sulk when the dispute breaks out. They cannot be the same person.[12]

Where does this leave us? If we were interested in continuity of consciousness for its own sake, without wanting to characterize the identity and difference of persons by its means, we might rely on the fact that remembering is something done by people (constituted as they are with the physical limitations they have) in order to under- write it as an equivalence relation. But it is the other way about. Our only reason here for insisting that *C must be an equivalence relation is precisely our desire to use it to characterize personal identity. In the absence of any commitment to that project, we might be content for *C to be (say) reflexive, transitive and non-symmetrical.

There is a clarification that the argument may require at this point. The foregoing objection to I_p depends on conceiving or conceiving of conceiving a delta in the stream of consciousness. It may be, however,

11. Cf. Hidé Ishiguro, 'The Person's Future and the Mind Body Problem' in *Phenomenology and Linguistic Analysis,* Wolfe Mays and Stuart Brown, eds, London, 1977.

12. Cf. Flew *op. cit.,* p. 67 and B. A. O. Williams, 'Personal Identity and Individua- tion' *P A S* 1956–57. Nor would it be right to insist on redescribing the situation as one where a single dissociated or scattered person did X and also, with another part of him, did not X. Such insistence might be based on an analogy with the way in which, without prejudice to his unity, a normal person can fidget with his left foot and not fidget with his right. There may be ideas of what a person is which allow this sort of redescription. But it is in the spirit of the Lockean notion, and of our own ordinary notion of person—the notion of a three-dimensional thing whose only genuine parts are *spatial* parts—to disallow it. When P_{t1} splits into Q_{t3} and R_{t3}, it splits into two *whole* persons, and Q_{t3} does not share R_{t3}'s consciousness of doing X. Even if Q_{t3} and R_{t3} both do X, their consciousnesses of doing X may be as distinct as if they were two people with no common origins at all. And they will communicate *inter-personally*. One need not refuse to make sense of the supposition that identical twins sometimes experience a strange community of consciousness in doing things. But both logically and actually they *can* do the same thing without feeling this community. And similarly with the race of creatures who figure in this fantasy. Such fantasies are not, however, destined to survive easily the scrutiny of possibility that is begun in section 7.

that, for persons properly understood, such a division is not in fact conceivable. But that will not necessarily invalidate the objection. For we may find that, if such a division is in fact impossible, then this impossibility really derives from the conceptual requirements on the individuation of persons: in which case the impossibility should be deducible from the right-hand side of I_p or the *C requirement. But it is not so deducible. Therefore I_p is at very best an inadequate elucidation of the identity of persons. Either then I_p is actually wrong, or else I_p is inadequate.

It was said that there were two difficulties in the *C condition as stated. The first, just completed, related to the formal inadequacy of *C. The second, to which I now come, is the need to fortify *C to play the role it was always intended to play. As it stands it comes nowhere near to pinning down that mental continuity which has always concerned the Lockean and constructionalist traditions. This is because it offers no plausible account of *error*.

Suppose that at t_3 I think that I vividly remember locking the back door, though the fact is that some well-disposed neighbour slipped the latch (at t_2) after I had gone off without locking up. Then, unless we are already possessed of a criterion of identity or something else to refute the memory claim itself, we seem to have:

(Wiggins who at t_3 imagines he remembers locking the door) *C (person who slipped the latch at t_2).

This is bad enough, but suppose that later at t_4 I begin to doubt that I locked the door, remembering that at t_3 I had supposed I vividly remembered doing so. Then it may be held

(Wiggins who doubts at t_4 that he locked the door) *C (Wiggins who thought at t_3 he remembered locking the door).

But then, whether I like it or not, *C must by the intended transitivity and symmetry hold (even as I doubt) between me and the man or woman who locked the back door. But here I don't have even what Locke intended by continuity of consciousness with the person who locked it. And insisting on the 'sufficiency of things' hedge that we introduced at the beginning of section 3 into the definition of C and *C, or stiffening the subjective requirements on remembering locking the door (the amplitude, stability, richness, etc., of the inner representation), will scarcely alter the position. The troublesome example itself could always be correspondingly enriched.

This is a fundamental objection. If we try to answer it by simply writing 'remembers' instead of 'really or apparently remembers' into the definition of C and *C, then we encounter the difficulty that identity may be already involved in deciding, in some cases, whether someone really remembers planting the fig tree.[13] The objection does not show that it is impossible to adjust the execution of the Lockean project while conferring some sort of a special role upon memory *among* other faculties. What it shows is that it will not do to define *C *in vacuo*—as if everything else could be determined thereafter—or without provision to relate a person and his actions in such a way as to say what it is for a person to own actions (Locke's phrase, *Essay*, Frazer, p. 479). And the proper response to the charge of circularity is surely now to describe what really remembering is and do this in the course of an exploration embracing not one but all of the typical Lockean cases of remembering *witnessing*, remembering *perceiving*, remembering *feeling*, remembering *thinking*, remembering *remembering*, remembering *suffering*, remembering *doing*. . . . The objection affords no proof that this will not suffice to make *C the stuff of a correct usable Lockean criterion of identity, with the range of decidable cases which we actually ascribe to the relation *is the same person as*. What is to be conceded at this point is rather that memory can only have a distinctive part to play (if there *is* a distinctive role for it) in concert with the whole range of faculties that are distinctive of persons; and that the elucidation of remembering is part of an ampler and more discursive investigation, an inquiry more concerned with descriptive verisimilitude, and less involved with invention or

13. This is to suggest that, however crucial a role the functions of remembering or intending may play in regulating the individuation of persons, considerations of identity must regulate the correct application of the predicate *remembers* X-ing.

To the critic who sees in this relationship of reciprocal regulation the chance of reviving Butler's objection to Locke, I offer the following *a priori* refutation of the generally received account of how clockwork functions in a timepiece. It is said that the mainspring unwinds, and in unwinding affects the hairspring. But it is also said that the hairspring affects the speed and manner of unwinding of the mainspring. How can that possibly be? If the normal operation of the mainspring presupposes the normal operation of the hairspring, how can the normal operation of the hairspring presuppose the normal operation of the mainspring? Well, it can and it does. Presupposition like mechanical regulation can be reciprocal. (Cf. below section 5.)

Some will hold that, whether the objection is answerable or not, here at last we have stated Butler's real objection. But it could only be Butler's objection if Butler meant by 'being conscious of personal identity' actually remembering doing something. The real authors of this objection, which I shall shortly revive in the form of an accusation not of circularity or absurdity but of non-effectiveness, seem to be B. A. O. Williams ('Personal Identity and Individuation', *op. cit.*) and A. J. Ayer (*The Problem of Knowledge*, Penguin, 1956, p. 196).

thought experiment, than most constructionalists have been ready to undertake—as well as being more deeply involved than they have envisaged in causality and in the physical constitution of organisms that experientially remember.[14] To define *C properly and fashion a better elucidation of personal identity than I_p is to start upon no smaller task than the description of a persisting material entity essentially endowed with the biological potentiality for the exercise of *all* the faculties and capacities conceptually constitutive of person-hood—sentience, desire, belief, motion, memory and the various other elements which are involved in the particular mode of activity that marks the extension of the concept of person. *Activity* is intended here in the sense of Chapter Three and of D(iv) of Chapter Two.

5. *The charge of circularity rephrased and reconsidered as a charge of non-effectiveness*

That Locke and so many others have concentrated on memory (and memory solely under its cognitive aspect) to the virtual exclusion of almost all the heterogeneous other things that are characteristic of persons and register in the stream of consciousness—the sensory and kinaesthetic aspects of experience, the play of the practical imagina-tion over possible outcomes, the constant surveillance of the fit of means to ends and ends to means, and all the other forward and sideways looking elements (not to mention the affective aspect of the backward looking component)—this, it may be said, is a lamentable, even pathological, symptom of much that is wrong with philosophy. Yes, perhaps. But nevertheless the charge of blindness or incompe-tence must not be allowed to obscure the Lockean claim that x is a person only if x has and exercises some sufficient capacity to remember or record sufficiently well from one time to the next enough of his immediately previous states or actions. That might prove to be true. But, because even this weaker statement gives a part of the purported essence of persons, it will still seem to impinge upon the question of their individuation. And some who wish to persist with Butler's objection will say that, in that case, one circularity should have been manifest from the outset. What about the *his* in 'enough of *his* immediately previous states and actions'? To this I reply that if there were really something illegitimate about the way in which the *his* turns up here in the Lockean condition, then there would have to

14. See *Longer Note* 6.14.

be something equally illegitimate about the way in which the pronoun *it* occurs in the following definition of a black box recorder: *a machine designed to record certain aerobatical data useful in case of accident befalling the aircraft that carries it.* I shall not try to add to Geach's criticisms of philosophers who have been unable to understand the occurrence of pronouns in a grammatical role analogous to that of variables.[15]

This confused objection does, however, lead into a better line of objection. This new objection claims that, contrary to what I have implied, no conceivable memory-involving improvement of I_p can operate *effectively*: 'Suppose P claims to remember planting the fig tree. We cannot settle the truth of his claim that he remembers planting the fig tree until we can establish by some criterion or principle independent of memory whether P is *identical* with the person (if any) who planted it. But then memory is doomed always to bring too little too late to determine any identity-question. For we must already have settled the identity-question by other means of determination before memory is allowed on to the scene at all. If the memory condition is an extra condition applied after it is already fixed by some criterion K *what* we are to trace through space and time, then either it contradicts K, or at best it restricts (determines some subkind of) the kind associated with K. Suppose K goes with *animal,* for instance. Then the memory-restriction may define *self-conscious animal.* But this', the objector will say, 'is going to create a very nasty situation for you. It is going to be possible for the victim of the car crash who loses his memory to be the same animal as the patient who walks out of hospital to start a new life but not the same person—even though both are persons.'[16]

So runs the objection: and every difficulty it deduces from the

15. See, e.g., *Analysis* 21, 3, 1961.

16. In rejecting this possibility, as the congruence of '=' obliges me to reject it, I distance myself yet further from Locke's own development of his theme. Locke tries to overcome the standard difficulties of C (amnesia, sleep, etc.) by distinguishing questions of identity of *man* from questions of identity of *person.* This is a thoroughly unsatisfactory part of his discussion. However well one makes the distinction between the concepts *man* and *person,* this can hardly show that nothing falls under both concepts (under which is John Locke?), or that identity can be so relativized as to make the two identity questions independent of one another. Instead I seek to show that, on an understanding that is both psychologically and biologically replete of what it is for a man to have a life, the concepts *man* and *person* are sortally concordant and determine for anything falling in the extension of both a unitary principle of persistence—a principle that Locke himself states admirably in the words: '. . . the identity of the same *man* consists in nothing but a participation of the same continued life, by constantly fleeting particles of matter, in succession vitally united to the same organized body'.

mistaken idea that memory must be an extra condition applied *after* another principle C has fixed an individuative kind is correctly deduced. (What is more we shall revive something from the objection in due course, though not in the form of a charge of non-effectiveness.) But, against the objection as it stands, and against the charge of non-effectiveness I have to ask what is this other and precedent principle or criterion K? It will be replied: bodily continuity. But on one reading of 'body' (interpreting it as standing for the abstract determinable *material substance*) the suggestion is in no way at variance with the proposal that is being explored. And on the other reading ('body of a human being') the respondent will have to explain how he is to avoid a conceptual obligation to count among present persons Jeremy Bentham, and even the Pharaohs, presumably more competently preserved. Bodily continuity (in the second sense of 'body') is not enough without life.[17] And surely sufficient exercise of the capacity for recall is conceptually connected with a particular mode of activity, and a whole cluster of vital functions and faculties of which Locke is entitled to argue that memory is one important member. His definition does not oblige us to say that memory determines identity questions autonomously; only that it contributes and, in conjunction with other considerations, is *crucially relevant* to our choice of continuity principle for determining the biographies of persons. What the objection really had to confront was a thesis about memory as part and parcel with other vital functions and faculties characteristic of persons. But against that thesis it simply begs the question.

The objection says: 'We surely cannot conclusively determine whether P is remembering planting the fig tree until we have independently established whether P is indeed one and the same person who planted the fig tree.' It sounds for a moment as if there is something in that. But why not the other way round? Put the other way round, the objection says: 'We surely cannot conclusively establish the identity or non-identity of P with the person who planted the fig tree until we have established whether, in cases like this, thinking he planted the tree, counts as remembering or not.' According to the neo-Lockean

17. It may be said that we can and do distinguish between the corpse of a man freshly dead—he is still here but dead—and his earthly remains. When ashes (say) are all that is left, then he is no longer there, it may be suggested. But the whole distinction which is relied upon by the objector is parasitic upon the point of distinguishing between life and death. Mere material continuity is not sufficient. And if life or its absence gives the *point* of these distinctions, then the *principal* distinction is between being live and being dead, and the best overall view will make existence or non-existence depend upon the principal distinction.

philosopher, there are cases in which this might be an almost equally good thing to say, or the only thing we *could* say. (Shoemaker's brain-transfer case is a dramatic example, but needlessly perilous. Suppose instead that a person Q loses large quantities of brain tissue in some hideous accident. Suppose that major surgery is undertaken; and that, taking advantage of the plasticity of brain function, a therapist then schools the person who emerges in all the facts of the life of Q before the accident.) If the back-to-front version has less weight than the first version—and no doubt it has—then we must remember that what is happening here is that we are ranging a whole battery of components of the continuity-cum-activity principle for persons against what is, on the neo-Lockean view, *only one component* of that principle. It would be premature to decide this issue. (See the five concluding sections of the chapter.) But the enemies of the Lockean conception have still achieved almost nothing.

6. *Two senses in which a person may be supposed to transcend his body, one correct, the other impossible*

We have neither reformulated precisely nor vindicated as sound and correct the neo-Lockean condition of continuity of consciousness. But no argument we have examined, nor yet any obvious extension of one, shows that every conceivable Lockean condition is either circular, or utterly absurd in the verdicts it delivers on cases, or void for non-effectiveness. Nor is the revised conception of the memory condition that we have arrived at redundant in the presence of some distinct physicalistic criterion. Whether plausibly or implausibly, the memory condition informs and regulates the continuity condition of personal identity, holds it apart from mere continuity of body, and leaves its distinctive mark on judgements founded in it.[18]

The answer to Butler also provides a way to draw together certain other data or phenomena. I have in mind the discomfort that almost everyone feels about any straightforward equation between himself and his body; the idea to which many of us are prey that the lifeless corpse is not the person; and the fact that there is something

18. Cf. *Identity and Spatio-Temporal Continuity*, p. 45, para. 2, and Part Four more generally, which goes on to claim, against one purely physiological view of the question, that the seat of memory and consciousness is not just one part of the body among others. So much seems right, but I no longer draw quite the same conclusion. See section 12 below.

absurd—so unnatural that the upshot is simply falsity—in the proposition that people's bodies play chess, talk sense, know arithmetic, or even run or jump or sit down. We bring these findings to the subject before speculation begins. The advantage of a neo-Lockean theory is that we do not need to force the facts to account for them.

A person is material in the sense of being essentially constituted by matter; but in some strict and different sense of 'material', viz. being definable or properly describable in terms of the concepts of the sciences of matter (physics, chemistry, and biology even) *person* is not a material concept.[19] The neo-Lockean activity-grounded principle of individuation for persons shows how it is possible for *person* to fail of materiality in that sense, and it shows that in a manner compatible with the strictest physicalism. For the continuity principle defines a material entity in the 'matter-constituted' sense of 'material', while leaving it possible for the concept *person* to be both primitive relative to the concepts that pull their weight in the sciences of matter and primitive relative to the concept *human body*. If we understand what a living person or an animal is, then we may define the body of one as that which realizes or constitutes it while it is alive and will be left over when, succumbing to entropy, it dies. (The insecurity of the argument from analogy, caught between gratuitousness and futility, like the instability of the scepticism it was meant to answer, must surely testify to the difficulties of reversing this order of elucidation.)

So much for an unexciting and satisfying way (reminiscent in some ways of the constitutive 'is' introduced in Chapter One) in which persons transcend bodies. But the still undiscredited possibility of Lamarckian memory, and the extension of this idea to delta formations in the stream of consciousness (neither of which possibilities appears to be excluded by a good account of memory *taken by itself*), will inevitably suggest another way. In exploring how this other way must subvert individuation, we shall resume an obligation that section 4 discharged incompletely. But by the end of this exploration we shall be even more strongly motivated to reappraise the claim of conceptual possibility. Anyone already half inclined to embrace some version of the naturalistic view of the concept of person mooted at the end of section 4, but fully aware of its vulnerability to certain kinds of thought-experiment, should now skip straight to the beginning of section 7.

19. Concerning definability in terms of chemistry and physics, see J. H. Woodger, *Biology and Language*, pp. 336–8, quoted at the head of Chapter Six. See also the analogous anti-reductive argument of *Longer Note* 1.11.

If lines of consciousness could divide—if the however exigent requirements for this to have happened seemed to be satisfied—then, it may be said, we should need at least a dual use of 'person'. There would have to be (1) a new use to denote a group-person or 'clone', whose members' consciousnesses all derived from a point in some common biography;[20] and (2) the residue of our present use, to denote individual mental continuants that act separately and communicate interpersonally. Call (2) the 'splinter' use. It seems that splinter persons will come into being either by birth or as the outcome of a fission, and will cease to exist if and when they either die or split. Consider then the following 'tree' of divisions in a consciousness originating from a person S:[21]

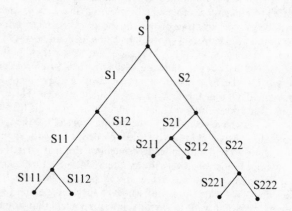

Note that in this diagram the S designations denote not nodes but arcs. The proposal is that, if the divisions represented by such a tree come to pass, then the *arcs* S1, S2, S11, S12 . . . are all different splinter persons. In addition, there is the clone or subclone person constituted of S111 and S112, the

20. Cf. *Identity, op. cit.* (Appendix) 5.7 and 5.6 and (Part Two) 4.3, p. 54. For clone-individuals, cf. 'Fruit trees are of two kinds: those which will set fruit with their own pollen, and those which will bear very little or no fruit at all unless cross-pollinated. Now all our cultivated fruits are propagated vegetatively by budding or grafting, or by layers, or cuttings; and therefore all the trees of a named variety form what is called a *clone*: that is they are parts of one single individual', p. 103, *Fruit Tree Growing,* vol. II (*Pears Quinces and Stone Fruits*) by Raymond Bush, Harmondsworth, Middlesex, Penguin, 1943.

21. For simplicity and because they raise special difficulties that contribute little to a general understanding of the subject, I exclude from consideration here the *fusion* of lines of consciousness.

distinct but related (sub)clone person constituted of that *plus* S11, the distinct but related (sub)clone person constituted of that *plus* S12 . . . and so on, enumerating at every point of division all arcs that lie beneath it until we get the whole archetype, the clone-person proper, comprehending S and everything that derives from S. On this use Smith is flesh and bone, but he has as members both individual (i.e. arc) members, and subclone members. He is a concrete universal, so to speak. Each arc or splinter-person bears here the same relation to the archetype clone as all individual Cox's Orange Pippin trees (which have the ancestral of the relation 'produced from a cutting of' to some original hybrid) bear to the clone or concrete universal that they perpetuate and jointly constitute, viz. Cox's Orange Pippin.

One quickly comes to think there is yet a third use of 'person' we should need in order to make sense of a mental entity's having personal memory of experiences before the splitting of the consciousness. Conception (3) of a person picks out all the distinct continuous paths that can be traced back to the original arc S, i.e. S→S111, S→S112. . . . Let us say these paths define life-histories. The reason why they are needed is this. Suppose a person Q remembers being the first to sail round the world single-handed, Q did navigate so, and Q was the first to do so single-handed. He was there throughout. But a branching may have intervened since this feat was executed. S1, say, may have been the splinter agent involved, but the splinter S1 is no longer. How then does Q survive? He is perpetuated by the splinters S11 and S12 perhaps. They authentically remember the feat, but the actual navigator cannot be identified with the splinters S11 or S12. Neither of these splinters is a splinter that was there at the sailing. Nor can the clone conception help. We want to say of whoever survives the splitting of S1 something we need not want to say of splinter members that branched off before the sailing. Nor again can any subclone, e.g. (S111 + S112 + S11 + S12), help us. For we may wish to say that the persons whom S11 and S12 represent or perpetuate, i.e. the life histories S→S111, S→S112, S→S12, think and feel in importantly different ways about the feat. In these different lives the feat may represent different things. Only the life-history gives us a way to say this.

Before we enter into any of the further difficulties or absurdities this project involves, it may be well to note how widespread in different cultures is the idea that persons may transcend not only particular bodies but even individual lives. Clifford Geertz has described the lengths to which the Balinese push the hypostatization of social roles, and the strange fusion of role and human being that is involved in their system of naming.[22] Perhaps the

22. The conception of person by which our own everyday life sets such store registers only in rarely used nonsense names. The names that matter are birth order names, kinship terms, teknonyms and status titles. Clifford Geertz, *Person, Time and Conduct in Bali* S.E. Asia Studies, 14 (New Haven, Yale, 1966).

Anyone who tries seriously to make something of the concrete universal conception should wonder whether to take his departure from an idea that Plato mentions in this connexion, but does not pursue: 'one and the same day is in many places at the same time and nevertheless is not separate from itself' (*Parmenides* 131[b3]).

concrete universal conception of person is an extant conception then. Maybe we could even discover it was our own conception if we let go of one nearly incredible feature of Geertz's account and allowed the individual conception to coexist with the generic or role defined conception of personhood. Within our own culture or a neighbouring compartment, J.-P. Sartre has written in his book about Flaubert:

> Un homme n'est jamais un individu; il vaudrait mieux l'appeler un universel singulier; totalisé et, par la même, universalisé par son époque, il la retotalise en se reproduisant en elle comme singularité.[23]

But there are serious doubts. If we want from the concrete universal conception only what the Balinese seem to have from some conception of that sort (if this is really what they have), then perhaps the clone or the life-history will serve to reconstruct it. For if this is all we want, then there is no question of building up a coherent historical record of the individual passions, thoughts and actions of an individual person. There is little or no provision for the individual or, as it were, perspectival aspect of human experience. The whole ordering of the events of human history is interpreted so far as possible in terms of the recurrence of generic types of doing or suffering.[24] And where there scarcely is such a thing as history, the idea of biography loses all purchase. It would be implausible to claim that the resultant conception of a person is utterly foreign to us. But if we take seriously as a thought experiment a world with persons liable to fission, and if we are anxious to hold fast to the *very thing* that made Locke's conception of a person interesting to us in the first place, then what we cannot abandon without forgetting completely the point of the exercise is our interest in constructing internally consistent, mutually consistent, indefinitely amplifiable, individual biographies. I suppose it might even be claimed that we could jettison the ideas of childhood, maturity and death if people were perpetuated after the manner of plants in a hedgerow. (Reduplication by fission would be scarcely very different.) But an interest in the Lockean conception commits us to try to preserve the possibility of an account of the formation of *individual* character—the path that a man picks through good and bad fortune to be what he in particular is. If so, the important question is: Can the three uses of 'person' be deployed somehow, singly or in concert, to salvage this individual conception—even in the description of a world of fissiparous persons? I shall try to demonstrate that they cannot.

Consider again the claim to have been the first person to sail single-handed round the world. Can the claim be reinterpreted to accommodate the fact there are that three equally good claimants, S→S12, S→S111 and S→S112, with differing attitudes to that feat? I see only one way. As made by any one of

23. *L'idiot de la famille: Gustave Flaubert de 1821 à 1857*, Paris, Gallimard, 1971.
24. Note in this connexion the account Geertz is moved to give of the Balinese tradition and practice of drama.

them, the boast must be read as the claim that there was once an as yet undivided life history that performed the feat, a life history having the fortified *C relation to all three of the life histories just mentioned, one of them being the claimant. The as yet undivided entity must comprise life-histories that *will* be separated as distinct life-histories but are at the time of the feat unseparated. And then the question is: What sort of a thing is a person if a life-history is a person? For there will prove to have been one period, before the separation, during which two or three of them were in the same place at the same time. (An idea much harder to accept than that of one place's being occupied by two things of *different* category or kind.) Unless our preconceptions about material objects are sadly astray, it follows that people are not only not human bodies, but not even material objects. Well, there are those who thought this all along. But how is Q, or any of the three life-histories that now represent him, and on the importance of whose remembering such things as the sailing single-handed around the world the Lockean motivation lays such stress, to conceive (how is he to make a notion for himself) of the person that he is?

There is only one answer I can think of: as a Leśniewskian sum or aggregate of person-moments or person-stages. The point about such Leś-niewskian aggregates is that distinct aggregates may have common consti-tuents, and that such aggregates will coincide as one person if, and only if, they have *all* their constituent person-moments in common. What is more, two, three or several Leśniewskian sums—this is their peculiarity—*can* be in the same place at the same time.[25] In this respect they are unlike material objects as we normally conceive of them. The trouble is that they are also much too unlike people. How is a person who is going to divide to conceive of himself as *two or three* people? Nor is this the only or the worst problem. Anything that is a part of a Leśniewskian sum is necessarily part of it. (Cp. Ch. Four, note 18.) But no person or normal material object is *necessarily* in the total state that will correspond to the person- or object-moment postu-lated by the theory under discussion. Finally look at the contrast between the predicates of ordinary material objects and the predicates of a Leśniewskian sum. An aggregate of this kind has its relevant properties derivatively from the properties of its constituent *moments*. But at least half of the things we want to say about persons cannot be even tortuously explained in terms of the states at an instant of person-moments. Consider for example *weak, clever, cowardly, a bad slip fielder, resolute, opportunistic, erratic, honest, a fair*

<hr/>

25. See David Lewis, 'Survival and Identity' in Amelie Rorty, ed., *The Identities of Persons*, University of California Press, 1976, who shows (in effect) how what I call within my framework the *C relation and the identity relation could be brought into line with one another by seeing persons as maximal *C interrelated aggregates of person stages. For criticism and discussion of Lewis's proposal see Derek Parfit, 'Lewis, Perry and What Matters', *ibid.*, and a review of this collection by Christopher Peacocke, forthcoming in *Philosophical Review* 1979. I am considerably indebted in the rewriting here of my previous criticism of the mereological conception of persons both to Lewis and to the review by Peacocke.

weather friend or the Emperor Galba's predicate *capax imperii nisi imperas-set*. It is true that (however unnaturally) we can see each of these as superven-ing on all the other properties of those Leśniewskian sums which are persons—*provided only* that we can first say which sums these are. And David Lewis claims that we can do this:

> if the [identity relation] is the [*C relation] we have . . . a non-circular definition of personhood . . . something is a continuant person iff it is a maximal [*C-interrelated] aggregate of person stages, that is . . . if it is an aggregate of person stages each of which is [*C-related] to all the rest (and to itself), and it is a proper part of no other such aggregate.

But this is not unproblematic. It seems to presuppose that we can say what a person-stage is before we come to say what a person continuant (i.e. person) is; and that *C can be explained independently of bringing into existence the elucidation of the persistence condition for persons. We have already come in an earlier chapter to doubt that such a project is as manageable as it may at first appear. By the time *C and 'person-stage' are fully intelligible we are already committed to a principle of individuation for proper continuant persons.

7. *Real possibility: the limits of personhood*

Such is the perplexity into which obsession with the Lockean condi-tion apparently forces us if we accept fission of persons as a concep-tual possibility. The possibilities or possible possibilities that the recent literature of the subject has been obliged to rehearse are not on the face of it marginal indeterminacies which, however capriciously we find we have to decide them, leave undiminished our confidence in our comprehension of what *is at issue* here. The conceptual possi-bility of a delta in the stream of consciousness jogs our whole focus on the concept of personhood. But, rather than jump to the conclusion that we have no idea at all of what we are about (in a case where maybe we should have a particularly good idea), let us go back to the beginning and ask: Is such a delta really a conceptual possibility?

Following Putnam and Leibniz, it was claimed in Chapter Three that any would-be determination of a natural kind stands or falls with the existence of lawlike principles that will collect together the actual extension of the kind around an arbitrary good specimen of it; and that these lawlike principles will also determine the characteristic development and typical history of members of this extension (or at least the limits of any possible development or history of such individuals).[26] To make the link with the problem we now face, let the reader first conceive for the space of a paragraph that the concept *person* is similar in the relevant ways to a natural kind concept. If that is supposed, then the first thing we can expect is that the sense of the sortal predicate 'person' will exempt us from counting as genuinely conceivable any narrative in which persons undergo changes that violate the lawlike regularities constituting the actual nomological foundation for the delimitation of the kind we denominate as that of persons. But then the thought we shall be tempted to pursue is that, if the *C relation is in any serious way involved in the identities of persons, and IF *person* is akin to a natural kind concept sufficing for the articulation and individuation of genuine continuant substances, then the spontaneous occurrence of delta formations in the stream of consciousness under the conditions presupposed to the individuation of persons will be nomologically excluded. If so then there must exist some condition for the existence of persons which excludes from *conceptual* possibility the division of any consciousness whatever that we can recognize as the consciousness of a person.[27]

Before we attend to the antecedent, the clause 'IF *person* is akin to a natural kind concept', or hasten to the conclusion that it will be easy to accommodate Leibnizian identity and the naturalist conception of personal identity to one another, it is important to point out that the nomological doctrine of kinds defended in Chapter Three, section 1 was aimed only at kinds that are unlike artifact and other kinds in having a scientifically palpable nature. Directly at least, it implied nothing about *person*. We have then to ask afresh: *Is* there some scientifically palpable real essence, some nature that is presupposed to a kind's being nomologically founded, which not only underlies in fact but also must underlie the kind *person* (must if members of it are to be subjects whom we can interpret, and react to in the way in which we react to what we recognize as people)? For unless some such case can be made, it is certain that it is futile to look in this quarter for a route by which the neo-Lockean or naturalist conceptions can escape from the problems of fission.

In the spirit of a bold attempt at a quick affirmative answer to the question how closely *person* resembles a natural kind concept, it

26. For the relation of lawlike principles to laws in the full or basic sense, see Chapter Five, section 2, objection (c). For the relation between the actual exclusion of fission, owed to the joint operation of such lawlike principles and f-accommodating conditions (in a sense there explained), and the conceptual exclusion of the fission of entities of a kind f whose existence and continuant status requires such laws and conditions, see Chapter Three, section 1 *ad fin.* and *Longer Note* 3.09.

27. See *Longer Note* 6.27.

might be said that it is no accident that we feel such certainty as we do feel that 'man' (*homo sapiens*), 'human being' and 'person' are co-extensive. It may be declared that, even granted the importance of the distinction between the sense and the extension of a predicate, there is still an overwhelmingly important *indirect* connexion between the interests with which these three different predicates are actually applied. It may also be said that it is a symptom of the strength of the lien between 'person' and 'homo sapiens', and a typical mark of the presence of something with most of the determinacy and specificity of a real essence, that it flies in the face of the innermost convictions of almost everyone to try to think of the persons we encounter in nature as having identities that are any less determinate than the identities of animals, or as posing identity problems that are for decision or reinterpretation in the way in which artifact-identities are for decision or reinterpretation when there is too much changing or exchanging of parts.

This is almost right, but there is one possibility that is passed over by this excessively quick way with the matter. What is more, the question has been begged against more than one kind of opponent. We shall come more easily at the truth, I believe, if we dismiss the bold answer and supplant it with a much more modest suggestion. I shall call it the animal attribute view. This sees *person* as a concept whose defining marks are to be given in terms of a natural kind determinable, say *animal,* plus what may be called a functional or (as I shall prefer to say) systemic component. Perhaps *x* is a person if and only if *x* is an animal falling under the extension of a kind whose typical members perceive, feel, remember, imagine, desire, make projects, move themselves at will, speak, carry out projects, acquire a character as they age, are happy or miserable, are susceptible to concern for members of their own or like species . . . [note carefully these and subsequent dots], conceive of themselves as perceiving, feeling, remembering, imagining, desiring, making projects, speaking . . ., have, and conceive of themselves as having, a past accessible in experience-memory and a future accessible in intention . . ., etc. On this account *person* is a non-biological qualification of *animal,* and, potentially at least, a cross-classification with respect to zoological classification across the grain, so to speak, of the evolution-based taxonomy. By this proposal it is not absolutely excluded (however lightly we take the suggestion in practice) that the extension of *person* should give hospitality to such creatures as chimpanzees or dolphins or even, in exchange for suitably amazing behaviour (explicable in the end, we are to suppose we should suppose, in neurophysiological terms), to a parrot. According to this view, a person is any animal that is such by its kind as to have the biological capacity to enjoy fully the psychological attributes enumerated; and whether or not a given animal kind qualifies is left to be a strictly empirical matter.

It is not impossible to find parallels for the suggestion. Consider the generic sortal-predicate 'vegetable', which has the same mixed character, formally speaking. A vegetable is any plant kind whose root or fruit or leaf is (a) savoury (b) edible by human beings. The set of all vegetables has as its subsets some but not all species of the *Cruciferae* family, some but not all species of the *Leguminosae* family, some but not all of the *Solanaceae* family, and any other species belonging to other families furnishing plants meeting both the conditions (a) and (b). (Again a *gopher* is any of several genetically unrelated burrowing animals.)

Here, and in the case of other parallels where there is no great theoretical or emotional issue, we can see very clearly. The functional specification is plain in sense and intention. It is not controversial, for instance, that any particular vegetable must belong to *some* particular natural kind. Whatever its natural kind is, it will belong essentially to that (or to some kind not much higher than that, cf. Chapter Four, section 9). If the concept *person* were like *vegetable,* and were not merely possibly but actually superordinate to more than one animal species, then the answer to the problem of divisions in the stream of consciousness could still be exactly as predicted at the beginning of section 7. Every person would belong to some natural kind that determined a sound Leibnizian principle of identity through change for some one kind of person (human-person, dolphin-person, parrot-person or whatever). There would be no one real essence of person as such; but every person could still have the real essence of a certain kind of animal. Indirectly, this would be the real essence *in virtue of which* he was a person. The real essences of the various kinds of persons would be for empirical investigation on the levels of biology and neurophysiology and psychology—even of history, economics, literary art (not excluding descriptive philosophy), and psychoanalysis.

This is the possibility to which I meant to point by the suggestion that, even if the concept of person did not correspond to a single natural kind, it might still be *akin* to a natural kind concept. But it is important just how small a concession it is to most of those who will have rejected the bolder first proposal, and how far short it falls of the liberalizations that have been envisaged. When this is plain, the case will appear for purifying the animal attribute view of all functionalist traits, and the natural complexity of that which makes persons the subjects of consciousness as we know it, and the objects of reciprocity and interpretation, will be manifest.

8. *The limits of personhood continued: and a formal difference between the* vegetable *and* person *concepts*

The functional specification under which various natural kinds of plants are collected up as vegetables holds no secret. We simply eat the root or the leaf and see whether the plant meets the specification, or not see. The corresponding animal attribute specification for *person* is not similarly transparent. Compared with what there is to understand, we know nearly nothing about the organization of the mental faculties in virtue of our possession of which those who dwell on the difference between *man* and *person* suppose that we account ourselves persons. The definition of *person* is not something we conceive for ourselves in the way in which we have conceived for ourselves the nominal essences for *hoe* or *house* and more or less effortlessly collect the extension in virtue of that. Nor is the proposed list of animal attributes quite like the nominal component of the definition that says what kinds of plant count as vegetables. Although we can begin a list of important attributes of people, and see how some faculties are nested in others, we have no firm grasp at all of how to *fill in the dots* in the proposed specification of what a person is. For reasons having little or nothing to do with vagueness and everything to do with the persisting obscurity of the interest of the classification 'person', we have no idea how to close off the list. That is one cardinal point. Even more important, the nature of the faculties definitely elected to the enumeration of attribute is not transparent to us in the manner of the nominal essence of, say, *house*. ('A shelter against destruction by wind, rain, and heat'. Aristotle, *De Anima* 403^{b3}.) That men need not have been the only persons is so far only a theoretical possibility.

There are still other questions to be asked before we redeploy the animal attribute proposal. Is the attribute component conceived as simply recapitulating and exhausting *all* the biologically and historically determined typical characteristics of *homo sapiens* as we know him? In that case, the question that is supposed to be at issue has been spoiled and tossed away already, and there will be precious little room left for non-human persons. The idea must rather be that certain particular attributes and attribute-ranges of men as we know them are to be thought important and necessary for being a person and that certain others are not insisted upon. In practice, what happens next is usually one of two things. Either the theorist settles for the conclusion that a person is any subject of *sufficiently many* important mental attributes (but the principle of counting attributes is *irremediably* obscure);[28] or he comes down so hard on certain particular attributes that he then puts in jeopardy the personhood of countless human beings.[29] The suspicion cannot help but arise that, if indeed *person* collects up natural kinds under a functional or systemic specification, and we do not rush things by ignoring the dots that we have left there, then this specification has to be constantly referred back to the nature of the particular class of actual persons who are men. Leibniz might have put the point by saying that in the first place the determination of the systemic specification is provisional and proportional to our knowledge—which is as one would expect—and that in the second place, just as certain marks of birth, shape and appearance have to stand proxy for the real essence of man or the concept *man,* so being a man or being a human being is the only thing that we can make stand proxy for what it is to be a person. We may also put the suspicion as Putnam will, if he is party to it: a human being is our only stereotype for *person.*

To these claims I think that the animal attribute theorist who embraces their conservative implications will want to add that here at last we begin to see the proper grounds for what has sometimes appeared to be only fear or prejudice, but now starts to seem the plainest good sense. This is our defensible or indefensible conviction that, however we may conceive of higher animals such as dolphins or

---

28. Mutate the mutanda here, and apply the argument against **D**(ix) in Chapter Two, section 8.

29. Really desperate expedients are here resorted to, even by subtle and unsolemn writers like Daniel Dennett. See 'Conditions of Personhood' in Rorty, ed., *The Identities of Persons*:

> Rawls does not at all intend to argue that justice is the inevitable result of *human* interaction, he does argue in effect that it is the inevitable result of *personal* interaction. That is, the concept of a person is itself inescapably normative or idealized [which appears in Dennett's view to exclude 'factual', and to be some property of a predicate that compensates it for deficiency in cognitive meaning, rather than a property that supervenes on its cognitive meaning]; to the extent that justice does not reveal itself in the dealings and interactions of creatures, to that extent they are not persons (p. 190). . . . The grounds for saying that the person is culpable . . . are in themselves grounds for doubting that it is a person we are dealing with at all. And if it is asked what could *settle* our doubts, the answer is: nothing. When such problems arise we cannot even tell in our own case if we are persons (p. 194).

horses or apes, such artifacts as robots and automata have no title to any kind of civil right—or even to the consideration that we ought to accord to the lowlier sentient creatures. For artifacts like these are not identified and individuated under concepts that are extension-involving (in the sense of Preamble section 7 and Chapter Three), nomologically grounded, or vital activity-determining; whereas extreme difficulty proves to attach to the project of diminishing the degree of extension-involvingness, *animal*-dependence, and even *man*-dependence, of the concept of a person. (For the meaning and import of these categories see again Chapter Three. I am supposing that the animal attribute theorist insists on the dots.) No weaker claim than that entered by the animal attribute view could do justice to the depth and passion of most people's resistance to the idea that automata can approximate to life or sentience, and it is certain that we still believe that, to have genuine feeling or purposes or concerns, a thing must *at least* be an animal of some sort.[30] Yet there are philosophers who think this is a prejudice, and there are other philosophers who doubt that anything at all can be extracted on this point from our present individuative preconceptions and practices, when we have not even encountered or tried to arbitrate a single case of divergence between the extensions of *man* and *person*.[31]

We need then to widen the scope and the appeal of the argument. And we need to recapitulate why it matters to the personal identity problem or to anything else which view of persons is correct. It will be simplest, however, to combine the fulfilment of this obligation with the fulfilment of the obligation to tie up one worrisome loose end that still hangs from sections 4 and 5.

30. I think that it should be emphasized that in this section and throughout this chapter, I use the nature/artifact distinction to mark the distinction between concepts that are nomologically founded and extension-involving on the one hand and concepts that lack this feature on the other—a regrettable semi-technical use. *Neither here nor in Chapter Three is any claim being entered that no higher animal or organism can be synthesized*—only that such a creature would have to represent, not an automaton, but a living open system renewing itself on the molecular level at the expense of its environment (and not, for instance, in equilibrium therewith in the manner of what we should now call an automaton). But then the creature would possess, corresponding with the sortal notion under which it was conceptualized *and concordant with that,* a nomologically founded empirically discoverable principle of individuation. See Chapter Three, section 2 *ad fin.* We should have made something that had *taken on a life of its own* (as we say).

31. Cf. Quine review (*op. cit.*), *Journal of Philosophy* 1972, of Munitz *Identity and Individuation.* 'To seek what is "logically required" for sameness of person under unprecedented circumstances is to suggest that words have some force beyond what our present needs have invested them with.'

9. *Amnesia reconsidered, and man as an animal*

The reader will have noticed that we never concluded the problem of the man who suffers total amnesia as a result of some appalling physical or mental shock and then begins life anew after a discontinuity that no effective *C condition could tolerate or let pass. The case is not impossible, still less counternomic, and there is no interference that detracts in any way from the victim's status as a natural thing existing in compliance with its kind concept.

There are at most four ways of appraising such a case.

(1) We may hold that it voids any application of the concept of person. But in practice, when people do lose their memory, we never adopt this view.

(2) We may attempt to do honour to *C by deciding that the man who begins life anew after total amnesia is the same organism or animal as, but a different person from, the man who lost his memory. This is a tempting but incoherent decision. (See the discussion of **R** in Chapter One.) If y is the same animal as x, and y is a person, then y is the person that x was. But then y is the same person as x.

(3) We may decide to say that, because y has no hope of playing x's role, y is a different person from x, and so (by Leibnizian logic) a different animal.[32] But here I shall venture my own opinion that, if anything stands in the way of the view, it is the violence this concession to the forensic and *C conceptions of person does to what in real life we actually want to say about amnesic people.

(4) The last or commonsensical view is that, *pace* the *C requirement, it is the same person and same animal throughout. This is the view that I favour.

I think it would be fair to subject an upholder of decision (3) to the following line of questioning: Since you allow the systemic component of the notion of person to dominate the *animal* element completely, and are more sanguine than the last section was intended to encourage anyone to be about the prospects of giving a coherent

---

32. Following the trail begun at Chapter Two, section 5 and continued at Chapter Four, section 9, I suppose that someone may hold that *animal,* of which *person* is a restriction, is not individuative at all, or not individuative in the same way as *horse, cat, man* or *person* are. What coincidence under the concept *animal* amounts to, it will be insisted, differs radically according to the kind of animal. Taking this view someone might, I suppose, extend the psychologistic Lockean individuative procedure and the *C requirement to animals as far down the evolutionary hierarchy as there can be psychologically or socially interesting differences between different members of a single species.

complete formulation of the psychological or systemic marks of the concept *person,* and since you are anxious to permit a *C condition to invade and reshape the biological principle of individuation of *homo sapiens,* why stop there? Why restrict this concession you have made to the demands of the forensic conception? What import does it have to insist that a person is an *animal* that meets this or that further condition? Why would you not allow an artifact to qualify as a person, provided it was programmed to satisfy fully the functional requirement that you have claimed to be the principal part of the definition of *person*? Why do you not retreat to a position where the concept *person* is no longer a hybrid concept like *vegetable,* but simply reduces to a complicated functional attribute that is completely specifiable? Seeing the problem of persons in the way you see it, one finds no rationale for choosing any particular point between decision (4), which is the verdict of the biological view of persons (as it is of the replete or naturalist view that amplifies or enlarges the biological view), and a purely functional conception of persons that will permit an artifact to qualify. Surely decision (3) marks an inherently unstable position, unless we rectify the rationale for it and reformulate this in terms that (in theory at least) allow room for persons who are *not* organisms.

By this route, as by the route indicated in section 8, we finally reach the same point. It must now at last be recorded that there are in reality many philosophers, some of them committed to the reduction of the psychological to the social and others engaged in other less radical and improbable projects, who are fully prepared to embrace the forensic or functional view in any case. Such thinkers will have been irritated to have been forgotten in the preceding two sections, and will have been anxious and impatient throughout this chapter to take to task champions of decision (4), champions of decision (3), and any other purists or reactionaries of the personal identity relation, for failing to see that the concept of person *is* a social concept and that identity of persons *is* to be arbitrated by standards matched in respect of pliability and adaptability to the social or forensic purposes that make work for the notion.[33]

33. Cf. J. M. Shorter, 'Person Identity, Personal Relationships, and Criteria', *Proceedings of the Aristotelian Society* 1970–71; Eric Matthews, 'Descartes and Locke on the Concept of a Person', *Locke Newsletter* no. 8, summer 1977, p. 9. These articles are representative of a much larger anti-naturalist tendency in the philosophies of man and person which is sustained by very diverse considerations.

To say that *person* is a social concept is to say that it is the concept of something social. Strictly speaking this is true—man is a political animal, etc.—but not anything strong enough for the purpose (which relates to individuating people otherwise than as

I do not know how to argue directly with someone who is prepared in full earnest to make the considered assertion that *person* is a social concept and social constructs are its compliants. I calculate that there is probably no direct argument that will have any efficacy if a philosopher is prepared to count for nothing the illumination that a naturalistic conception can throw upon the perplexity we are caused by thought-experiments involving such things as the interchange of brains or their parts and the 'carbon copy' replication or duplication of skills and memories.[34] For me, or for anyone who is willing to be party to the doctrine of individuation that the naturalistic conception of persons makes possible, it seems immensely important that, at the limit, such thought experiments denature the human subject, and create the prospect that, in place of an animal or organism with a clear principle of individuation, we shall find some day that we have an entity whose identity has become a matter not of discovery but of interpretation (or even stipulation). But up to this point it has not been my concern to seek to *demonstrate* to anyone apt to respond differently to it that the prospect of individuative confusion is a frightening one. The object has not been to make the case against thinking or doing any of the things that figure in these thought experiments, but only to understand and explain by reference to general considerations of identity and individuation why even theoretical exercises of this sort have subjected us to the strain of thinking of ourselves as clones, as concrete universals, or as parts of one another. Perhaps this strain is in some obscure way good for us.[35] But it now seems that, to finish the argument or reach out to those who

animals). Hence the attraction some have felt to go beyond saying that person is a concept with marks (in Frege's sense) that are social and to say instead that persons are *social constructs*. This is not the thought that the concept *person* is a social construct in the special sense in which all concepts are social constructs. What is presumably meant is rather that it is socially determined which marks are to be reckoned to be integral to the concept *person* and which not integral. That again might be true, on a slightly circuitous literal interpretation. What I dispute is that we have so much freedom here that we can invent and reinvent at will (or can even reinterpret) the *principle of individuation* for persons.

34. See Bernard Williams, 'Are Persons Bodies?' in S. Spicker, ed., *The Philosophy of the Body*, Chicago, Quadrant Books, 1970; also N. Miri, 'Personal Identity and Memory', *Mind* Jan. 1972.

The possibilities or possible possibilities corresponding to these thought experiments may or may not be inconceivable *modulo* the basic or derived laws of the physical world; but they disrupt the expectations on which individuation depends and they disturb the application of the generalizations about the relation of animal and environment whose instantiation by substances sustains definitely their status as persons. (Cf. *Longer Note* 3.09, paragraph 4.)

35. As Derek Parfit has in several ways suggested. Cf. his 'Personal Identity', *Philosophical Review* 1971.

view with maddening equanimity what the individuative naturalist views with profound unease, an identity purist must digress and respond in its own terms to the challenge that the social construct theorist has issued. He must essay the indirect approach and try his hand at drawing out all the social and philosophical *implications* (in bourgeois, totalitarian and other political conditions) of treating the concept of person otherwise than as a peculiar restriction of the natural kind concept *animal*. The social construct theorist is right to point to the conceptual importance of the role of the notion of a person in social and moral philosophy. Indeed that is his sole argument. But it is not excluded that there is serious oversight or error in the instant deduction that he is so eager to make from the fact of this importance. If this can be shown, then the naturalist view of persons can be purged of all associations with the functionalist view of them.

10. *Persons as social constructs and persons as given*

Suppose that we dispense with the animal component in the animal attribute elucidation of *person* and assert cheerfully that specification by some finite number of attributes, fixed *without* essential reference to human beings just as they are, captures every mark that is essential to the concept of person. What we then have to imagine is a state of affairs in which all conceptual constraints whatever (including moral or normative constraints of conceptual provenance and important discriminations of importance) will be founded in the finite systemic specification of person; and a state of affairs in which nothing prevents the interpretations of speech, conduct and the thoughts that lie behind the desires that lie behind conduct, from being founded in a conception of personhood perceptibly narrower and certainly simpler than that implicit in our present (however conservative and obscurantist) mode of interpretation of these things.[36] Now here one is bound to wonder what change it would bring to the theory and practice of politics, if all inquiry and all description came to be organized by a conception of human personality that was focused only by a systemic specification, rather than by the idea of something that we can try to discover about, and may even be surprised by. What sort of differences would flow from this reorientation? And what options would it foreclose?

Both negatively and positively, possibility is very important in

36. See *Longer Note* 6.36.

politics. One aspect of its importance that is partially concealed from most self-styled political realists is that in the real world most of the desires of the majority of human beings are conceived in circumstances—and are conceived *for* circumstances—in which these human beings have good reason to try to imagine some variation (even if they have little practical encouragement to sustain this effort, beyond mere resentment, into understanding of what is and is not genuinely conceivable for the actual world). I admit that only an imaginative citizen or a real statesman will have the vision and stamina to visualize, in the complete pictures that are required, what this or that variation of circumstances would really mean, in respect of gains and losses and in respect of its answering or not answering to needs and desires. But it will be a great pity if we make this the reason to impoverish in advance the whole conception of political possibility that is presupposed to this highly necessary (however rare) exercise of the imagination—as if to extend the blessing of theory to what may up to now have seemed only a *practical* shortcoming of the managerial or social engineering cast of mind, which narrows down to the supposedly familiar and controllable the range of thinkable futures, and then plans busily to optimize the quantity and distribution of desire-satisfactions. It is typical of a man of this cast of mind to seek to project forward into the future that we fondly suppose to be open very particular present desires—desires that we have conceived (or given the particular form that specifies them for satisfaction) only in reaction to circumstances that relatively few of us have good reason to see as affording much choice. We should sympathize with the manager (or speculate realistically how to dispense with him). But we should not sympathize with him to the point of jeopardizing the statement of what is theoretically unsatisfactory or arbitrary in such projection. It is one thing to say that it is *hard to know* what alternative forms desire would have taken under other circumstances, or what standing concerns underlie the desires that particular circumstances provoke. (Provided this is seen as a curb on how ambitious or officious managers ought to be, it will also afford them some defence against the dissatisfactions of their subjects.) It is another thing altogether to legitimize what have seemed like real failures of political and social imagination, and to cut down to size the very idea of real political possibility, by the official endorsement of a systemic (finite list of non-extension involving attributes) conception of persons. Not only does this reduce the theoretical subject matter of morals and politics and limit the range and variety of counterfactual speculation that this subject matter can be expected to sustain; and not only does it reduce drastically (for the same reasons) the scope for real criticism of the actual works of social engineering that ought to have held in check by a healthy respect for the partly imponderable real essence of actual persons: it will also license a state of affairs in which there was absolutely nothing except fear of confusion to obstruct proposals for modifying or reinventing even the *accepted* specification of what a person was—just as we constantly and effortlessly modify and re-fashion through time certain institution- and artifact-concepts.

This book is hardly the place to try to argue utterly from scratch with those already enamoured of all the views I seek to oppose here, still less with those who make a good living by ministering to the conception that the only relevant discrimination for any time *t* between the different possible outcomes for the time *t* will have to be with respect to the total and distribution of the satisfactions of desires existing at *t*, and the temporally discounted 'net present value' at *t* of all satisfactions actually projected by the managers of society for times after *t*.[37] I should be foolish to forget that this view of rationality is entertained by countless intelligent men. I suppose that, with certain saving inconsistencies (and reduced into theoretical but perfectly mythical order by 'the' social welfare function) it is the basis of the Utilitarian theory of public rationality. (The common intellectual property of left and right, that is, as well as of all middle persuasions not sustained by a genuinely pluralistic vision of political values or political and human possibilities.) And maybe I am simply wrong to think that in the end this position can be shown to be as arbitrary and irrational as it is dispiriting and destructive of all meaning.[38] But to those still prepared to try to imagine in a little more detail what is being envisaged—or to those who want more from political philosophy or from politics than works of social engineering—I would put forward this thought: When the nature of human beings is not determined from outside us, because it can be freely reconceptualized and reinterpreted at any time (and the relevant finite set of attributes

37. Even less then is it the place to try to show that there is no coherent notion of desire which sees desires themselves as transparent self-announcing raw data for the manager or statesman, and not as needing to be understood and interpreted in the light of all the thoughts that they involve—and the thoughts themselves as needing the backing of human nature for their interpretation. (See *Longer Note* 6.36.) One crucial question is whether there is (what I doubt there is) a universal *a priori* theory of rationality that a manager or cost-benefit theorist can avail himself of for interpretive purposes.

38. For an attempt at the first and easiest phase of the complex assault which would have to be launched against this position, see my 'Deliberation and Practical Reason', *Proceedings of the Aristotelian Society* 1975–76, or the amplification of its later sections given in J. Raz, ed., *Practical Reason*, Oxford University Press, 1978.

can be reformulated to some significant degree independently of what persons are really like), the potentiality of human beings enjoys a diminished conceptual status. In fact it is dubious that there *is* then anything more to be made of human nature than the sum of what registers at the level of explicit situation-relative desire and actual human behaviour. But surely what we ought to have wanted was a theory of human nature which, at one and the same time, would organize positively our notions of human potentiality and describe discursively, with a view to the improvement of our understanding of possibility and the rendering serious of our attempts at criticism of decisions and institutions, what it is about men as empirically given organisms which interacts with historical situations to produce the thoughts and feelings that make desire itself interpretable and intelligible.

In a book about identity that has made an extensive though semi-technical use of the notion of nature, I think that the most that anyone could expect or want from me on this theme is one sufficiently deliberate gesture towards the character of the linkage that comes to light here between the problem of the individuation and the physical nature of persons on the one hand, and the problem of human nature and the foundations of ethics and politics, on the other.

11. *Nature and naturalism*

In this book 'nature' has stood for 'physical nature' and that complex of significant properties by which a substance instantiates genuine laws that furnish the materials for a Leibnizian principle of existence, persistence and identity for members of the class associated with the nature. It is for philosophical investigation what the connexion is between nature so conceived and the psychological nature or natures of men. It is surely no accident, though, that in this chapter it has proved completely impossible to disentangle the physiological and the psychological components of the identity principle for persons. I am persuaded that the relation of the two notions of nature is that the psychological nature of man with which moral philosophy is concerned is *supervenient* on the notion of nature we have associated with the criterion of identity.[39] Deferring the whole difficulty of proving

39. Cf. Donald Davidson, 'Mental Events' in Foster and Swanson, eds., *Experience and Theory*, Duckworth, 1971. Note that Davidson could be right about the supervenience of the mental on the physical and my own contention could still be wrong; and that supervenience covers a number of different possibilities.

this, it is crucial to the position I should defend to distinguish two very different roles, one an explicit role and the other an inexplicit but much more important role, played in moral philosophy by the notion of nature. Without this distinction, both my individuative naturalism and the position I have taken up concerning the linkage of metaphysical and axiological questions will seem to depend on *ethical* naturalism,[40] a position no moderate cognitivist of my persuasion could find tempting (and utterly distinct from the individuative naturalism here defended as a thesis of philosophy of mind). In the presence of this distinction, however, I hope that this position will seem to accord with what almost everyone thinks he already knows.

I begin with the explicit role. One of the philosophical roles of the notion of human nature is to organize arguments from facts about historical circumstance and time-relative possibility to judgements of human need. Similarly, but in a slightly different and more explicit way, the notion figures in arguments about the distinction between the basic needs of human beings—what always, because of their nature, they must have to flourish—and all their other appetitive states.[41] Such forms of argument are not absolutely without relevance to the topic of this section.[42] But the nature-based model of argument, forceful though it is within a small and definitely circumscribed area,

40. Ethical naturalism in the sense in which G. E. Moore rejected it, namely the view that 'good' is reducible by predicates standing for the physical or natural properties of things, or by some complex of such predicates. It is a misreading of Moore to interpret him as having given an early version of later arguments to the effect that 'good' falls on the worse side of the *cognitive/non-cognitive, objective/subjective, factual/non-factual* contrasts. Supervenience without reducibility reconstructs very well, I think, Moore's thesis that 'good' stands for a non-natural property. I am putting together here, without the approval of either, Donald Davidson, *op. cit.,* 'Mental Events' and A. T. Kolnai, 'The Ghost of the Naturalistic Fallacy', forthcoming in *Philosophy* 1979–80.

41. Both contentions are argued for in an unpublished thesis of Sira Dermen of University College London. That the elucidation of need involves the idea of necessity, situation, and the good is prefigured in one sense of 'necessary' elucidated by Aristotle in *Metaphysics* Δ. 5.

42. Nor are the distinction between what depends upon the variable and what depends upon the naturally invariable elements in human life, and the distinct distinction between what is here and now readily modified and that which is not, foreign to ordinary men or the subjectivity of their most unreflective experience. Both are indispensable to practical thinking in a world of scarcity. In practice, the distinction between a need and a merely appetitive state seems to be conceptually inaccessible for a utilitarian manager. Obviously, wherever this is so, he can hardly interpret the everyday behaviour he surveys as expressive of the distinction. Indeed when his concept of person has lost any determinate centre of gravity (can be anything at all he makes of it) his methodology does not require the additional reassurance that 'there is no such thing as human nature'. (A slogan that is not in fact to be attributed to Karl Marx, I understand, and is inconsistent with his theories.)

has been generalized by Ethical Naturalists and Eudaemonists far beyond what it will bear. And the real and overwhelming importance of human nature is its inexplicit role, to which I turn next.

In the strict and interesting sense of 'natural', values are not part of the natural order; nor are value properties perceptible by the senses in the relatively straightforward way in which artifactual properties are. Their discrimination depends on a complex set of beliefs and concerns, variously formed, refined and adjusted, that human beings *bring* to the apprehension of the natural order. But, if that is so, then the question arises why we should suppose that different human beings will bring even remotely similar beliefs and concerns to this apprehension. It suddenly seems not boring and familiar but familiar and surprising that men understand one another readily when they converse about values and that they can prolong dialogue indefinitely and discursively, with some appreciable prospect of moving nearer to agreement. It is even more surprising that human beings who belong to one culture or to neighbouring cultures can *widen* the scope of an argument in some fair confidence that this is more likely to promote than to destroy mutual intelligibility. The familiarity of these facts should not lead us to ignore them or take them for granted. What we have to ask here is: What grounds this agreement, and what makes the expectation of intelligibility and a shared discrimination of an enormous range of value properties as justifiable as in practice it is?[43] And what are the *enabling conditions* for a shared mode of criticism to have evolved even to the point it has now reached—the point, that is, where it is easier to attain what John Rawls calls 'reflective equilibrium' on certain matters of good and evil than on certain supposedly scientific ones,[44] and where judgements about good and evil can be made confidently enough to form some part of what gives meaning to human life conducted within all sorts of human association? I should argue that the answer has everything to do with human nature and

43. Concerning agreement, L. Wittgenstein, *Philosophical Investigations,* § 242, and Donald Davidson, 'Radical Interpretation', *Dialectica* 1973.

44. It would surely not have been enough to bring this about for a finite number of normative or evaluative 'axioms' to have been socially imprinted. Compare Aristotle *N.E.* 1137^{b19}. Axioms or principles susceptible of finite expression cannot be what sustain the community of reaction that mutual intelligibility requires, extending as this does across such an indefinite multitude of relatively independent questions lying in an indefinite multiplicity of modalities of good and evil. Nor can any complex of discriminations that could be taught, so to speak, from scratch sustain it. Again, even in concert, axioms and complexes of discriminations taught from scratch could scarcely create or sustain what Strawson has called the participative attitude. (Cf. 'Freedom and Resentment', *Proceedings of the British Academy* XLVIII, 1962.)

nothing to do with what we could get from the functional attribute view of what a person is.

I should make it clear that in asking what grounds all these things or what underlies the sharing of discriminations and modes of criticism, I am not asking for a non-circular explanation of their existing. Rather I am pointing to the fact that any ample theoretical description of what is involved by them will have to speak of a shared set of underlying human concerns and affective attitudes; then I am claiming that the account will have to articulate these concerns and attitudes by reference to the actual features of the world with which they engage as their objects, described by the theorist in substantially the same terms as participants use;[45] and finally I am insisting that the description will have to organize and specify these concerns and attitudes themselves, not by enumeration, but by an account of how historical and environmental circumstances *combined* with the nature of men as biological organisms to generate them. The fact that there is no non-circular account of what it is about human nature and biological constitution that has made all these concerns and attitudes possible, or issued in different places in such different forms of human activity and association, should not lead us to suppose (what simply does not follow) that everything can stay comfortably the same—that our however moderate actual prospects of a measure of agreement and mutual comprehension can endure—even when the species-specific foundation on which human nature is supervenient is seen as irrelevant and the nature of human personhood is seen as something that is simply for *us* to decide to modify or refashion.

I shall conclude with three points this attempt to remind the social construct theorist of the neglected significance of what he may either profess not to understand or claim is simply obvious and not denied by anybody. First, the constitution that is seen in its causal relations with the contingencies of human history and geography is a constitution supervenient on contingencies of human *biological* constitution.[46]

45. It does not tell against this claim that, within the tolerance permitted by the possibility that a theorist has indeed *interpreted* his subjects' utterances, the theorist can disagree with his subjects about the exact extension of their terms (e.g. correct mistakes); nor does it tell against it that, to the extent that this is compatible with the theorist's grasping the *point* of their predicates, theorists and subjects can diverge in affective attitudes and in the *senses* they attach to their respective predicates. The crucial point is only that the explanation which the theorist offers employs essentially a predicate tied systematically to the *same reference* and *same extension* that his subjects discriminate. For this requirement see section V of my 'Truth, Invention and the Meaning of Life', *Proceedings of the British Academy* 1976.

46. If it were not then even the interpretation of speech might be nearly inconceivable. Cf. L. Wittgenstein, *Philosophical Investigations*, p. 223.

Secondly, the impossibility that I allege, that the theorist should discharge his explanatory task without reference to the same extensions as his subjects discriminate, mirrors on the level of the theory of interpretation and explanation a conclusion to which one is already forced on the level of the phenomenology of the apprehension of value.[47] And, thirdly, I would emphasize the proper relation of the first two points. It is almost impossible to conceive how human engagement could survive extinction of the idea of values as something that in some serious sense we discover (out there, so to say) in the world. But for the idea of the discovery of the extension of value predicates to subsist it is not necessary that the perception of values should be utterly independent of what human beings are like. It is only necessary—and here we return to the place from which this whole excursus was entered upon—that what human beings are and what concerns they make their own should to *some* significant extent be determined by something *independent of what human beings decide to make of themselves.* But then again it appears that the functional account of what a person is cannot suffice, given as it is by a finite list of non-extension-involving attributes. For seeing ourselves only under the aspect of such a definition, a definition that is so much up to us that individuation itself becomes a matter of interpretation, there is no way for us to see the value-properties of other things and other people in the world *as* independent of ourselves—not even in the limited way in which they have to be independent in order to be taken seriously as values and as something *discovered* to us by our concerns. Values and concerns will be mere projections. If this is right, then, when we consider the social construct theory, we find ourselves driven in another way to the conclusion that it will be the final state not of freedom but of meaninglessness that we shall have attained when we arrive at the point where the limits of the class of persons are no longer supplied from outside us, and where there is no answer independent of ourselves to the question what we are or even who we are and what matters to us.

This then is where I claim that the theory of individuation, the theory of interpretation, and the observation of human morality and the phenomenology of value all lead. It has never been proved that the whole structure of values as they appear to us is not an illusion. But it is especially clear that it need not be an illusion if we can make something of human nature as one part of the ground of that limited but indispensable propensity to anthropocentrically objective agree-

47. Cf. 'Truth, Invention and the Meaning of Life', *op. cit.*

ment that enables us to enjoy our however limited community of concepts and mutual intelligibility in evaluative and deliberative judgements; and if, second, we can connect this notion of human nature with the notion of nature with which the theory of individuation is concerned. If freedom and dignity and creativity are what we crave, we shall find more promise of these things in the Heraclitean prediction 'You would not find out the bounds of the soul, though you traversed every path: so deep is its *logos*' than in the idea that it is for men to determine the limits of their own nature, or mould and remake themselves to the point where they can count as their very own creation.

Whatever the reader thinks of the argument or the conclusion, he must take note that the concept of nature, or the idea of a shared human neurophysiology and a psychology which is supervenient on that, does not play here the unconvincing speaking part assigned to it by Ethical Naturalism. It plays a mute, causal, or enabling role, at which not even the cognitivist philosopher who first exposed the naturalistic fallacy would have needed to cavil. Everything is what it is and not another thing. Persons are a class of organisms, and they are identified under concepts that are nomologically conditioned. Whatever else they may be, they are things in nature. Artifacts, on the other hand, which are not in or of nature but often beneficially displace nature, are not identified under concepts that are nomologically conditioned. Meanwhile the values recognized by persons, being the outcome of the impinging of the external world upon persons constituted as persons are constituted, are *sui generis* (which is not to say that they are beyond sense perception) and irreducible to any terms belonging to a natural category. No theory of ethics or politics will prosper by contradicting these unremarkable and unremarked truisms, or seeking to diminish the role that human nature plays within them.

12. *Conclusion: the abandonment of the *C condition; a small amendment to Locke; and an inconclusive postscript on the brain.*

It is time to summarize conclusions. Decision (3) at section 9 is the wrong decision, using 'person' in the sense in which we still employ it. For (3) is unstable and vulnerable to invasion by the artifactual view, against which my claim is that by *person* we mean *a certain sort of animal,* and for purposes of both politics and morality that is the best thing for us to mean. As for decision (2), it is on pain of madness that we shall try to see ourselves as both *homo sapiens* and something with a different principle of individuation. Decision (4) remains, and is manifestly correct. The hospitalized amnesiac, or Nijinsky even at the last stages of madness, are the same man and the same person, however close the breakdown of the *C condition may suggest that they have come to the threshold of actual extinction.

What then about the *C condition? Its critics have been wrong to maintain that the *C proposal was absurd or circular or non-effective. The one thing wrong with the *C condition was that for purposes of certain actual decisions it seems incorrect. It represents one of the illusions of which the pronoun 'I' is so productive. But the critics of the *C condition have overlooked how easily the main project out of which it arose can be repaired. Let us rewrite Locke's famous sentence, and say that a person is any animal the physical make-up of whose species constitutes the species' typical members thinking intelligent beings, with reason and reflection, and typically enables them to consider themselves as themselves, the same thinking things, in different times and places, ... And, after the attributes mentioned in section 7 have been transcribed in an empirical spirit, let us supply the lacunae, which we marked there by dots, by drawing upon the indefinite and extensible fund of our knowledge of men, *knowing* that we shall never close off the enumeration or evaluate once and for all the relative importance of the various differentiae.

Memory is not then irrelevant to personal identity, but the way it is relevant is simply that it is one highly important element among others, both in itself and in its association with other components, in the account of what it is for a person to be still there, fully *alive*. It plays its part in determining the continuity principle for persons, as opposed to bodies or cadavera, but (as Butler rightly said, for the wrong reason) it will scarcely furnish a necessary or sufficient condition of identity, survival or persistence.

On this account the bearing of memory on individual problem cases, over and above what has been said, is very uncertain. But here as everywhere my primary concern is to put problems of identity onto a broader basis of theory and relevant information, not to attempt to issue a set of decisions. So far as brain transplants are concerned, a responsible review of all the arguments and thought-experiments that have been essayed in the swelling philosophical and medico-fictional literature could not, if it were made in the light of the theory of individuation outlined in this chapter, evade, simply by explaining the source of the perplexities they create, all the problems posed by surgical and mechanical intervention. Some of these no doubt fall just short of imperilling the application of *person* and concepts related to *person*. Here I only add, to what I have said about breaches of the normal relation between animal and environment, that we should take nothing for granted about how well we really understand brain transfers of the kind described by Shoemaker. How do we fit the brain to the physiognomy of the new body which is to receive it? How is the existing character expressed in the new body? We are deceived by the high-quality of the actors and mimics we see on the stage if with the help of greasepaint and props they have made us think this is as (relatively) simple as the transposition of music from one instrument to another.[48] With so much said I shall leave the last word with Swift:

> When Parties in a State are violent, he offered a wonderful Contrivance to reconcile them. The Method is this. You take a Hundred Leaders of each Party; you dispose them into Couples of such whose Heads are nearest of a Size; then let two nice Operators saw off the *Occiput* of each Couple at the same Time, in such a Manner that the Brain may be equally divided. Let the *Occiputs* thus cut off be interchanged, applying each to the Head of his opposite Party-man. It seems indeed to be a Work that requireth some Exactness; but the Professor assured us, that if it were dextrously performed, the Cure would be infallible. For he argued thus; that the two half Brains being left to debate the Matter between themselves within the Space of one Scull, would soon come to a good Understanding, and produce that Moderation as well as Regularity of Thinking, so much to be wished for in the Heads of those, who imagine they came into the World only to watch and govern its Motion: And as to the Difference of Brains in Quantity or Quality, among those who are Directors in Faction; the Doctor assured us from his own Knowledge, that it was a perfect Trifle. (*Gulliver's Travels*: Book III, *A Voyage to Laputa*.)

48. Cf. Williams 'Personal Identity and Individuation', *op. cit.*

Longer Notes

Longer Notes

0.02. *Identity symbolism* It is objectionable perhaps from the point of view of purest purity of formalism to have one and the same sign, ' $=$ ', occurring, as it will here, both in the two-place predicable ' $x = y$ ' and in the distinct three-place predicable that is indispensable to the consideration of the 'same what?' question, viz. ' $x \underset{f}{=} y$ '. But this will not confuse anyone in practice. The notational point is neglected pending the final resolution of the minor but vexed question whether there is a clear sense in which ' $x = y$ ' is logically prior to ' $x \underset{f}{=} y$ ' or logically posterior to it or neither.

If ' $x = y$ ' is the logically prior idea, then ' $x \underset{f}{=} y$ ' is not merely equivalent but *definitionally* equivalent to '((fx) & (fy) & ($x = y$))'. (Never mind the question of synonymy.) If ' $x = y$ ' is logically posterior to ' $x \underset{f}{=} y$ ', then this conjunction just mentioned is not the *definition* of ' $x = y$ '; even though, given Leibniz's Law for relative identity, ' $x \underset{f}{=} y$ ' will turn out to be *strictly equivalent* to '((fx) & (fy) & ($x = y$))'. The strict definition of ' $x = y$ ' will be ($\exists$f) ($x \underset{f}{=} y$), an equivalence we can only *articulate* at the second level, it seems. The very free use that the arguments of Chapter One make of the equivalences $(x = y) \equiv (\exists f)\ (x \underset{f}{=} y)$ and $(x \underset{f}{=} y) \equiv ((fx)\ \&\ (fy)\ \&\ (x = y))$ is not meant to be committal with respect to the very difficult, and possibly not very important, issue of definitional priority, and is intended as equally uncommittal with respect to epistemic priority. I retract all claims I have ever made to have resolved or even identified properly the issue of logical priority. See further Chapter Two, footnote 2, and *Longer Note* 2.03. The free use of the aforesaid equivalences is *not* of course uncommittal with respect to the subjection of ' $x \underset{f}{=} y$ ' to Leibniz's Law. For this, however, some argument *is* offered.

0.03. *Second-level readings* It may be complained here that the second-level reading would commit one to reading, not only ' $a \underset{f}{=} b$ ', but also all first-order sentences like 'Man (Socrates)' in second-order terms, e.g. as 'Socrates falls under the concept *man*'. I think that, if one were actually committed to it, this kind of Platonism would be both harmless and reducible; but it is doubtful that there is such a commitment, and well worth remembering that it would be possible to minimize disturbance to the first-order framework that almost everyone regards as preferable if such quantifiers as ' $\exists$f' were taken substitutionally (a reading that all the substantive claims advanced in this book are proof enough against vagaries of interpretation to allow, provided we think in terms of possible extensions of English to augment the predicates of the first level). The cardinal point though is that sentential forms like 'a and b are the same *what?*', 'a and b are the same something', 'Socrates is something', and 'there is something Socrates is', are already *provided* for in English and all of a piece with old friends like 'there is something I am and you are not, viz. an admirer of Hegel' (cf. M. A. E. Dummett, *Philosophical Review* LXIV, 1955, pp. 96–107 and *Philosophical Review* LXV, 1956, pp. 229–30; also *Frege: Philosophy of Language*, London, Duckworth, 1973, ch. 7). Perhaps we do have to see these as second-order assertions in English given in forms such as ($\exists\phi$) ((I am ϕ and you are not ϕ) & (ϕ = what it is to be admirer of Hegel)). But it is the existence of such English locutions that helps to make the idea of a second-level predicate calculus intelligible. Just as 'Socrates is something' means something already, before we light upon the formalism of '($\exists$f) (f Socrates)', so surely does 'a is the same something or other as b' mean something well before we represent it as '($\exists$f) ($a =_f b$)', or as speaking of a and b having the relation ' = ' restricted to the extension of some sortal concept or the other.

0.04. *Geach on 'the same f'*   Geach has criticized criticisms directed from an absolute or Leibnizian standpoint at his non-Leibnizian relative reading of 'a is the same f as b'. He has found fault on at least three counts: (a) they presuppose the conception of individuals as qualityless particulars; (b) they presuppose some sort of synonymy between 'a is the same f as b' and 'a is an f, b is an f, and a is the same as b'; (c) where they attempt to escape from the charge (b), they are involved in an incoherent account of $a =_f b$. (See Geach's review of Griffin's *Relative Identity* in *The Times Literary Supplement* for November 1977.)

I do not think Geach could urge criticism (a) against the position taken up in this book.

To (b) I respond by reserving my right to doubt *synonymy* and by treating with a caution at least equal to that which Geach has recommended (see the beginning of his article 'Ontological Relativity and Relative Identity') the question whether ' = ' or '$=_f$' is logically prior. It does not matter very much to the claims advanced in Chapter Two about the role of sortal concepts in determining principles of individuation whether option (i) or option (ii) of *Preamble*, section 6, is chosen. And it would not matter very much how swiftly option (ii) proved to involve the chooser in option (iii). If the relations of 'the same' and 'the same f' require a second-level statement for their explicit articulation, just how surprising should that seem, given that it is simply a fact that we have in English both 'is the same' and 'is the same f', and given therefore that the problem of the relation of these is not a gratuitous unnecessary or self-imposed problem?

To (c) I respond by pointing out that it is a curiosity of Geach's view of 'is the same f as' as primitive that it makes it much harder to understand some of the informal remarks made by his allies, and by the supporters of the view that identity is relative. When they ask 'a is the same *what* as b', or assert that to exist is to be *something*, such abstraction is not provided for by option (iv).

1.09. *Relative indiscernibility* If there were a satisfactory statement of the f-indiscernibility of f-identicals then, for one who believed, with Noonan (*op. cit., Mind* 1976, p. 569) that he could conceive of the possibility that x should be the same man as y without being identical with y, or that x should be the same river as y without being identical with y, it would appear circular to pass back and forth, as I do in Chapter One, between $a = b$ and $(\exists f)\,(a \overset{=}{_f} b)$, or to claim, as I do, that Leibniz's Law holds not only for the relation $x = y$ but also for the relations $x \overset{=}{_f} y$ and $(\exists f)\,(x \overset{=}{_f} y)$. But Noonan offers no systematic account of the *being the same* f relation, over and above equivalence. This might not matter very much, and a non-Leibnizian $x \overset{=}{_f} y$ might be a harmless plaything, if Noonan allowed that it is $x = y$ that does all the work. But that is not at all his position. He denies for instance that it is classical identity that is linked with predication in the truism that if x is an f then x is identical with some f. (See Ch. One, note 18.) Indeed it is unclear to me not only what he thinks the relation is between '$a = b$' and '$a \overset{=}{_f} b$', but even whether there is any role he is prepared to assign to classical or unrelativized identity. What is it then which supports substitution arguments *salva veritate*? Or how are we to dispense with all of these?

For a confessedly unsuccessful attempt to restrict congruence by defining a class Δ_f of predicates such that Leibniz's Law assumes the qualified form:

$$x \overset{=}{_f} y \supset (\forall \phi)\,(\phi \in \Delta_f \supset (fx\ \&\ fy\ \&\ \phi x \supset \phi y)),$$

see Nicholas Griffin, *op. cit.*, pp. 140–1. 'It is difficult', he writes, 'to know for each f what goes into Δ_f and what stays out.' After what he expressly declares to be a partial account, he concludes: 'This characterization of Δ_f is somewhat clumsy but simplifications are not easy to find. Attempts to link Δ_f with the significance range of [the predicate that stands for the sort f], for example, have failed.'

1.10. *Synchronic and diachronic identity* For a purported demonstration that identity through time is not real identity, made by arguments certainly exempt from all the usual confusions of sameness and similarity (exposed as such by, e.g., V. Chappell's admirable 'Sameness and Change', *Philosophical Review*, vol. LXIX, Jan. 1960), see D. Gabbay and J. M. Moravcsik, 'Sameness and Individuation', *Journal of Philosophy*, vol. LXX, no. 16, 1973. (Cf. Goodman and Carnap cited at notes 22 and 25; John Perry, *Journal of Symbolic Logic* 35, no. 3, para. 4.) Consider, Gabbay and Moravcsik suggest, the sentence

(6) The young woman I met eight years ago turned into the senior lecturer whom I met last year.

and its 'restatement'

(8) The young woman I met eight years ago is the same as the senior lecturer I met last year.

'Since they are equivalent', they say, 'substitution in one should have the same result as the same substitution in the other. If we substitute in (6) on the right side the expression we have on the left ["The young woman I met eight years ago"], and if we construe the expressions as simply referring to the woman, then we get

(11) The young woman I met eight years ago turned into the young woman I met eight years ago,

which is false. . . . When we perform the same substitution in (8):

(12) The young woman I met eight years ago is the same as the young woman I met eight years ago,

the result fails to be equivalent to (11) . . . (12) taken naturally is a truism, but (11) is not. This shows that the "is the same as" in (8) has a sense distinct from identity; it also shows the need for interpreting the referring expressions in (6) and (8) as denoting stages of entities instead of the entities themselves. Of course, once we construe the referents as stages, the sameness involved cannot be identity.'

Comment. The argument would depend on its own conclusion if the 'equivalence' of (6) and (8) were founded in the supposed synonymy of 'is the same as' (in the sense hoped to be proved separable from ' = ') and 'turns into'. To avoid this begging of the question, the argument must be understood as depending on some relation of 'overall synonymy' between (6) and (8) *taken as wholes,* or on their necessary equivalence. But from the fact that they are equivalent as wholes and equiform in respect of the verb, it does not follow at all that these verbs should have been equivalent in sense. As is pointed out in *Reference and Generality,* p. 61, by Geach, who calls the genus to which this specimen belongs the 'cancelling out' fallacy, one could demonstrate by these means that '. . . killed Socrates' and '. . . was killed by Socrates', and '. . . killed . . .' and '. . . was killed by . . .', meant the same, e.g. by reference to the overall equivalence of the sentences 'Socrates killed Socrates' and 'Socrates was killed by Socrates'.

Such attempts as Gabbay and Moravcsik's are to some extent encouraged by the distinction that some writers have made between synchronic criteria of distinctness and fully-fledged criteria of *identity.* See B. A. O. Williams, 'Personal Identity and Individuation', *Proceedings of the Aristotelian Society* 1956–57; and G. E. M. Anscombe, 'The Principle of Individuation', *ibid.* Suppl. vol. 27, 1953. This matter is pursued further in section 7 and footnote 16 of Chapter Three.

1.11. *Four-dimensional talk*   Champions of the four-dimensional approach to these questions usually start out with the explanation that the diachronic concatenation relation that they are preparing to define is to hold between some such entities as that-horse-at-midnight-1.4.1968 and this horse-at-noon-12.12.1970. Geach has criticized this approach very severely. See 'Some Problems About Time', *Proceedings of the British Academy* 1965. It seems to me that the most important deficiencies are: (1) the difficulty of understanding just how an adverbial phrase like 'at noon 12.12.1970', occurring in such a context as 'The vet attended the horse at noon 12.12.1970', can attach to the substantive instead of the predicate 'the vet attended . . .'; and (2) the scale and programmatic obscurity of the disruption or reconceptualization that some four-dimensionalist philosophers would visit on all the natural language predicates truly applicable to three-dimensional substances but not, as the predicates seem to stand, truly applicable to four-dimensional items.

There is one obvious way to remedy these deficiencies, and this is to make the transition to the four-dimensional language openly by such stipulations as this: the thing-moment this-horse-at-noon is to consist of the set of all space-time quadruples 1_i, 1_j, 1_k, t such that t is noon and 1_i, 1_j, 1_k is a point occupied at t by the matter which at t constitutes this horse. The four-dimensional counterpart of this horse is then to be the series of all such thing-moments for all times during which this three dimensional horse exists. (Some choices will then have to be made about how to define, for thing-moments or their series, the predicates that will be true of them whenever a certain familiar predicate is true of the three-dimensional continuant.)

Note that, in the proposed definition of thing-moment, the continuant language designation 'this horse' plays an essential role. The same applies within the definition of the four-dimensional counterpart. If someone were to make the non-obligatory (and I think incorrect, see Chapter Six, pp. 168–9) claim that a certain familiar continuant horse was identical with a particular specified series of thing-moments, then the words 'this horse' would occur essentially on both sides of the '$=$', if the claim were written out in full. With this recipe, there is no question of giving an autonomous description in pure four-dimensional terms of the relevant set or series of sets of quadruples, and then saying that *this* entity is or represents the horse.

Choosing consciously this particular route we may see the four-dimensional theory as an enrichment of the ideology and ontology of ordinary continuant talk. The definitional priority of the continuant language, in which the construction of four-dimensional counterparts of three-dimensional continuants is founded, is instantly and unreservedly conceded by anyone who candidly adopts it. And nothing is claimed about the identity of the entities articulated within the three-dimensional and four-dimensional schemes.

It would be a gross misunderstanding of what I have just implied about thing-moment and temporal cross-section analyses of identity sentences to take the remarks as directed against four-dimensional talk *as such*. I have suggested rather that there is nothing whatever wrong with it. Physics arises from the desire to explain at the deepest possible level the physical phenomena of motion, impact, etc. It has proved that the three-dimensional Aristotelian way of thinking is unequal to that task. In its unsupplemented state, the ordinary language of three-dimensional continuants is unequal even to the task of describing adequately for these purposes the most familiar physical events and processes. The case for enriching natural language was overwhelmingly strong here. But only some snobbery that fastened on the more finished parts of physics to the exclusion of all else could blind a man to the fact that, give or take a little, the old three-dimensional language is the language of much of biological science, the language of the physics laboratory itself, and the language of aerodynamics and other 'applications' of physics. Nor could the pure space-time language, as it is employed by human beings, be brought into being, or invested with its proper significance, without some of the introductory explanations needing to lean on the crutch of the three-dimensional language. It is interesting that in practice the crutch is often retained, and that the predicates of the three-dimensional language are frequently permitted to stay on in the everyday language of science. No confusion results from this mixture. One should not take at their face value the claims that this retention is 'unofficial' It could only be unofficial if the three-dimensional theory were either reducible to or interpretable within some four-dimensional theory. But to achieve either reducibility or interpretability it would need to be possible to find, for every predicate F in the continuant language, a true biconditional $A \equiv B$ such that (1) A was constructed with the help of F and without the help of expressions not belonging to the continuant language itself; and (2) B was constructed from expressions belonging to the four-dimensional language and from no expressions belonging only to the portion of the continuant language that was to be reduced or interpreted. If such biconditionals could be formulated we could raise the question whether the true biconditionals were derivable from a four-dimensional theory or would need to be added thereto. (For Tarski's distinction between these possibilities, and the distinction of reduction and interpretation, see for instance J. H. Woodger, *Biology and Language,* Cambridge, 1952, pp. 271–3). But, at least on the proposal for clear and open enrichment that I have commended, we could not even formulate biconditionals which met the first condition.

The problem that confronts those who set the wrong sort of store by four-dimensional talk, and tumble over themselves to contract the unnecessary obligation to represent three-dimensional talk as covertly four-dimensional, is to describe the function which, term by term and predicate by predicate, maps arbitrary sentences of four-dimensional talk onto everyday continuant talk; and then to reproduce in pure four-dimensional talk the logical connexions holding between everyday continuant sentences. The truth is, though, that it is simply a mistake to suppose that we *must*—if we are with a clear scientific conscience to continue to speak of them at all—identify the persisting entities articulated by the three-dimensional world-view with those articulated by the four-dimensional. The two kinds of entity simply do not complete for room in the world (see *op. cit. Preface* (1)). Their mutual relations are not unintelligible or the slightest bit unsayable. It is in the linkage of the two articulations of reality that there resides some of the enormous importance of the category of *event*, the category of *process*, and the category of *stuff*.

Physics refines the ordinary notion of stuff. But, unlike the category of thing, the category of stuff remains stable when the four-dimensional view is introduced and is continuous with the everyday category to which belong honey, chocolate, mud, etc. Even when we are *en route* to the physical theory of the elements, the criterion for strict identity is the same. (No addition or subtraction, see Helen Morris Cartwright, 'Quantities', *Philosophical Review* LXXVIII, 1969). There is a similar point at issue—for all that its interpretation is more and more theoretical—when the question is whether this and that are the same quantity of stuff. Scientific conceptions of stuff are a natural refinement of the everyday conceptions of stuff. I suspect that the same goes for *event* and *process*. But I have claimed that this does not apply to the concept of *continuant*. Note, for instance, that for continuants, as opposed to pure mereological constructs out of matter, it is impossible (and, again, as unhelpful as it is unnecessary) to formulate any principles of conservation.

1.19. *Constitutive 'is'* Sidney Shoemaker (*Philosophical Review* LXXIX, Oct. 1970, 'Wiggins on Identity', reprinted in Milton K. Munitz, ed., *Identity and Individuation,* New York, New York University Press, 1971) rightly suggests that an analogous procedure needs to be applied to 'That piece of bronze is the statue I told you about' and suggests, again surely rightly, that in this sentence the 'is' may be satisfactorily marked off from identity by the paraphrase 'is composed [at *t*] of the same matter as', a symmetric (and presumably transitive and reflexive) *tensed* relation. My cavil against this attempt to specify further the purport of the constitutive 'is' concerns the assertion which he makes *en route* to his own paraphrase and against mine, that 'it does not seem right to say that it [the statue] is composed of a *piece* of bronze—and still less that the piece of bronze is composed of a statue'. In my usage of 'compose' and 'constitute', a usage suggested by mereology (but which I believe to agree with the underlying logic, stripped of pragmatic accretions, to which the expressions conform in English) there is nothing actually wrong with saying what Shoemaker thinks it is not right to say. And identity is even a special case of constitution. For any *x*, *x* composes *x*. But neither *x* composes *y* nor *y* composes *x* nor the conjunction of these sentences actually entails '*x* = *y*'. See Chapter Three, footnote 16.

1.24. *Mereology and 'content identity'* Mr Risto Pitkänen (see 'Content Identity', *Mind* LXXXV, no. 338, 1976, p. 265) objects to the whole argument, and says of what is written here

> This argument betrays a serious misunderstanding. It does not follow from any calculus of individuals that a sum-individual ceases to exist if some or even all of its parts, proper or improper, are physically broken ... there is no reason to assume that the sum-individual, X, which consists of parts of J, disappears just because a part of it, J, is broken.

But Mr Pitkänen's remark really makes my point over again for me. There are two possibilities. By the first, the mereological construction uses the notion of jug J. In that case the construction is derivative, and does no independent work. Naturally it yields no type-(4) case. The other possibility is that we obtain the 'atoms' of the mereological construction in a different and more interesting way—e.g. from our understanding of the concept of 'stuff'. We then work, not down from the jug J to jug-parts which can themselves be shattered and destroyed, but *up* to the jug from these atoms—none of which ceases to exist just because the jug ceases to exist. There is then a real point in the construction. But then X does *not* cease to exist just because J does. X may be 'content-identical' with J. This is Mr Pitkänen's concern (never mind my doubt at p. 93, n. 16). But for the reason he himself gives the life-histories principle excludes the Leibnizian identity of X and J and the Leibnizian identity of J and C.

1.29. *Hume's church*   Hume goes on in tell-tale manner to say: 'But we must observe, that in these cases the first object [*sic*] is in a manner annihilated before the second comes into existence; by which means, we are never presented, in any point of time, with the idea of difference and multiplicity; and for that reason are less scrupulous in calling them the same.' Hume has less interest than we ought to have in pressing the point I am about to make because, having distinguished respectable strict 'numerical' identity from what he variously dubs 'imperfect', 'specific', 'fictitious' identity (the lamentable ancestor, I suppose, of 'genidentity', and a notion which on one occasion he even calls a perfect notion of *diversity*), he can then afford to let you say whatever you please about the disreputable second notion. But we must insist—*either* we make up our minds to say the building was annihilated *or* we do not make up our minds so.

If we do say the building was annihilated then a certain building seems to be found in existence after it lapsed from existence. It is easy to avoid this absurdity. Here are two or three different ways. First take 'church' in its first and third occurrences in 'the present church is the same church as the old church' to mean 'building'. Take the second occurrence of 'church' to signify what can persist when a congregation loses its church building. Mark this latter sense by capitals. Thus the sentence signifies something like 'the present church building embodies/realizes/houses the same Church as the old church building embodied/realized/housed'. If this really is a way of reading the sentence that we are concerned with, then, there must be some 'is' of 'realization' which extends the 'is' of constitution. (Here cf. (μ) later.) To add to the sentence 'the new church building is the same Church as the old church building' the qualification 'but it is not the same *building*' imports a zeugma at 'is', which reverts the second time round to its ' $=$ ' sense, with consequential change in the grammatical role of the expression following 'same'. A second way is to take 'church' to mean 'Church' throughout in the affirmative sentence 'the present church is the same church as the old church', and to take the addition 'but it is not the same building' as importing a zeugma at the subject place: '. . . but the new *building* is not the same *building* as the old'. Third, let 'church' mean building at its first and third occurrence and behave in the titular fashion and unlike a proper covering-concept at its second occurrence, as it was supposed 'land mark' might behave in (γ) (meaning say 'whatever building houses such and such a congregation'). We lose the type-(5) identity-statement whichever analysis we adopt.

If we do not make up our minds to say that the church was annihilated then either we do not know what to say about the example, or we say that it was not annihilated. It is then false that the new church is not the same building as the old one. It is the same, and has simply been repaired and remodelled. That is what we have decided to say.

Again the rebuttal does not depend on its being a hard and fast question how 'church' behaves in the example. As before, the example cannot be permitted to survive by poising itself ambiguously between mutually exclusive alternatives.

2.03 *Quine and the Identity predicate*   Professor Quine shows how any first-order theory with '=' and a finite store of other monadic and polyadic predicates contains the resources to eliminate '=' as a primitive sign in favour of a complex predicate constructed out of all the other predicates of the theory. Cf. *Word and Object* (Cambridge, Mass., MIT, 1960), p. 230. If this reduction were cited in evidence against **D** or against my claim that '=' is primitive, then I should reply that in the first place it scarcely measures up to the set of objections to the community of properties and relations account of identity that I have already filed; and that in the second place it does dubious justice to the evident univocity of '*x* is identical with *y*'. Suppose that, for each of several languages unlike English in having a clearly delimited set of predicates, we frame by exhaustion its surrogate identity predicate, and then replace with that the extant '=' predicate. What do the surrogates that we have framed for the various languages have in common? Each expresses a certain congruence with respect to the predicates of the particular language into which it is introduced. But so long as we restrict ourselves to that which can be expressed in first-order terms, or that which can register *within* definitions of this sort, we cannot express what makes each of them an identity or congruence predicate. Quine's method makes what sense it does for us by its surreptitious allusion and dependence upon an idea which is essentially second-order. This is the idea that we can supplant identity by a relation S defined in terms of all the first-level predicates of the language in such a way that (aSb) iff, for any ϕ, $\phi a \equiv \phi b$.

There is a third point. John Wallace has shown that the method of reducing '=' yields even stranger results than any that Quine himself has countenanced. (See Chapter One, footnote 7, for references to Quine. For Wallace see *Philosophical Grammar*, Stanford University Ph.Dd., 1964, published by University Microfilms Ltd, Ann Arbor, Michigan, U.S.A., 1969. See pp. 80ff.) Applied to a theory with the three unanalysed predicates '*x* is a forest', '*x* is a tree' and '*x* grows in *y*', Quine's proposal forces the truth-value false upon the sentence 'In every forest there grows more than one tree'. A defender of the method may claim that such troubles will disappear so soon as we consider first-order theories with expressive power more closely approximating to that of English. Wallace suggests that the claim of eliminability should be rephrased as follows: if a theory has a finite number of unanalysed predicates, then a finite number of predicates can be added to the theory so that in the resulting expanded theory what we usually intend by identity is eliminable by the prescribed method. But now, for purposes at least of the evaluation of the idea that identity is something supervenient on other properties and relations or can be reduced or explained in terms of them, everything depends on what predicates *are* added in order to force the desired truth-value upon sentences involving the constructed predicate that is introduced in lieu of '='. The appearances can only be saved in fact if monadic and polyadic predicates presupposing place-time- or thing-individuation are supplied. It is upon *these* that identity will be supervenient. We are scarcely left with a refutation of the thesis that identity transcends all definition, reduction or analysis.

Quine's unsympathetic attitude (*vide* Chapter One, footnote 1) to the claim that if *a* and *b* are the same then there must exist an answer to the question *same what?* is strange, unless he still identifies it with **R** or assimilates it to some weird doctrine of the semantical incompleteness of '*a* is *b*'. See his review of *Identity and Individuation* (ed. M. K. Munitz, New York University, 1971) at *Journal of Philosophy* vol. LXIX, no. 16, 7 September 1972.

> When we do propound identity conditions for bodies, or persons, or classes we are using the prior concept of identity in the special task of clarifying the term 'body' or 'person' or 'class'; for an essential part of the clarification of a term is clarification of the standard by which we individuate its denotata. (Cp. p. 860, "Worlds Away", *J. Phil.* 1976.)

This is exactly right; at least by my doctrine it is. What is strange is to find the author of those words rejecting **D** when the rationale of the *same what?* question, at least as I see it, is so essentially bound up with the clarification of the standard by which the denotata of an identity sentence are individuated. The point at issue may seem to turn on Quine's 'we are using the *prior concept* of identity'. But a defender of **D** who has rejected Quine's reduction of identity is just as well placed as Quine to say that an identity or coincidence concept (whether $x=y$ or $x\overline{\underset{f}{=}}y$, it makes no odds) pre-exists all particular *principia individuationis*. That is the role of the schema given toward the end of section 1 of Chapter Two. He is even better placed than Quine to exploit the interrelations of substance and identity to effect the elucidation of the one by the other.

I cannot forbear to mention one other anomaly in Quine's position. In his paper 'Identity' (read to the British Association for the Philosophy of Science, summer 1974) Quine gives an account of the genesis of the idea of identity according to which identity begins 'embedded in the ostensive teaching' of sortal terms: embedded in 'same apple as', 'same dog as', before it ascends to the full blown relation. Perhaps this concedes enough actually to settle the issue I have preferred to leave unresolved at *Longer Note* 0.02. See also p. 59, *The Roots of Reference* (LaSalle, Open Court, 1974).

2.08 *Ultimate sortals; and the arguments of Tennant and Stevenson for* $D(ii)$ A sortal concept that is not too high to be individuative of x is called in Chapter Two, section 5, an ultimate sortal for x if and only if it restricts no other sortal concept that is individuative of x. But the argument of that section and its neighbours is intended to dispense with the supposition that for every individual there is an ultimate sortal for it.

From the premiss that every sortal concept restricts some highest sortal concept, *plus* the premiss that cosatisfiable sortals are corestrictive, Neil Tennant gives what I have not given, a formal proof of $D(ii)$. See *Journal of Philosophical Logic* 6, 1977, pp. 223–31. I have learned much from Tennant's work and comments on Chapter Two, and I ought to have learned more. But, in the absence of $D(ii)$ itself, it is not a perfectly straightforward matter to justify either of his premisses. For the first see the dubious argument of note 40 of *Identity and Spatio-Temporal Continuity*, p. 71. The second is not independent of the claim (advanced at p. 33 of *Identity and Spatio-Temporal Continuity* in a defective proof of $D(ii)$) that all cross-classifications that all pairs of sortal concepts can impose on an object must be subordinate to some autonomously individuative sortal concept. (The cross-classifying concepts, that is, must both restrict some common and autonomously individuative sortal concept which resolves the cross-classification.) I see only two ways of justifying such an assumption. One depends on the argument that is being advanced in the text for $D(ii)$. For the other, which depends on prohibiting *all* cross-classification, see *Longer Note* 2.09.

Somewhat similarly, in a manuscript called 'Extensional and Intensional Logic for Sortal-Relative Identity', Leslie Stevenson takes as an axiom (his A.4) the principle that if two sorts overlap then they are both sortal subsets of another sort. He can then provide a formal argument for the conclusion that the relation of being corestrictive between any two sorts f and g—let us represent this as 'f^g', following Tennant—is an equivalence relation over non-empty sorts (for reasons that will become apparent in Chapter Three empty sorts can be ignored): Suppose f^g and g^h. Then for some sort j we have f restricts j and g restricts j; and for some sort k we have g restricts k and h restricts k. g is non-empty, and whatever is in g is in both j and k. So j and k overlap. But then they are corestrictive and j^k. But 'restricts' is transitive. So f^h. Symmetry and reflexivity are obvious.

2.09 *Cross-classification*   The assumption that, if two natural kinds have common members, then either they coincide or one is a subkind of the other is commonly made in the relatively scant modern philosophical literature of this subject. Cf. John Wallace, *Philosophical Grammar*, p. 74–5: 'Natural kind predicates are arranged in a hierarchy. If K_1 and K_2 are natural kind predicates, then either (i) every K_1 is a K_2 or (ii) every K_2 is a K_1 or (iii) no K_1 is a K_2. An *infima species* is a natural kind predicate K_1 such that, for any other natural kind predicate K_2, either every K_1 is a K_2 or no K_1 is a K_2. Everything in the universe falls under at least one, and thus under exactly one, *infima species*.' Similarly in *The Axiomatic Method in Biology*, Cambridge, 1937, p. 42, Woodger defines a hierarchy as a relation **R** which is asymmetrical, one-many, has one and only one beginner, and is such that its converse domain is identical with the terms to which the beginner stands in some power of **R**. See also Richmond Thomason, 'Species, Determinates and natural Kinds' (*Nous* vol. III, 1969, pp. 95–101):

> A taxonomic system S will consist of a set of elements—the natural kinds of S—and a relation $<$ on these elements—the relation of species to genus. We will stipulate that . . . for all natural kinds a, b and c of S: $a <$ a; if $a < b$ and $b < c$ then $a < c$; and if $a < b$ and $b < a$, then $a = b$ . . . Taxonomic systems are characterized by a property which is not in general possessed by semi-lattices: no natural kinds a and b of a taxonomic system overlap unless $a < b$ or $b < a$. The principle of disjointness holds because the natural kinds of a system of classification may be conceived of as obtained by a process of division. The universe is first divided into disjoint sorts (e.g. *animal, vegetable* and *mineral*) then these are further divided into disjoint sorts, and so forth. . . . [M]icrobes [however] appear to be both animal and vegetable. I would prefer to regard such anomalous cases as not falling under the original scheme—e.g. as *neither* animal nor vegetable—thus preserving the principle.

So far as I can judge, there is real promise in Thomason's lattice-theoretic approach to taxonomic systems: but it would be better not to accept his account of classification, and better to replace his disjointness condition by a weaker condition requiring only that every classification be resolved at some higher but properly sortal level. For there are cases where cross-classification is indispensable, and indispensable for compelling theoretical reasons. One such case is illustrated by the figure

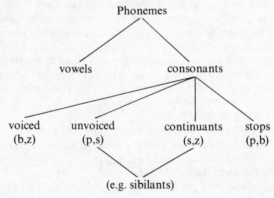

There is no way of rearranging this to expel cross-classifications and achieve the identificatory advantages of a 'key' without breaking up theoretically significant groups. (Cf. p. 80 of Noam Chomsky, *Aspects of the Theory of Syntax,* Cambridge, Mass., MIT, 1965). Another case where it would be a pity to exclude cross-classification is across animal species themselves. If we are interested in evolution and speciation, in what came from what and why, then no doubt genetics (and ultimately molecular biology) must be at the root of what we inquire into. Genetics must organize our taxonomy. But perhaps not everything we shall want to know in order to reconstruct a coherent story of evolution can be intelligibly or usefully stated at that level. We may need to compile our account from quite disparate levels of inquiry not excluding geology, climatology, geography and even (conceivably) history. Now consider the phenomenon of the morphological convergence upon the forms of diverse and genetically remote species by the South American and Australian marsupials, which speciated over and over again to take advantage of the relative lack of competition from other orders or genera and to profit from all the possibilities offered to them on those continents. There is a real point in speaking of the marsupial wolf, the marsupial rodent, the marsupial mole, etc., even though the terms *wolf, mole, rodent* do not have their usual taxonomic sense or purpose here. In this deviant but illuminating extension of their use, these terms now impose a cross-classification upon animals. Again, I suppose, it is a real possibility that ethology might have to reclassify animals across the grain of a genetically based taxonomy. *Cetacea,* for instance, may not, relative to *all* interests, possess a uniformity of behaviour commensurable with their close genetic affinities. For some ethological purposes, perhaps, some members of that genus may need to be compared with creatures that are not mammalian at all. And all of them in certain important respects resemble non-mammalian creatures more closely than they resemble most mammalian ones. It is no criticism of taxonomy that it must ignore such facts, but that does not make them unimportant. Cf. also Howard Kahane, 'Thomason on Natural Kinds', *Nous* IV, 1970, especially p. 410.

That zoological sortals have appeared to philosophers to form a hierarchy properly subject to Thomason and Wallace's overstringent conditions probably results from the evolutionary character of the material that the zoologist has been called upon to bring into order.

Admittedly, not all taxonomists have been evolutionists. But, as their relevance has become clearer, questions of evolution have only sharpened an antecedent appreciation of such structural features of organisms as the fusion of scaphoid and lunare in all *Carnivores* however diverse. Even before its evolutionary significance is understood, one may see that such a feature *must* be important without yet knowing quite *why* it is important. Surely, on any adequate view, the two concerns, with evolution and organization, are not opposed but *presupposed* to one another.

The hierarchical arrangement of zoological sortals in a species-genus tree diagram results from the formal relationship between this kind of diagram and the evolutionary dendrogram from which, in the presence of other information and decisions, it can be transcribed. But this hierarchical arrangement seems to rest on a wholly contingent fact—the one-many property, within the common subject-matter of pre- and post-Darwinian taxonomy, of the relation 'evolves into' in the field of animal species. (Even here sibling species such as the fruit flies, *Drosophila pseudoobscura* and *Drosophila persimilis* might count as some sort of exception; and perhaps it is not utterly impossible, even if it is genetically nearly inconceivable, that the phenomenon of convergence within quite diverse species should give rise to the same difficulty.) Although zoology provides the most imposing and striking example of a system of sortal classification, its rather special formal character has over-impressed perhaps.

It is true that, if all taxonomies were set up by a method of dichotomous division, then all classes separated on any particular level would be disjoint, and overlapping would be simply impossible at any level. Indeed any taxonomy would be instantly recognizable as a tree, or a hierarchy in Woodger's sense. But such a gain is quite illusory if it is achieved by dichotomy. You cannot say what a thing is by saying what it is not, for at least half of the terms on such a tree would not be sortal terms. This and the other objections have been well known since Aristotle (cf. *De Partibus Animalium* 642^{bs}ff.), indeed since Plato (cf. *Politicus* 262^D). See p. 121ff. of H. W. B. Joseph, *Introduction to Logic,* 2nd edn, Oxford, 1916. The real reason for holding that cross-classifications must be resolved lies neither here nor in the properties of zoological sorts (nor for that matter in Aristotle's doctrine of the unity of definition and the recoverability of the species from the last differentia), but in the argument in Chapter Two for **D**(ii). See also *Longer Note* 2.10.

Cross-classifications that are resolved under a higher sort do not ultimately disturb a system of natural kinds. It is always (say) animals that are under study; and different classifications will not import different identity or persistence conditions for particular animals. There is no reason, however, to rule out *a priori* one other possibility: this is that the matter to be discovered in a certain place at a certain time may sometimes be usefully categorized at such widely different levels of explanation or theory that these categorizations are not commensurable with one another at all. There need be no common or agreed identification of what is there. This does not imply disagreement between identifications. It implies distinctness in the entities identified. Radically different kinds of thing may co-occupy some portion of space. (Cf. Chapter Five *passim.*)

2.10 *Overlapping of sortal concepts, supposedly without agreement in the corresponding principle of individuation* Nicholas Griffin has complained about this demonstration that it assumes that no two substance sortal concepts can overlap. Cf. *Relative Identity,* p. xi, and note 18, p. 84.

In dealing with sortals subordinate to ultimate sortals Wiggins is prepared to avoid 'unrealistic and absurd prohibitions on cross-classification' (*Identity and Spatio-Temporal Continuity*, p. 33). . . . He gives an example from Chomsky's *Aspects of Syntax*, p. 80, to illustrate cross-classification among sorts. (Footnote 39, *Identity and Spatio-Temporal Continuity* [see now *Longer Note* 2.8].) It is surprising that he assumes without argument that such features do not extend to ultimate sortals.

But there is no question of merely assuming. The defects and obscurities in the version of the argument that Griffin criticizes in his chapter five have long since been recognized by those who want nevertheless to accept **D**(ii). (See p. 112 in Shoemaker, *op. cit.*, *Philosophical Review* 1970.) But Griffin appears to have misunderstood the status of all arguments of the kind offered by Stevenson, Tennant or myself for **D**(ii). They are not intended to consolidate arguments of the kind given at Chapter One, section 2 and section 7 example (λ), for seeing '*x* is the same f as *y*' as absolute or Leibnizian. The intention is exactly the other way about: it is to base **D**(ii) upon the absoluteness of identity, independently credited, and upon any other beliefs that are indispensable to our actual ontology and conceptual scheme. See the argument of Chapter Two, sections 4 following.

The reason why any two sortal concepts under which one individual entity falls must be restrictions of some common sortal concept—why any two cosatisfiable concepts are corestrictive—is given by the argument in the text. Either the two sortal concepts are finally subject to the same individuative principle, or they are not. If they are subject to the same principle then it must be possible to find or frame a sortal concept that they both restrict. If they are not finally subject to the same individuative principle, then we are not guaranteed against the possibility of contradiction (**R**) or indeterminacy if we trace an entity under these distinct individuative principles, which (in so far as they are not concordant) potentially disagree at some point.

2.11. *Indeterminate particulars*   I should certainly allow that there were indeterminate particulars lying outside the direct ambit of the argument for **D**(ii). For instance, there are numerous temporally indeterminate terms that we employ in order to talk about matter or stuff. We speak of bars of soap, pats of butter, lumps of cheese, pools of water, pots of stew and so on. It is not clear exactly what to say about these terms. So far as persistence and reidentification over time is concerned, their status is manifestly inferior to that of the fully fledged continuants that fall clearly inside the scope of **D**(ii). It seems plain that a good account of them will not regiment them, or force upon them the well-drilled ways of true substances, or the equally well-drilled ways of quantities in the sense of Russell or Helen Morris Cartwright. (See her 'Quantities', *Philosophical Review* Jan. 1970; because the criteria of identity through time for strict quantities exclude the diminution of the amount of stuff that is in question, a bar of soap is not the same thing as a quantity of soap, in the strict sense.) I imagine that a good account will illuminate rather the various purposes that give a point to our use of such terms, and will show how these purposes make it possible for us both to live with temporal indeterminacy and to tolerate the fuzziness of identity questions, diachronic *and* synchronic, concerning the irregulars that fall under them. Some of the same difficulties may arise in a relatively milder form with artifact terms. (See below Chapter Three, section 4.) Artifact terms are not exactly like such lump-mass terms, but maybe a clear treatment of the one will help to liberate us from the preconceptions that make it difficult for us to give a clear account of the other. When we have this we shall also know what to make of the difference between orderly biological thing-kinds and less orderly kinds, such as *mountain, hill* or *puddle*. Perhaps a mountain or hill is best seen as approximating to something like a great *lump* of rock and earth, for instance. Maybe a puddle approximates to a small *stretch* of water. Such terms seem to lie on the borderline between true substance terms and what might be denominated lump-mass terms. It is not a formal but a scientific question, however, whether a sufficiently rich theory is forthcoming to resolve the indeterminacies and possible individuative arbitrariness of putative natural kinds such as *lake* or *spring* or *mountain*.

3.09 *Coinciding and splitting*   1. In a fuller treatment than mine, more will need to be said to protect the Chapter Two thesis that x and y's f-coinciding (i) entails the community of the properties of x and y, and (ii) precludes the intervention of *splitting*. It may be necessary to incorporate in the account of f-coinciding, for given sort f, not only the holding of the laws and lawlike norms whose holding is presupposed to the instantiation of the kind f, but also some stipulation against certain kinds of abnormal and extreme interference with those environmental and other conditions under which specimens can be treated and individuated as individual continuants. A full treatment of (ii) could scarcely be achieved outside an adequate philosophy of biology, or without a lengthy inquiry into the identification, and then the significance for the theory of individuation, of the environmental conditions under which the animals and plants that we are prepared to treat as individual substances will maintain themselves homeostatically as living organisms, and are adapted to pursue systemically integral and individual existences within the norms of coming to be and passing away which are associated in the world as it is with their particular species.

2. It is important that, so far from being a mere escape-clause violating the *Only a and b* Rule justified in sect. 4, Ch. Three, a determination for a given kind of what constituted normal environmental conditions would be (i) kind-specific, (ii) a matter for empirical inquiry, and (iii) such as to sustain certain subjunctive conditionals. In so far as individuation was a concern for this determination, it would have access to the formal properties of Leibnizian identity, and could deploy these in advance of a detailed account of the norms of the persisting and coinciding of f-specimens. There is nothing circular about this. There is nothing arbitrary either. Contrast the stipulation theory treated in *Longer Note* 3.19.

3. For the application of all this to persons, see Chapter Six, section 7

following; and for the problem of the twinning of a zygote see *Longer Note* 6.27.

4. Students of philosophy are taught to shun, as remnants of bankrupted scholastic philosophies (which I have a more selective and correspondingly keener interest in condemning than those who opt here for comprehensive condemnation—cf. Chapter Four, footnote 27 and principle Θ), concepts like that of the *normal* or the *characteristic*. It is a historical fact that these concepts have been wildly abused and exploited to make many absurd and empty claims that may be here passed over in silence. But the serious and pertinent point, which should motivate a fresh attempt to elucidate them in realistic post-Darwinian terms, is that there are some scientific purposes for which they are needed, and that students of philosophy are never supplied with the recipe for rewriting essential occurrences of these predicates in those definitions and assertions which are both true and indispensable to biological science. An undirected search, by one with no technical knowledge of where to look, rapidly gleaned a crop of examples of which I shall transcribe only two.

> Regulation denotes the extensive power embryonic forms of life have to continue a normal or approximately normal development or regeneration in spite of experimental interference by ablation, addition (implantation), exchange (transplantation), fusion, etc. . . . The processes thus revealed operate in all embryos to a greater or lesser extent. (Needham, *Biochemistry and Morphogenesis*.)

> The DNA . . . functions as the information store, which contains a permanent record of the individual's organizational potential. However, the characteristic activities of the individual, and furthermore his specific activity at a given time, depends upon which sections of the information encoded in the DNA are being expressed and also the relative rates at which the information contained in the various sections is being transcribed. Thus the activity which we hold to be characteristic is not expressed by describing DNA alone, since the interchanges between the organism and the environment are the factors that determine what sections of DNA are to be transcribed at a particular time and the rates of transcription. (J. Z. Young, *An Introduction to the Study of Man*.)

5. I expect that it may be necessary to emphasize that, in stressing the irreducibility of these occurrences of 'normal' and 'characteristic', I am not saying absurdly that an abnormal f-specimen is not an f. At most the thesis of Chapter Three commits me to saying that the norm for an f is (a) nomologically conditioned and (b) *that by reference to which* the distinction between being an f and not being an f at all is determined.

3.19. *Identity in the absence of a rival candidate* What has been said in the literature on this topic has mostly concerned personal identity. Much of it has been directed at Bernard Williams's celebrated example ('Personal Identity and Individuation' *Proceedings of the Aristotelian Society* LVII, 1956–57) of a twentieth-century man with a convincing semblance of all of Guy Fawkes's memories and character. Many philosophers have suggested in reply to Williams that we should simply stipulate that, *provided* that there is no other claimant, or no other equally plausible claimant, the man counts as Guy Fawkes.

At first sight the proposal looks even worse than it is. For it seems to be straightforwardly circular to stipulate that the man is Guy Fawkes provided there do not exist two *different* claimants. But this is no difficulty for the stipulator. Leibniz's Law provides a sufficient criterion of difference, even though it provides none of sameness. So we can tell claimants apart by their qualities. The objection will then become: what if distinct candidates are qualitatively identical? The stipulator's reply to this question will be that in that case the distinctness will have to be established by reference to spatio-temporal position. Against this, at last, the objector can make a fair point on Williams's behalf: this throws us back onto a framework of material things needing to be individuated by a more autonomous set of individuative procedures—e.g. the procedures defended in Chapter Two. Which takes us right back to the place where we started.

That is the first difficulty. The second difficulty arises from the following question: if we want to follow the stipulationist's advice and make the ruling of identity between the plausible claimant and Guy Fawkes, how far in space or time do we first have to search for a rival claimant? There is no limit, unless we have a theory about the genesis and behaviour of the kind of thing in question. The only theory we do in fact possess is one about how persons move and persist *as embodied*. But this theory the 'no distinct rival candidate' theorist (like every other kind of play-it-by-ear theorist) is already engaged in undermining. So too are we, if we allow the latter-day claimant any title at all to be Guy Fawkes. (It is no use saying that it is most unlikely that there is a competitor. It was unlikely that there would be even one seriously plausible twentieth-century claimant, but why, if there were *one,* would another one somewhere be so very strange or unlikely?) In the presence of the better sort of evidence of continuity 'the f at t_i = the g at t_j' appears (unless there is a very peculiar choice of f or g) to be a decidable sort of proposition. If the proposed criterion were correct, however, then its decidability in principle would be much more mysterious than we normally find it to be.

The third difficulty (see Chapter Three) is that, if the stipulation theorists had their way, then it would have to make sense to say to the Guy Fawkes claimant: 'If it hadn't been for that other fellow, who appears to be just as good as you are at reminiscing about attempts to blow up the Palace of Westminster, *you* would have been Guy Fawkes.' Even those who doubt that, if one is Guy Fawkes, one is necessarily Guy Fawkes must find this idea hard to take seriously. Cf Williams's discussions in 'Bodily Continuity and Personal Identity', *Analysis* 21, 1960, a discussion independent of modality but all of a piece with the idea that identity is the kind of relation that holds, *if* it holds, of necessity. (Which helps to distinguish identity from any degree you like to mention of similarity.) See also G. C. Nerlich, 'Sameness, Difference and Continuity', *Analysis* 18, 1958, and 'Continuity Continued', *Analysis* 21, 1960; and C. B. Martin 'Identity and Exact Similarity', *Analysis* 18, 1958. For the opposite point of view see, e.g., J. M. Shorter, 'More about Bodily Continuity and Personal Identity', *Analysis* 22, 1962; and Bruce Langtry, *Australasian Journal of Philosophy* vol. 53, no. 1, 1975.

3.22 *Artifact identity and problems of vagueness* When we face such questions we have to decide a question that is vague. When was the original artifact finally lost to the world? We can make a decision to count a time *t* as the very last moment of the original object's existence and refuse to nominate any moment as the first moment of the completion of the replacement of the object. Or we can make our decision the other way round. (The problem lacks the determinacy of the first moment of motion versus last moment of rest problem—on which see 'The *De Re* "Must" ', *op. cit., Preface* (5)). What the vagueness of the problem in no way justifies us in doing, however, is to decide it *both ways round,* with original and successor both overlapping and violating the regulative principle that two concrete substances of the very same kind cannot be in exactly the same place at exactly the same time (Cf. Locke, *Essay* II, 28.1: 'We never finding, nor conceiving it possible, that two things *of the same kind* should exist in the same place at the same time, we rightly conclude that, whatever exists anywhere at any time, excludes *all of the same kind,* and is there itself alone.')

There are certain to be people who will object against me that there would be nothing to prevent one from *defining* a new and previously unmentioned entity—an entity whose first moment of existence was after the first moment of the original artifact and which *spanned* the period in which lay the rationalizing Dedekindian cut just described. This object survived well into the lifetime of the successor of the original object, they will say, and does occupy the same place at some of the same times as was occupied by the original artifact and the entity that the rationalizing criterion counts as its successor. And so much the worse, they would say, for the discussion in Chapter Three.

So long as we hold onto the regulative principle, the only possible defence of the Chapter Three proposal is to show that the overlapping entity is ill defined. But surely it *is* ill defined, being the temporal counterpart of spatially incongruous entities like the animal Tib, which is Tibbles *minus* his tail, even though Tibbles has a tail (Cf. my 'On Being in the Same Place at the Same Time', *Phil. Review* 1968, op. cit. *Preface* (1)). It is in the nature of artifacts to come into existence by being made. This is one of their few near-lawlike features. We can of course define the mereological aggregate which is this or that parcel of matter, but this is not the artifact. If we are interested in *artifacts* we have to look for them, and find out when they were made and when they were finally destroyed or dissipated. We cannot settle the date of their manufacture by a definitional decree.

In these connexions I have wondered whether what I have said agrees or disagrees with Kripke's extremely brief footnote 18 'Naming and Necessity', *op. cit.,* 'where the identity relation is vague it may seem intransitive. . . . It seems . . . utopian to suppose that we will ever reach a level of ultimate basic particulars for which identity relations are never vague and the danger of intransitivity is eliminated. The danger does not arise in practice so we can ordinarily speak simply of identity without worry.' The last remark quoted seems obviously correct. But I hope, by describing some of the safety mechanisms which could operate to protect our conceptual practice, to have removed all semblance of vagueness ever resulting in the identity relation's even *seeming* to be intransitive. It is not so much that the identity relation is vague as that vagueness and indeterminacy infect the question of *where the boundary is* beyond which we cannot apply the notion safely.

3.24. *Reply to an objection to the deictic–nomological doctrine of natural kinds*   1. It is in the spirit of the view of natural kind substantives that we have traced back from Putnam and Kripke to Leibniz and Aristotle to predict that, as physical theory progresses, a point will be reached where substance kinds originally specified by something tantamount to a direct or indirect deictic/nomological method will be redefined in a new way that is at once nominal *and* scientific, in fact real—but real in a sense that is barely provided for by my usage, since the new way is not clearly deixis-dependent. It is true that by my usage the new definitions can count as real—cf. *Preamble,* section 7—just to the extent that I can still insist that they are found, or are corrigible, in a manner that is residually or indirectly extension-dependent. But it may seem that, so soon as this sort of redescription becomes possible, the distinction of extension-involving and not extension-involving loses its whole importance.

2.   To anyone who advanced this objection, I should reply that the fact—if it were a fact—that it was possible in some cases to supersede our distinction between extension-involvingness and its opposite would scarcely demonstrate the dispensability of the distinction for the cases that I have been principally concerned with (viz. ordinary macroscopic persisting substance, not theoretical entities or elements of chemistry and physics). Still less could the new option demonstrate the dispensability of the distinction for purposes of understanding the conceptual cum individuative scheme that *makes possible* the complete definitions—or causal definitions as Leibniz calls them at *Nouveaux Essais* III, 3.18—that accrue to a science when it is on the way to completion.

3.   There is one yet more important respect in which the distinction between the extension involving and the not extension involving predicates lives on after the arrival of real or causal definitions. Even when expanded scientific definitions supplant deictic nomological ones, we shall be able to recover and redescribe what is almost the same distinction by using a new *ratio divisionis*: that between concepts that have theoretically rich and significant real marks and concepts whose lack of theoretical significance makes the

answer they give to the *what is it* question theoretically bare and nomologically utterly unspecific.

4. I hope that the points urged in paragraph 2 above will go some way to cover the case in science that several people, including Hugh Mellor (cf. 'Natural Kinds', *British Journal of the Philosophy of Science* 28, 1977) and Bernard Williams, have urged me to consider (though both stuffs and theoretical entities lie outside the self-imposed limitations of this book). The case is this: on the basis of the deictic and nomological determination of a structure of kinds like the periodic table, further possibly unexemplified kinds or elements can be given an abstract specification.

[A] Some archetypal natural kinds have the wrong archetypes; [B] others have none at all. Consider elements high in the periodic table that do not occur in nature and have never been made. We have names for them, but there may never be archetypes to constrain our use of the names. Even if specimens eventually appear, the discovery, creation or synthesis of previously unknown fundamental particles, elements and compounds can surely be *predicted*. The term 'neutrino' applied to just the same particles when it was used to predict their existence as it has applied to since their discovery. (Mellor, *op. cit.*)

[B], which is the immediate question, I shall treat first. [A] will be treated in paragraphs 6–8.

5. Under [B] I would remark that this possibility depends upon a sort of cantilevering process (a phrase I borrow from Gareth Evans) which would be impossible in the absence of the whole going concern that I have tried to describe. It is true that, given all the support that the going concern provides, there is nothing to prevent a name from being introduced in such a way that it appears at the outset simply to abbreviate a description that a scientist arrives at on the basis of this theory, speculatively. But even here the new description is corrigible by reference to the extension *if* such can be found, produced or manufactured. The onus of match is from the description to the extension *if there be one.* And, where the element is indeed unexemplified, we are surely in a second best position—most especially from the point of view of testing the predictions that Mellor speaks of. Even under the special circumstances he adduces of elements very high in the periodic table, and even where the status of the name is provisional, it will not quite do to treat the name as simply standing proxy for the description that elucidates its meaning. The name *aspires* to the normal condition that has been described by Putnam and Kripke and to home upon that to which it answers—upon something that is however remotely and indirectly identifiable.

6. Concerning Mellor's point [A], and the need for the deictic/nomological doctrine to make room for correction of first conceptions of a natural kind term's extension, see section 1 of Chapter Three, especially the passage to which footnotes 5 and 6 are annexed; and see Leibniz's anticipations at *Nouveaux Essais* 4, vi.4 of the difficulties that Mellor finds in Putnam's

example of water on Earth and Twin-Earth (in 'The meaning of "Meaning" ', *Mind, Language and Reality* vol. 2, Cambridge, 1975, pp. 215–71—an article I have nowhere appealed to, preferring, *vide* footnote 1, Chapter Three, the more economical and less easily sidetracked argument of his first article on this theme). Particularly pertinent is Leibniz's discussion of the options that would exist if it were discovered that more than one stuff-species answered to the name 'gold', which we had previously treated as a specific stuff-name (and wanted to continue to treat as specific—contrast 'jade').

7. As regards natural kinds being defined by the wrong archetypes. Mellor asks what is to be made by Putnam of isotopes of elements, especially when these occur naturally in actual samples that have been used to fix the references of element names.

It is undeniable that the extension of 'chlorine' included both isotopes before their discovery and so presumably includes both isotopes now. What Putnam must say is that chlorine [has] been found not to be a natural kind after all, but rather [a] mixture of natural kinds (*op. cit.,* p. 303).

But there is no 'must' about it, and this is a different sort of case from water on Earth and Twin-Earth, and from jade and jadeite. Here the proper reaction is not to split the reference, or correct the first *deixis,* or purify the original conception of the extension of the element, but rather to elaborate upon the role of the *nomological* component in reference-determination.

8. In fact, so far from undermining Putnam's doctrine of kinds, the special questions that arise where the fundamental properties of atomic weight and atomic number diverge illustrate vividly the virtues of the theory. Nothing is better consonant with the theory than the resolution of these questions in the idea that what matters is what is fundamental in the explanation of chemical reactions. (That is the electron shell, and the atomic number.) The doctrine explains and rationalizes the decision not to split the element into two natural kinds. What happened was a reasoned decision in favour of a notion of relevant similitude that embraces both isotopes under one element.

9. It may be instructive to compare Putnam's account with W. V. Quine's. See 'Natural Kinds' (work cited at footnote 2 of Chapter Three): 'Things are similar in the . . . theoretical sense to the degree that they are interchangeable parts of the cosmic machine revealed by science. . . . More literally could things be said to be similar in proportion to how much of scientific theory would remain true on interchanging those things as objects of reference in the theory.'

10. I will conclude with a remark about Frege and a remark about Leibniz. (i) The opposition Mellor sees between Frege's semantic theory and Putnam's and Kripke's account of natural kind substantives is partly illusory. See references cited at Chapter Three, footnote 3. What is at issue is *at most* a correction in detail to the account of how particular classes of expression make their contribution to truth-conditions. The framework of the theory of sense and reference is unaffected. (ii) For Leibniz a real

definition is a definition that proves the possibility of something's satisfying it. (This is not to be confused with the idea that a real definition is one which is guaranteed free of mistakes.) His usage and mine are linked as follows: a substantive which requires an elucidation that is extension-involving in my sense is precisely a predicate that admits or requires real definition in his sense. For a substantive such that any definition of it is *corrigible* by reference to compliants must also be such that it *can* have compliants.

4.02 *Possible worlds and identity* 1. The regulative maxim to dispense entirely with possible worlds arises not from any settled aversion to these— that would be as premature as uncritical enthusiasm—but from the conviction that possible world construction in the manner of Saul Kripke can begin only at a point after the resolution of the questions of identity and essence that I am concerned with. It would also appear that, if what follows is correct, then such vexed questions as the identity of origin must be resolved by means independent of possible world construction.

2. A possible world, if it corresponds in the way Kripke envisages to a *supposition,* is incompletely specified (radically indeterminate in fact) if no identification is given of the entities supposedly referred to or mentioned in the supposition that it corresponds to. It will be recalled that this is how the otherwise intractable problem of identifying individuals across worlds is resolved. To identify the supposition (the relevant world) we need to know *already* which entity is which within it. (Unless for some reason nothing hangs on this, and an arbitrary individual will do. But then we are outside the ambit of any interest in identity as such.)

3. In making this claim of the priority of ' = ', I associate myself with (even if in the claims of the next paragraph I shall trespass beyond) Kripke's own wise and commonsensical observation that possible worlds are not things we discover or observe with a telescope, but are constructions of ours; and that they are projections from the suppositions that *we* make and set ourselves to explore. What that must imply is that, if some supposition concerns a certain individual (some possible world contains a certain individual), then it is up to the supposer to specify which individual it is. He does not read off—indeed, if he needed to, he could not read off—from the text of his own supposition which individual is involved in the supposition. (There is an affinity here with the case for the irreducibility of identity as that is argued at *Longer Note* 2.03.) I draw the conclusion that those who use the method of possible worlds to determine the answers to questions of necessity and identity or necessity and origin are using a mistaken method. (Whether or not they are reaching conclusions that are true. About necessity of origin I am a militant agnostic.)

4. Note that there has been no suggestion yet that we have complete freedom in this matter of supposing, or possible world construction. But an inquiry into the limitations upon such constructions will only confirm the contention that questions of identity are logically prior to the questions about the canons of possible world construction.

5. It is agreed between Kripke and any essentialist of my kind that we are not free to construct any world we wish, and that we cannot exploit the postulational or constructional approach to worlds and individuals in order to insert just any individual we please into any arbitrary role or kind in any old possible world. Unless anything can be anything—and the demonstration of **D**(ii) in Chapter Two was meant to show the high conceptual cost of that idea (compare sections 9 and 11 of Chapter Four)—it is not open to us to construct a possible world in which Julius Caesar is a clay pipe or a paddle steamer or the number fifty-seven. But then I think it follows that the required understanding of the restrictions on possible world construction has to be supplied from outside the theoretical framework of possible worlds. What is surely required is the extension and application of the ideas which have already given us **D**(ii) of Chapter Two and all the other individuative principles recently proposed to the reader's natural understanding of identity. When this extension and application is complete, however, and when our essentialism is extended to embrace a certain principle of the necessity of identity (see section 3, Chapter Four), it will provide for those who require it the best possible *intuitive* justification of Kripke's apparatus for possible world construction.

4.11. *The Barcan proof of the necessity of identity*   Cumbersome though it now appears, our form of the Barcan derivation removes two other difficulties from the orthodox formulations of the necessity of identity.

1. First, a minor difficulty is removed because there is no question, in the NEC version, of a necessary *truth*'s having the contingent consequence of the existence of the evening star, or of the inference from '*Fa*' to '*a* exists' needing to be impugned. 'H is necessarily P' is not put forward as a necessary truth. It is a truth about *de re* necessity.

2. Second, the restricted scope of NEC also removes what seemed once to be a more intractable difficulty. At least in the □ version by which Prior, Lemmon and Quine made it known to the philosophical world, Miss Barcan's proof was wide open to the charge that, when one forms the predicate *necessarily identical with x* (which is taken to determine a property and then argued to belong to *y* if it belongs to *x*), the proof is involved in the manufacture of a very dubious property. For if 'necessarily (. . . = Hesperus)' can turn out true or false of Venus, depending merely on how that planet is referred to—and the position of the sceptic was precisely that he was sure that the resulting sentence *does* turn out as false if 'Phosphorus' is put into the open place—, then evidently 'necessarily (. . . = Hesperus)' expresses no genuine condition on objects and determines no property of any kind. (Cf. Cartwright, *op. cit.,* at Chapter One, footnote 8; also Ayer 'Internal Relations', *Proceedings of the Aristotelian Society* Suppl. vol., 1935.) In that case 'necessarily identical with Hesperus' determines no property that is even a candidate to be transferred *à la* Leibniz from Hesperus to Phosphorus. In response to this objection the only way to prove *necessarily identical with Hesperus* to be a genuinely Leibnizian predicable was, I think, to find a form

for the open sentence '____ is necessarily identical with . . .' which was manifestly *de re* and in which the surface structure of the English adverb 'necessarily' was carried across into a logical form in which terms are *shown* falling outside the scope of that adverb.

3. I say this was the only way to proceed because otherwise, unless the contingency theorist is half convinced already, the argument moves round and round in a circle. There are many philosophers who are quite unconfused about the difference between necessity and *a priority* but share the late E. J. Lemmon's conviction that the theoremhood of '$x = y \supset \square (x = y)$' must at all costs be avoided.

4. The necessity theorist may say to the sceptic: 'Surely if Hesperus = Phosphorus in the actual world, we cannot construct a possible world in which Hesperus is Z without *ipso facto* making Phosphorus Z.' But the contingency theorist can justifiably reply that the $\square$ version of the theorem is already packed into the conception of possible worlds that delivers this result and delivers Kripke's conception of a rigid designator. And he was not party to that conception.

5. The sceptic, confronted with the fact (cf. the Russellian approach of Smullyan, 'Modality and Description', *Journal of Symbolic Logic* 13, 1948) that he cannot prove the dubiety of the credentials of necessary identity predicates by reference to the sensitivity of the context 'necessarily (___ = . . .)' to different definite descriptions, may perfectly fairly reply that there is no scope ambiguity in proper names, and that proper names suffice (in the manner exhibited in the previous paragraph) to make his point. Proper names are not uniformly intersubstitutable in 'probably' contexts. So why should they be in the for all one knows equally opaque 'necessarily' contexts? One would scarcely wish to be able to prove by a proof similar to Miss Barcan's, simply replacing the sentence operator 'necessarily' by the sentence operator 'probably', that if x is y then probably x is y. But again the best response (I hold) is a derivation with the argument place for a term standing outside the 'necessarily' context. See now my *Preface, op. cit.* (9).

4.24. *Conceptual limitations upon existence and conceptual limitations upon change when once existent* Essentialists have sometimes presented their theories in such a way as to create the impression that they confuse with one another the questions in each of the following pairs.

A.1. Could this set have had different members?
A.2. Could this set change its members?

B.1. Could this rat have been a toad?
B.2. Could this rat turn into a toad?

The need for the distinction between these questions is urged by Kripke at 'Naming and Necessity', footnote 57. If the questions that are paired here were conflated it would be all too easy to use the Leibnizian theory of section

9 to answer *no* to B.2, or to take over and adapt, for purposes of answering *no* to A.2, an argument of Richard Sharvey's, *op. cit.* note 17, p.113:

> Any apparently variable class [e.g. the class of Supreme Court Justices] would have to be identical (at any given [1969] time) to some class that does *not* change its members [e.g. the 1969 class of Supreme Court Justices]. So that at that time Leibniz's Law would be violated. Therefore such a variable class cannot exist . . . indeed, in virtue of Leibniz's Law, there is a strong sense in which there can be no such thing as temporary identity.

One might then represent these arguments as entailing the answer *no* to A.1 and B.1. That would short-circuit the whole line of argument that is pursued in Chapter Four.

Neither A.1 and A.2 nor B.1 and B.2 mean the same; and, so far from depending on the conflation, the argument of Chapter Four is aimed directly and specifically at the questions A.1 and B.1. It is a bonus of this particular procedure, however, that a negative answer to A.1 and B.1 smooths a road to the correct and negative answer to A.2 and B.2. For the questions are related thus: whether a thing can submit to a certain kind of change or not depends on what it essentially is.

It may also be as well to reassure the reader that nowhere in Chapter Four is there at work the illusion that 'it is false that anything can be just anything' entails 'of each thing it holds that there is some substance predicate that it must satisfy'. We are arguing separately in section 9 and elsewhere, recapitulating **D**(ii) of Chapter Two, that the latter is true. And, as a bonus, the argument that is to be presented illuminates *why* it is false that anything can be just anything.

One more clarification of the argument of Chapter Four is in place. Of course the inconceivability of Julius Caesar's not being a man is not logical inconceivability. The point of calling a sentence a logical truth in the narrow sense is that its denial can be shown by logic alone to involve contradiction. A logical truth is a truth forced upon us by the meanings of the logical constants. By this criterion not even 'all bachelors are unmarried' qualifies. Because logical necessity in the useful and strict sense is exigent, the species of possibility which is its dual is hopelessly permissive. 'But it's logically possible that not-Q' is the principal weapon in some analytical or Humean philosophers' armoury. It is a useless one though—unless they mean by 'it's logically possible' 'it's conceptually possible'. But that is nearly always the *question at issue,* and one may need to have thought into the *implications* of Q to decide that question. Logic alone (in the serious or strict sense) will seldom suffice for that. Where available, definitions can help supply what is needed. But we have claimed that individuals such as Caesar have no explicit verbal definition. We are now exploring what in effect plays the constraining role in our thinking about the entity Caesar that a definition plays in constraining thought about bachelors. And we must not not be browbeaten here by the scornful contempt of those who prefer to this labour the lighter work of simply asserting of almost anything they please that they can conceive almost anything at all of it.

4.32. *Necessity of constitution*   At his footnote 56 of *Naming and Necessity*, Saul Kripke gives an argument for the necessity of constitution which is quite different from the arguments for the necessity of origin that we have tentatively rejected at footnote 22. The argument is a separate and formal argument: If we allow that $A \supset \square \Diamond A$, then $a \neq b \supset \square (a \neq b)$. For suppose (1), $a \neq b$. Then by $A \supset \square \Diamond A$ we have (2) $- \Diamond - \Diamond (a \neq b)$. Now suppose (3) $- \square(a \neq b)$. Then we have (4) $\Diamond (a = b)$. Then, by $(a = b) \equiv (\square (a = b)$ and the intersubstitution of logical equivalents, (5) $\Diamond \square (a = b)$. But this gives (6) $\Diamond - \Diamond (a \neq b)$ which contradicts (2). (3) is to blame. So on the supposition of (1) we have $\sim$ (3), viz. $\square (a \neq b)$. Therefore $(a \neq b) \supset \square (a \neq b)$.

Given $(a \neq b) \supset \square (a \neq b)$, then, Kripke's argument goes as follows.

Let 'A' be a name of a table, 'B' name the piece of wood from which it actually came. Let 'C' name another piece of wood. Then suppose A were made from B, as in the actual world, but also another table D were made from C. . . . now in this situation $B \neq D$; hence, even if D were made by itself, and no table were made from A. D would not be B.

For if $B \neq$ table D, wood D is necessarily not table D.

If I venture to reject this argument too, it is because the constitution relation which holds between A and B and between C and D is presumably a tensed relation. Identity and difference are not tensed, and need to be sharply distinguished from constitution. (See Chapter One, especially sections 6, 7, and footnote 17).

5.15. *Discrimination without identification*   Michael Ayers ('Individuals without Sortals', *op. cit.*, pp. 114–16) took issue with this opinion, as it first figured in *Identity and Spatio-Temporal Continuity*, on the grounds that it seemed to him to make impossible the singling out of something as yet unidentified; and on the grounds that such unidentified things can in any case be singled out 'as natural unities or natural structures which come into existence, continue to exist, and cease to exist quite independently of any conceptualizing on our part, [the] principle of unity in each case [being] causal'. (Cf. Eli Hirsch, 'Physical Identity', *Philosophical Review* 1976, pp. 360–1: 'a child raised on a farm who has never seen a car. . . . [is] shown a blue car moving across an open field . . . [he] is immediately in the position to say "that big blue thing (with the four round black things on the bottom) is moving across the field" '.) So far as mind-independence or realism goes, and so far as the importance of causal principles of unity is concerned, I hope it is clear that the disagreement that Ayers seems to have expected simply does not exist. The point that Ayers seems to me to overlook in his optimistic use of a primitive notion of 'natural unity', and in his pessimistic view of the conceptualists's chances of describing naturally and correctly the singling out of an as yet unidentified thing, is that, if a man picks up some strange thing and, not yet knowing what it is, keeps it in his pocket or his desk drawer, then the diachronically stable mode of persistence which it promises or exemplifies *cannot help*, in the kinds of case Ayers describes, but provide the man with the assurance that (∃f) (f is a well defined thing kind, and this strange thing belongs in f). On our account of singling out it is perfectly possible for a thinker to qualify as singling something out, as being in the right *rapport* for that, without *knowing* what he is singling out or having any in the context informative answer to the question what he has singled it out *as*. (Cf. MacIntyre, 'Essence and Existence', *op. cit.*, note 24, Chapter Four.) It will be illuminating to compare generally with the question of discrimination without identification the fact that one can observe (directly) one event make another happen and witness thereby (on the neo-Humean view) the exemplification of a nomological regularity of which nevertheless one has no inkling (cf. Donald Davidson, 'Causal Relations', *Journal of Philosophy* 1967).

The theory that Ayers is criticizing was not in the first instance a theory of recognition or perceptual discrimination at all. (Though the truism that there is no such thing as a merely determinable thing ready to be dressed and undressed with different suits of conceptual clothes must no doubt have certain *implications* for such a theory, and no theory must entail that there are things which there cannot be.) The theory Ayers attacked was a theory of identity—of what it it is for this entity to be distinct from that entity, and of the determination (which turns out to resist all characterization by a simply spatial or simply spatio-temporal theory) of the boundary between an entity and everything distinct from it. Only by implication does it contribute anything to a psychological theory of individuating *thinkers* or of sentient *articulators* of things. Still less then can it either be or entail a particular theory of *perceptual* discrimination. (The only reason why in practice the theory seems to mention the intelligences which do discriminate things is that, being the theory it is, the theory embroils questions of identity and difference with substance-concepts, and substance concepts are, in a certain way we have described and qualified, the property of intelligences.)

With this said, though, let me respond in its own terms to one more remark that Ayers makes (p. 117):

No observer who becomes acquainted with what goes on from pupation to emergence [of a house fly] could rationally take it to involve the cessation of the existence of a maggot or indeed of any *thing* whatsoever from any conceivable point of view. For on the assumption that he is not simply mistaken about the general character of the underlying causal process (as he might have been had he observed the emergence of an ichneumon wasp from a parasitized pupa), he has witnessed a continuity and nothing else. . . . [1] The recognition of the fact of continuity is logically independent of the possession of sortal concepts; whereas [2] the formation of the sortal concept is at least psychologically dependent, in normal cases, upon the recognition of continuity.

In so far as [1] falls within our purview at all (being about recognition), it would appear in the light of the theory of individuation to be false. We have accounted for the only thing that might suggest it was true. [2] overlooks that ever-present possibility, *mutual* dependence.

6.14. *Experiential memory and the conceptual claims of physicalism*   In 'Remembering', *Philosophical Review* 1966, Deutscher and Martin point out that even if A did (say) plant a fig tree in a certain spot at a certain time, A's thinking he remembers planting it is not enough to establish that A remembers doing so. He may have forgotten the actual planting. If someone has told him about it later, then A may have subconsciously imagined the planting; and, even as he imagined it, he may have forgotten that he knew about the action only from another person's account. (Cf. Grice, 'The Causal Theory of Perception', *Proceedings of the Aristotelian Society*, vol. 35, 1962, to which both this *Longer Note* and the analysis of memory at *Identity and Spatio-Temporal Continuity*, pp. 45, 55 and footnote 55, are indebted.) This is a real if remote possibility. What is required then, in addition to the right kind of agent-centred inner representation on A's part, is that there should be a causal relation between A's planting the tree and his subsequent memory-representation. This is a sufficiently familiar point. What is original in Deutscher and Martin's contribution to the subject is to have demonstrated, as a conceptual contention, that it was impossible to define the *right sort* of causal connexion between an incident and the memory representation of it without recourse to the notion of the memory trace. (This may be conceived under the specification 'the normal neurophysiological connection whatever it is, between rememberings and the incidents of which they are rememberings'. This is not a circular procedure: but even if it were circular that would not matter for present purposes, which relate to the *necessary* conditions of remembering.) Deutscher and Martin carefully explore a multiplicity of alternatives to the explicit memory-trace account of the causal connexion between incident and experiential memory of incident. They show that none of these accounts can simultaneously allow for the possibility of *prompting* and define the particular sort of *operativeness* we are looking for between incident and representation.

In their physicalistic tendency these arguments about memory have important parallels with what seems to hold of other faculties that are distinctive of persons. If we are to make the distinction we believe we want to make between perception and misperception, for instance, there has to be something independent of what is subjectively given in perception to fix the *position* of the perceiver. What else can fix it but the body of the perceiver? Somewhat similarly, it seems to follow from Deutscher and Martin's analysis that experiential memory is inconceivable without some matter on which a trace or systematic change is imprinted by the original incident, and which may carry the resulting state forward to the time when the person involved recalls that event. And what Deutscher and Martin lighted upon when they criticized 'if . . . then___' analyses of the conceptually requisite causality was, I think, a completely general difficulty in pinning down by conditionals the character of any mental disposition. (For a more careful statement of this contention see my 'Towards a Reasonable Libertarianism' in T. Honderich, ed., *Essays on Freedom and Action,* London, Routledge, 1973, p. 49. And see more generally Juan-Carlos D'Alessio, 'The Analysis of Dispositional Concepts', D.Phil., Oxford, 1968, to which I am indebted. For the body-involvingness of pain, for instance, see *op. cit. Preface* (7).) A disposition is the sort of thing which can rest latent, be revived and refreshed, and is at the disposal of its owner to use under all sorts of different circumstances or not to use. It is impossible to conceive of memory causality by analogy with action at a distance as a transaction over a matterless gap between the external world at one time and a mind at a later time. The more one tries to conceive of such a thing the less it can satisfy him. And it scarcely improves things to think of the memory trace as an immaterial imprint on immaterial stuff. This can only help to the extent that immaterial mind is made intelligible by being *modelled* on the material, and distinguished from it only by the apparently vacuous contention that it is immaterial.

6.27. *Person-fission and person disassemblage: some further considerations*

1. The naturalistic discussion of these problems in section 7 of Ch. Six may be supplemented by Wollheim's psychoanalytical discussion of the fission problem. (See *op. cit.,* at footnote 3, Chapter Six.)

2. It should be noted that the problem of person fission that section 7 is concerned with is a problem of the splitting of lines of plenary consciousness and has nothing to do with any problem of the twinning of a zygote. It is true that on my view of *person*—see the revised Lockean conception at section 12—there is much to be said for counting a *fetus* as a person and for tracing persons back in the direction of the zygote. But the zygote is not conscious and if there were a problem about it, it would not be the problem of section 7.

3. Once we recognize that, like many other substances, persons need not begin to exist at a point which is specifiable absolutely definitely, and that it is not in any case circular to use the *general* notion of distinctness to make a conceptual ruling that persons do not come into being before the point at which twinning is nomogically possible—see Chapter Three—it is dubious at least that the splitting of a zygote does represent a serious problem of individuation.

4. It may be objected to me that neither the modified Lockeanism of section 12 nor the naturalistic view of persons as a kind of organism given in section 7 can be defended in the purely cognitive terms in which I have principally chosen to defend them. For it may be said that they entail a view about such things as the normative issue of abortion. But I should assert that in fact they lack all normative implications (in the only relevant or proper sense of 'normative': implications concerning *what ought to be done, what ought not to be done* or *what neither ought nor ought not to be done*). It is true that the view of persons as organisms that sections 7 and 10 jointly determine might greatly assist someone who wished to spell out what exactly was bad

about abortion—the destruction of something with a certain distinctive set of potentialities. But they do not imply any answer to the question whether or not this evil can be outweighed, e.g. by the evil attaching to the quite special (indeed unique) circumstance of one person's being lodged firmly inside an unwilling other person, in radical dependence (as Judith Jarvis Thomson puts it) on her life system.

5. If Wollheim's psychoanalytical discussion of fission is right, and equally if my biologically oriented discussion is right, then it is by the approach that musters conceptual importance for nomological and factual findings, and not in any muddled neo-Aristotelian identification of the person with the living and functioning intact body, that the answer will be found to such puzzling thought experiments as that which is given by Bernard Williams in 'The Self and the Future', *Philosophical Review* XXXIX, 1970.

6. It should be said that Williams's positive view, which is that persons *are* their bodies, is innocent of all the desperate obscurities of a neo-Aristotelian contention that a person is an intact living-body but ceases to exist before the body ceases, on death. (The theory of individuation defended in Chapter Two definitely excluded this. It is unclear how a mere hyphenation, 'living-body', can restore it as a possibility.) For Williams, a person *is* a body that is living, and the concept *living* is a normal restriction of the sortal concept *body*. After death the person continues to exist, dead, just as after demobilization an Anzac continues to exist, a civilian. (Cf. Ch. Two, sect. 5.) The disadvantages of Williams's view are rehearsed in the second paragraph of section 6 and fourth paragraph of section 5 of Chapter Six. These disadvantages are my reason for preferring, to Williams's view, a view that treats *body* not as collateral or superordinate to *person* or *animal,* but as derivative from it.

7. In my terms the moral of the paradox that Williams has put forward in 'The Self and the Future' can be put as follows. The theory and practice of individuation of persons break down, not only if we ignore the various nomological dependencies of the sortal concepts under which we single things out, but also if we fail to comprehend the vulnerability of the whole theory and practice of individuation in the face of interventions that pass, in a way in which ordinary medical treatment does not pass, too far beyond certain limits. These limits are the conditional limits of personal life in the only form in which we can certainly conceive it. For the idea that normal f-accommodating conditions are presupposed to the practices of individuation that are required to give sense to the questions we ask about individual instantiations of f, see Chapter Three and *Longer Note* 3.09. It does not just happen to be the case that the autonomy and adaptability of organisms (admittedly very extensive in the case of higher organisms) falls short of being unlimited.

6.36. *Radical interpretation and human nature*   1. In so far as the argument of sections 10 and 11 is more obscure or incomplete than can be helped, it will serve a purpose to formulate as clearly as I can one tenet that exerts a partly perhaps concealed regulative and suggestive influence on the whole tendency of those sections. This is that in prosecuting the going concern of interpretation, and extending this to the languages of people previously unknown to the rest of civilization, we do not allow nature in its interaction with environment to float completely freely, as Peter Winch puts it (*Ethics and Action*, p. 79) 'like a currency with no fixed parity'.*

2. Following on W. V. Quine's classic treatment of these themes in *Word and Object* (Cambridge, Mass., 1960), Donald Davidson has described vividly the interpenetration of belief and meaning. Davidson encourages us to think that holding alien beliefs relatively constant in the light of what the world presents to a subject's experience and exercising charity (which Grandy, *op. cit.*, will encourage us to commute to *humanity*), we may hope to escape from the circle that he finds here and 'solve' for meaning. I think this idea of holding belief relatively constant gives a good first approximation to an account of radical interpretation—on a preliminary or simplified view of 'the world'. But on a more complex view of the problem and of what the world is, one must take into account not only what the world presents to the experience of subjects but also their interests and their *focus* upon that world. How else can we guess what the world *presents* to them? But now we have to reckon with an inextricable interpenetration of the alethic or propositional attitudes and (broadly speaking) the affective attitudes. (See my 'Truth, Invention and the Meaning of Life', *Proceedings of the British Academy* 1977). And we have to start to envisage radical interpretation's proceeding through a succession of approximations which, at some points, will involve holding belief relatively constant in the light of what the world presents to the subject's experience *taken together* with the concerns of the subject. But then we can only break out of the circle of belief, affect and meaning if, in advance of any particular problem of radical interpretation, we think we know more than nothing not only about the world but also about men in general.

3. Presented with the human form we entertain immediately a multitude of however tentative expectations. We interpret the speech and conduct of the remotest human strangers in the light of the maxim that we should interpret them in such a way as to ascribe beliefs, needs and concerns to them that will diminish to the minimum the need to postulate *inexplicable* disagreement between us and them. We entertain the idea, unless we are irremediably conceited or colonialist in mentality, that there may be something we ourselves can learn from strangers about the true, the good and the rational (though there is no theoretical need to push this process of mutual accommodation any farther than it will go). In the absence of a belief in such a thing as

* Cp. here David Lewis, 'Radical Interpretation' in *Intentionality, Language and Translation*, edited by J. G. Troyer and S. C. Wheeler, *Synthèse* 27, 1974. On interpretation more generally, see Richard Grandy, 'Reference, Meaning and Belief', *Journal of Philosophy* 1973; Gareth Evans's and John McDowell's Editorial Introduction to *Truth and Meaning: Essays in Semantics*, Oxford, 1976; and § 1 of McDowell's article *(ibid.)* 'Truth Conditions, Bivalence, and Verificationism'; D. Davidson *Dialectica* 1973.

human nature, I do not think there is any idea of inexplicable error or disagreement that is available to us. Nor could we regard the human form as a clue to so much. We ought to check ourselves in a way that we do not and cannot here check or restrain ourselves.

4. Arguments for the proposition that there is no such thing as human nature often rest on premisses about the inconceivability in a pure or socially unconditioned form of anything we can recognize as human nature. It is not necessary to dispute the truth of the premiss. What is wrong is only the argument for the conclusion. It is indeed essential to the normal development of human beings that they should live in society, and different societies may indeed be very different. But those who seek to build on this premiss should note that an analogous argument would proceed from the non-existence of objects exempt from the forces exerted by other objects, and from the diversity of such forces, to the unacceptability or uselessness of the idea of inertia and of Galileo's principle that, if left to itself, a moving body will move with uniform velocity in one and the same direction.

Bibliography

*Selected Writings on the Individuation and Identity of Substances**

ANSCOMBE, G. E. M., 'The Principle of Individuation', *Proceedings of the Aristotelian Society*, Suppl. Vol. 27 (1953), 83–96.

ARISTOTLE, *Categories*, esp. Chs 1–5.

—— *De Generatione et Corruptione*, Bk I.

—— *Physics*, Bk I, Chs 7–9; Bk II, Chs 1–3.

—— *De Anima*, Bk II, Chs 1–4.

—— *Metaphysics*, e.g. Bk V, Chs 6, 7; Bks VII, VIII, X.

AYER, A. J., *Philosophical Essays* (London: Macmillan, 1954), Ch. 2, 'The Identity of Indiscernibles'.

AYERS, MICHAEL R., 'Individuals Without Sortals', *Canadian Journal of Philosophy*, 4 (1974), 113–48.

BARCAN MARCUS, RUTH, 'Essential Attribution', *Journal of Philosophy*, 68 (1971).

BENACERRAF, PAUL, 'What Numbers Could Not Be', *Philosophical Review*, 74 (1965), 47–73.

BLACK, MAX, 'The Identity of Indiscernibles', *Mind*, 61 (1952).

BRODY, BARUCH A., 'Why Settle for Anything Less Than Good Old-fashioned Aristotelian Essentialism?', *Nous*, 7 (1973).

BURGE, TYLER, 'Mass Terms, Count Nouns and Change', *Synthèse*, 31 (1975).

—— ['A Theory of Aggregates', *Nous*, 11 (1977), 97–118].

BUTLER, JOSEPH, *First Dissertation* to the *Analogy of Religion*.

CARTWRIGHT, HELEN M., 'Heraclitus and the Bath Water', *Philosophical Review*, 74 (1965), 466–85.

—— 'Quantities', *Philosophical Review*, 79 (1970), 25–42.

CARTWRIGHT, RICHARD, 'Identity and Substitutivity', in MUNITZ, MILTON K. (ed.), *Identity and Individuation* (New York: New York University Press, 1971), pp. 119–33.

—— ['Indiscernibility Principles', *Midwest Studies in Philosophy*, IV (1979), 293–306].

—— 'Scattered Things', in *Analysis and Metaphysics; a Festschrift for Roderich Chisholm* (Dordrecht: Reidel, 1975).

CHAPPELL, V. C., 'Sameness and Change', *Philosophical Review*, 69 (1960), 351–62.

* Compiled late summer 1979 after correction of galley and page proofs. Square-bracketed items were seen too late to influence the text. I gratefully acknowledge the advice in Aristotelian matters generously given to me here and elsewhere by M. L. C. Nussbaum.

CHISHOLM, R. M., *Person and Object* (London: Allen & Unwin, 1976), esp. Ch. III, App. A and B.

COBURN, R., 'The Persistence of Bodies', *American Philosophical Quarterly*, 13 (1976).

DUMMETT, M. A. E., *Frege: Philosophy of Language* (London: Duckworth, 1973), esp. pp. 130–1 and Ch. 16.

—— 'Does Quantification involve Identity?', in LEWIS, HARRY (ed.), *Peter Geach: A Profile* (Dordrecht: Reidel, 1980).

EVANS, GARETH, 'Identity and Predication', *Journal of Philosophy*, 72 (1975).

—— ['Vague Objects', *Analysis*, 39 (1978)].

FRAASSEN, BAS C. VAN, 'Essence and Existence', *American Philosophical Quarterly Monograph*, 1977–78.

FREGE, GOTTLOB, *The Foundations of Arithmetic*, trans. J. L. Austin (Oxford: Blackwell, 1950), sect. 62.

FURTH, MONTGOMERY, ['Transtemporal Stability in Aristotelian Substances', *Journal of Philosophy*, 75 (1978), 624–46].

GEACH, P. T., *Logic Matters* (Oxford: Blackwell, 1972), pp. 238–49, 302–17.

—— *Reference and Generality* (Ithaca: Cornell University Press, 1962), esp. sect. 31–4.

—— 'Some Problems About Time', *Proceedings of the British Academy*, 1965.

—— 'Ontological Relativity and Relative Identity', in MUNITZ, MILTON K. (ed.), *Logic and Ontology* (New York: New York University Press, 1973).

GOODMAN, NELSON, *Problems and Projects* (Indianopolis: Bobbs Merrill, 1972), Pt IV.

GRIFFIN, NICHOLAS, 'Ayers on Relative Identity', *Canadian Journal of Philosophy*, 6 (1976).

—— and ROUTLEY, R., 'Towards a logic of relative identity', *Logique et Analyse*, 1979.

HACKER, P. M. S., ['Substance: The Constitution of Reality', *Midwest Studies in Philosophy*, IV (1979), 239–61].

HACKING, IAN, 'Individual Substances', in FRANKFURT, HARRY G. (ed.), *Leibniz: A Collection of Critical Essays* (New York: Doubleday, 1972).

HAMPSHIRE, STUART, 'Identification and Existence', in LEWIS, H. D. (ed.), *Contemporary British Philosophy* (London: Allen & Unwin, 1956), 3rd ser., pp. 191–208.

HERACLITUS, Diels fragments B1, B12, B47, B91, B125, in DIELS, H. and KRANZ, W., *Die Fragmente der Vorsokratiker* (Berlin, 1951).

HOBBES, THOMAS, *De Corpore*, Pt II, Ch. 11, in MOLESWORTH, WILLIAM (ed.), *The English Works of Thomas Hobbes* (London: John Bohn, 1839–45), Vol. I.

ISHIGURO, H., 'Leibniz and the Idea of Sensible Qualities', in BROWN, S. and VESEY, G. (eds), *Reason and Reality* (London: Macmillan, 1972).

—— *Leibniz' Philosophy of Logic and Language* (London: Duckworth, 1972), esp. Chs I, IV.

KRIPKE, S., 'Naming and Necessity', in HARMAN, G. and DAVIDSON, D. (eds), *Semantics of Natural Languages* (Dordrecht: Reidel, 1972).

—— [*Naming and Necessity*, rev. ed. (Oxford: Blackwell, 1980)].

—— 'Identity and Necessity', in MUNITZ, MILTON K. (ed.), *Identity and Individuation* (New York: New York University Press, 1971).

LEIBNIZ, G. W., *Nouveaux Essais sur l'Entendement Humain*, esp. Bk II, Chs 23, 27; Bk III, Chs 6, 10, 11.

—— *Discourse on Metaphysics.*

—— *Correspondence with Clarke*, esp. Leibniz's fifth paper. sect. 21–6.

—— 'Disputatio Metaphysica de Principio Individui', Gerhardt (ed.) *Die Philosophischen Schriften* IV, pp. 15–26.

—— 'Meditationes de Cognitione Veritate et Ideis', Gerhardt IV, pp. 422–6.

—— *Correspondence with De Volder*, see the selection at pp. 515–39 in LOEMKER, L. E. (ed.), *Philosophical Papers and Letters* (Dordrecht: Reidel, 1969).

LEWIS, DAVID, 'Survival and Identity', in RORTY, A. (ed.), *The Identities of Persons* (University of California Press, 1976).

LOCKE, JOHN, *Essay of Human Understanding*, II, xxvii.

—— Reply to the Bishop of Worcester's Answer to his letter, *ad finem.*

MACINTYRE, ALASDAIR, 'Essence and Existence', in EDWARDS, PAUL (ed.), *Encyclopaedia of Philosophy* (New York: Macmillan, 1967), Vol. III, pp. 59–61.

MORAVCSIK, J. M. E., 'The Discernibility of Identicals', *Journal of Philosophy*, 73 (1976), 587–98.

MUNITZ, MILTON K. (ed.), *Identity and Individuation* (New York: New York University Press, 1971), contributions of CARTWRIGHT, RICHARD, KRIPKE, S. and SHOEMAKER, SYDNEY.

NOONAN, H., 'Sortal Concepts and Identity', *Mind*, 87 (1978).

—— 'Wiggins on Identity', *Mind*, 82 (1973).

PARFIT, DEREK, 'Personal Identity', *Philosophical Review*, 80 (1971).

PELLETTIER, J. F., 'A Bibliography of Recent Work on Mass Terms', *Synthèse*, 31 (1975).

PERRY, JOHN R., 'The Same *F*', *Philosophical Review*, 79 (1970), 181–200.

POPPER, K. R., 'The Principle of Individuation', *Proceedings of the Aristotelian Society*, Suppl. Vol. 27 (1953).

PRATT, VERNON, 'Biological Classification', *British Journal of Philosophy of Science*, 23 (1972).

PRIOR, A., 'Things and Stuff', in *Papers in Logic and Ethics* (London: Duckworth, 1976), pp. 181–6.

—— 'Time, Existence and Identity', in *Papers on Time and Tense* (Oxford: Clarendon Press, 1968), pp. 78–87.

PUTNAM, HILARY, 'Is Semantics Possible?', *Metaphilosophy*, 3 (1970); also in *Mind, Language and Reality* (Philosophical Papers, Vol. 2; Cambridge: Cambridge University Press, 1975).

QUINE, W. V. O., *From a Logical Point of View* (Cambridge, Mass.: Harvard University Press, 1953), esp. pp. 65–79 ('Identity, Ostension and Hypostasis') and pp. 139–59 ('Reference and Modality').

—— *Set Theory and its Logic* (Cambridge, Mass.: Harvard University Press, 1963), esp. p. 13.

—— Review of Geach, P. T., *Reference and Generality*, in *Philosophical Review*, 73 (1964), 100–4.

—— 'Natural Kinds', in RESCHER, N. (ed.), *Essays in Honour of C. G. Hempel* (Dordrecht: Reidel, 1969).

—— Review of MUNITZ, MILTON K. (ed.), *Identity and Individuation*, in *Journal of Philosophy*, 69 (1972), 488–9.

—— 'Worlds Away', *Journal of Philosophy*, 73 (1976).

—— 'Intensions Revisited', *Midwest Studies in Philosophy*, II (1977).

QUINTON, A., *The Nature of Things* (London: Routledge & Kegan Paul, 1972), Pt I.

SHOEMAKER, SYDNEY, 'Wiggins on Identity', *Philosophical Review*, 79 (1970).

—— ['Identity, Properties and Causality', *Midwest Studies in Philosophy*, IV (1979), 321–42].

SHWAYDER, DAVID, 'Man and Mechanism', *Australasian Journal of Philosophy*, 41 (1963).

SLOTE, MICHAEL, ['Causality and the Concept of a "Thing"', *Midwest Studies in Philosophy*, IV (1979), 387–400].

SMART, B., 'How to Reidentify the Ship of Theseus', *Analysis*, 32 (1972), 145–8.

—— 'The Ship of Theseus, the Parthenon, and Disassembled Objects', *Analysis*, 34 (1973), 24–7.

STEAD, G.C., 'ΟΜΟΟΥΣΙΟΣ ΤΩΙ ΠΑΤΡΙ', *Studia Patristica*, III, Band 78 (1961).

STEVENSON, LESLIE, 'Extensional and Intensional Logic for Sortal-relative Identity', *Logique et Analyse* (forthcoming).

—— 'A Formal Theory of Sortal Quantification', *Notre Dame Journal of Formal Logic*, 16 (1975), 185–207.

—— 'Relative Identity and Leibniz's Law', *Philosophical Quarterly*, 22 (1972), 155–8.

STRAWSON, P. F., *Individuals* (London: Methuen, 1959), esp. Ch. Four.

—— 'Chisholm on Identity Through Time', in KIEFER, H. E. and MUNITZ, MILTON K. (eds), *Language, Belief, and Metaphysics* (Albany: State University of New York Press, 1970), 183–6.

—— 'Entity and Identity', in LEWIS, H. D. (ed.), *British Contemporary Philosophy* (London: Allen & Unwin, 1976) Vol. IV.

—— 'May Bes and Might Have Beens', in MARGALIT, A. (ed.), *Meaning and Use* (Dordrecht: Reidel, 1979).

TARSKI, ALFRED, 'Foundations of the Geometry of Solids', in *Logic, Semantics, and Metamathematics* (Oxford: Oxford University Press, 1956), pp. 24–9.

WALLACE, JOHN R., 'Philosophical Grammar' (Stanford University, unpublished doctoral dissertation, 1964), pp. 80–3.

WILLIAMS, B. A. O., 'Personal Identity and Individuation', *Proceedings of the Aristotelian Society*, 57 (1956–57).

—— 'Bodily Continuity and Personal Identity', *Analysis*, 21 (1960).

—— *Problems of the Self* (Cambridge: Cambridge University Press, 1973), papers 1–5.

WILSON, N. L., 'Space, Time and Individuals', *Journal of Philosophy*, 52 (1955).

WOODGER, J. H., *The Axiomatic Method in Biology* (Cambridge: Cambridge University Press, 1937), Ch. III, p. 1, and Appendix E (by Tarski), p. 16.

WOODS, M. J., 'Substance and Quality' (B.Phil., Oxford, 1959).

—— 'The Individuation of Things and Places', *Proceedings of the Aristotelian Society*, Suppl. Vol. 37 (1963), 203–16.

—— 'Identity and Individuation', in BUTLER, R. J. (ed)., *Analytical Philosophy* (Oxford: Blackwell, 1965), 2nd ser., pp. 120–30.

Index

For breakdown and supplementation of entries like 'coincide', 'sortal concept', 'identity', etc., see Table of Contents (p. ix) and Contents for Longer Notes (p. 190). Names occurring solely in the Bibliography are not cited here.